THE STONE KILLER

A Hoodlum Reaches For God

By Ronald J. Lawrence

The Stone Killer
A Hoodlum Reaches For God
by Ronald J. Lawrence

Printed in the United States of America

ISBN 9781619042971

Unless otherwise indicated, Bible quotations are taken from the New American Standard Bible. Copyright © 1977 by The Lockman Foundation.

www.xulonpress.com

PROLOGUE

Deadliest Of The Deadly

The loud banging on the door seemed from a sledge hammer rather than a fist. I cautiously opened it and the bulky man grinned broadly.

"Hi! I'm Jesse Stoneking. FBI. Glad to meet you." Then the booming chuckle and the bone shattering handshake. His laughter was raucous, yet charming and contagious, part of his charisma.

Jesse Eugene Stoneking could have been a politician, a businessman, an entertainer, anyone who lived a straight, reputable life. But he was the notorious, predatory high-level hoodlum and merchant of death who became an unlikely, deep undercover FBI informant. He intrigued courtrooms for two years with his underworld exploits and eventually decimated organized crime in St. Louis.

It was the summer of 1986 and we were in a motel in rural central Illinois where I explored his life for three days. He had been an enigma. As an investigative reporter for the St. Louis Post-Dispatch specializing in organized crime, I wrote about many of the top gangsters, but I had heard little of him until he surfaced two years earlier. Intelligence authorities had few files on him. He had kept a low profile, staying in the shadows most of his criminal life.

Built like a bulldozer, his mere presence was intimidating. He was 5 feet, 10 inches tall and weighed 200 pounds, his bulging muscles obvious. His fists were hammers that beat men into submission.

Framed by coal black hair, his face seemed a solid chunk of granite. His eyes were just as potent weapons. They could be piercing like a stiletto or innocent as a baby's, depending on what he wanted them to convey.

All of that contributed to his reputation as the worst of the worst, the greediest of the greedy, the deadliest of the deadly, an underworld baron. Much of his life had been a chronicle of sin and depravity.

Death was no stranger to Jesse Stoneking. Even when it stalked him it was an opportunity to prove his virility. Killing was a way of life, violence a means to an end. To him, "cracking people" was how to achieve manhood. His nickname, the "Stone Killer," wasn't undeserved and enhanced the image of the dreaded gangster he needed to project.

He was a ferocious enforcer who feared no man. Cross him, lie to him, steal from him, challenge him and you likely will take up residence in a grave. That was why as the contemporary Al Capone he almost killed five men in his own Valentine's Day Massacre.

An adept burglar, he plotted his scores with the precision of a brain surgeon and the tenacity of a drill sergeant. With scams, he was a virtuoso of duplicity and intrigue. Those qualities made him a consummate thief, one of St. Louis' most intrepid and innovative money-makers who stole several million dollars in just a few years, giving him the life of luxury and influence he craved.

It was why Jesse walked with the high and the mighty, the elite of organized crime, and was a power figure destined to become an outfit boss. He was held in great esteem by the powerful Chicago Syndicate and the St. Louis Mafia, whose don took him on as a colleague and gave him a murder contract.

Jesse was in hiding when I was granted an exclusive interview by his Federal Bureau of Investigation handlers. He gave me some of the most sensational stories of my career, unlocking the mob's vault containing a wealth of secrets and exposing his own deep, dark self.

I wanted to learn what made a big-time gangster tick, a task I assumed would be difficult as pulling teeth. It wasn't. He opened his soul and disclosed the real Jesse Stoneking, not a camouflaged and sugar-coated one. He was candid about even the most hideous aspects of his criminal and personal lives, some shocking. He wasn't reluctant to admit his culpability and he didn't try to mitigate it.

I warned him if he was untruthful just once I would walk away from him. I asked him questions the answers to which I already knew. Not once did he lie to me then or over the coming years, although deceit once was a talent. His FBI control agents vouched for his integrity. I assumed he didn't want to be branded a liar. That would tarnish the new, honorable image of himself he needed to create.

I insisted nothing he told me would be off the record. I didn't need a confidential source no longer connected, just news stories from an identifiable source. The only felony I assumed he never would admit was murder for which there is no statute of limitations. I was wrong.

Jesse was somewhat unique as an organized crime informant. Jimmy "The Weasel" Fratianno, Henry Hill, Salvatore "Sammy the Bull" Gravano and others snitched after they were arrested. The information they possessed was their bargaining chips for less time behind bars.

Jesse used that to gain freedom from prison, but he stayed on the streets for two years, facing dangers and death, trapping friends and enemies alike. Few other working informants of such stature in the underworld in the Midwest and who wreaked such damage to organized crime have been acknowledged publicly by the government.

Readers will witness the duplicity and treachery of the mob and its operatives, the planning of murders, the lethal struggles for control of the underworld that made St. Louis the "bomb capital" of America. They will participate in the execution of a high-stakes robbery that almost got a police officer killed and caused the Mafia to put out murder contracts. They will live the life of a hoodlum, feel his emotions and desires, frustrations and panic.

I depict Jesse Stoneking no less than what he was and no more than what he became. It is about a man who walked the thin line between life and death, decency and perversion. And it is about a man who discarded his lucrative, evil past and took on a new life, the arduous journey back to God.

I concluded Jesse bared his soul to me and disclosed his terrible secrets as his way of atonement. He was making peace with God, himself and the world he had brutalized and swindled for so many years. Perhaps God wanted his hidden life to be out in the open. Only He knows.

Jesse carried a lot of heavy baggage he had difficulty unloading, causing his conscience to wage war with him. God had to reconstruct him, destroy the old before building the new. God allowed adversities into Jesse's life to get his attention. And it did! But could Jesse survive?

The only actual names I use are those who have been identified publicly in court or in the media as members of organized crime, who were named as Jesse's associates or who were convicted of crimes as a result of his undercover work. Names of other individuals are changed. The identities of his children are excluded to protect them, although I use the names of his two wives.

Many of the events, especially criminal, discussed are factual as Jesse related them. Some never have been disclosed and others are based on news stories and other articles I wrote; law enforcement and court documents; several thousand pages of transcripts of conversations recorded by Jesse and of my interviews with him; court testimony; and FBI wiretaps.

I interweave his emotions and his struggles to find God as he described them, often during recollection of his criminal past. At times, I divulge my emotional reactions to what he told me and my effort to help him. Most of Jesse's personal observations before he became an informant, during and afterward were reconstructed to the best of his memory.

Some of the dialogue quoted contained obscenities which I deleted because of the religious nature of this writing.

Let us explore Jesse Stoneking the villain before we look at Jesse Stoneking the Christian. There is a lesson there for all of us.

CHAPTER ONE

A Hit Coming Down

It was a little after 1 a. m. that summer night in 1988 when swarthy, ruggedly handsome Jesse Stoneking and his wife, Dorothy, stepped onto the front porch of his mother's house in St. Louis County. Rain-laden black clouds punctuated by the crack of thunder and the flash of lightning forebode an approaching storm.

Storms were much of what Jesse's life was of late. One crisis after another, threats to his very existence, countless burdens that would break the spirits of most men. His wasn't shattered yet, but how long could it remain intact? How often he prayed to God about it, just as he had before visiting his mother that afternoon, and he knew the Lord was with him.

Jesse surveyed the neighborhood, as he did wherever he was, especially at night. He was in hostile territory and there were shadows where danger could lurk, hiding places for a sniper to blow him away, but he detected little out of the ordinary, nothing alarming. Death surely wasn't stalking him tonight.

Vigilance was second nature to the "Stone killer." It was how one survived in his world. One of his first lessons long ago when he enrolled in the school of crime was anticipating trouble was to be prepared for it. Survival now demanded no less.

Jesse and his mother had been estranged for too long and he had to rebuild their relationship. He kissed her on the cheek and held her close to him. "I don't know when I'll be back, Mom," he whispered. To tell her differently would be a lie and he no longer could do that. Deceit had dominated his life too long. Truth must prevail. He would be on the run and he didn't want her to know why.

"You just be careful now, honey," she said, looking deeply into his eyes, tears filling her own. "I need to see you again. We have to get back together again. Love you. son."

"Love you, too," he said as he stepped off the porch and started toward his car at the curb.

Bombs were the favorite death tools of the St. Louis mob and Jesse had learned much about them. He retrieved a flashlight from the car and crouched, shining the light underneath. No bomb was secured to the underside.

He next checked the hood and the trunk. The threads he had attached to them were intact. His car was hot-wired so anyone connecting a bomb to its electrical system would become his own victim. It was an explosive device detonated by remote control from a distance he feared most. A few years earlier he came within seconds of being hit that way. He had taken every precaution he could and now it was safe to leave.

As Jesse drove away, a dark colored sedan eased out of the shadows down the street behind him, its headlights off. He detected it immediately. He increased his speed. So did the sedan. Its headlights came on. He slowed and so did it.

He was under surveillance! But by whom? The law no longer had any interest in him. His car had an Illinois license plate registered in his alias at an address in a rural community far away where he lived until two days ago.

No one, especially the mob's hit squads, would know he would be here today. Where his mother lived would be unknown to the outfit. She now used her maiden name. Then he remembered his cover had been blown by his trusted friend, his former partner! He surely wouldn't sell him out. Or would he?

Jesse turned into a side street and the sedan followed. He tried evasive maneuvers he had used before to shake tails by government agents and his enemies, but he couldn't lose them. These guys were no amateurs. The sedan slowly closed in. He couldn't let them come within shooting distance. He returned to the thoroughfare, now deserted.

He instinctively reached under the seat for his .45 automatic, his "guardian angel," his faithful companion for many years, but it wasn't there. He didn't have it anymore. He had gotten rid of it as a promise to God that was part of his reconciliation with Him. If he had a gun, he would maneuver them into a trap, get the drop on them and confront them, shoot it out if he had to. He had been trapped before and the two assassins died.

Once again he was vulnerable, but he stayed calm. Dorothy was silent. He saw the fear on her face, but said nothing to comfort her. It wouldn't do any good.

The speedometer hovered at 50 miles an hour. The chase car was half a block behind now. The only way they could get to him would be to force his car to a stop or slow down. He wouldn't allow that.

He had to get to the other side of the avenue and head in the opposite direction. The median was covered with large shrubbery and trees. He would have to use a cross street.

They would assume he was armed and they would unleash a firestorm of gunfire if they could get near enough. He laughed sarcastically to himself. Where was a cop when you needed one! He would welcome a traffic ticket now. Even arrest.

The fuel gauge showed the gas tank was only a fourth full! He couldn't go far on that. He cursed his negligence. To run out of gas would be his death warrant. Never did he allow the fuel to get that low. That was a critical part of his survival plan. The need to flee, just as now, often came without advance notice.

Up ahead, a semi-trailer was heading in his direction. It was what he needed. He waited until it was 100 feet away. Without slowing, he yanked the wheel hard to the left and made a turn directly in front of it.

The tires under him screeched in agony and the car, balancing precariously on two wheels, almost overturned. The driver of the truck slammed on the brakes, the bulky vehicle jack-knifing and blocking the intersection.

As Jesse accelerated in the opposite direction the sedan stopped. The street lamps and the truck's headlights momentarily illuminated the driver, a convicted killer, a member of a cabal that had tried to whack him before. He couldn't see the passenger.

And then Jesse was gone. He now had the few minutes he needed to lose them. And to live!

Dorothy sobbed convulsively, her panic obvious. He put his hand on her shoulder. "It's okay now," he said, but his words were of little comfort.

A mob hit had been coming down. It had been a long time coming. He had eluded the attack dogs and denied them their reward. But had he shaken his past? It almost caught up with him. Could he live with that or would it torment him? Who eventually would pull the trigger on him?

The reality of what nearly happened gripped him. Dorothy surely would have been killed with him. The hitters would have cared little about her. Then an icy chill careened through his body as an even more terrifying vision came to him. It was of their three children's bullet riddled bodies. At the last minute they had decided not to bring them and left them with a relative away from the metropolitan area. Would he have caused their deaths, too?

It was too horrendous to contemplate. Four loved ones, his own flesh and blood, might have died because of him. That family members always have neutrality in a mob hit is a fallacy. Witnesses aren't allowed to live. Anger raged through him. He wanted to strike out and retaliate in kind, but he no longer could do that. At another time, in another place, he would have without a second thought. It would have been expected of him, a matter of honor.

Then Jesse realized he hadn't saved himself and Dorothy. God intervened and rescued them. His prayers had been answered in the Lord's time and in His manner. He thanked God and prayed for further protection he knew he would need.

For much of his life, Jesse had accepted death for what it was - a liability of his chosen profession if he was on the receiving end, an asset if he was dealing it. "I never thought anything about cracking a guy," he told me. "It never bothered me. So what? It was just something you had to do. I figured the guy deserved it. There was something to be gained by it. But I'd never kill somebody for no reason at all."

But his past finally was catching up to him as he knew it would one day. The "Stone Killer," the bully of the mob who once inspired fear and envy now was the object of scorn. The deadly hunter had become the hunted, fair game for the mob's kill squads. He was running from those who once ran from him. His debt to the outfits almost had been paid in full, reparations made with his blood. He had no idea where or when he would stop fleeing. If he ever would. But run he must.

Reap What You Sow

Jesse called me a few weeks later. He found refuge in Wickenburg, Arizona, a small town in the desert not far from Phoenix. It surely would be a haven for him and his family, where he could find peace at last.

I was concerned about him. Could he retain the stability he needed in his life, that only offered by God? Or would his conscience dominate him? I knew he was turning his life over to Jesus, but he had to travel a difficult, treacherous road full of potholes and false detours.

He told me his close call with death that night was prophetic. "I know they're gonna get me some day. You see, it says right there in the Bible that you're gonna reap what you sow. So I guess that's true because God says it. I'll get a bullet in the head some day. It'll happen for sure one day. God will get His evens."

"Jesse, you know God doesn't work that way," I said. "He doesn't get His evens with someone like you who's come back to Him. He's forgiven you through Jesus. Sometimes it's hard to see Him helping you. He doesn't always do it the way we want it and when. He does it His way at His time. He sometimes wants us to use our adversities as stepping stones to greater love for Him, greater faith in Him and not stumbling blocks to self-pity."

"But look at what almost happened to me and Dorothy. You don't realize how close we were to being killed. A wrong turn. A couple miles an hour slower and we'd both be in caskets. You wouldn't be talking to me. You'd be going to our funerals."

I laughed, not derisively, but encouragingly. "Almost happened? But it didn't, did it, Jesse? Why do you think it didn't? Good luck? God was looking out for both of you."

"Yeah, I know that. This dummy isn't thinking straight. I've already thanked God for saving us."

As a teen-aged boy, Jesse dedicated his life to Satan and crime instead of to Jesus Christ he once worshipped. Now, he wanted to return to Jesus.

CHAPTER TWO

From God to Mob

J esse Stoneking didn't casually drift into crime for the lack of anything better to do or for the fun of it. He plunged headlong into it with a passion and commitment when he was just 14 years old. And his grandfather escorted him there.

To Jesse, rebellion was how to get even with the world and those close to him, especially his parents, who treated him unfairly. It was an opportunity to pursue riches and respect he was being denied. How better to show God wasn't needed in his life?

Jesse spent the first nine years of his life in a run-down, sparsely furnished second-floor flat on the south side of St. Louis. His father was a cab driver whose meager earnings never went far enough. Food was simple and Jesse wore used clothing. His father was a strict disciplinarian and Jesse called him a "square-john," not a complimentary description.

His parents bought a house in Belleville on the eastern edge of the metropolitan area. It wasn't elaborate but it was roomier than the apartment. His father claimed the suburban environment would shield his children from temptations of the big city so they could lead honorable, productive lives.

The deprivation in his early life festered in Jesse. It bred unrestrained greed that would drive him through much of his adult life.

By the time Jesse was 12, he was heading in the opposite direction of crime and to God. He attended Mass regularly, was a proud, dedicated choir boy and went to a Catholic school. He read his favorite book, the Bible, daily. His parents were proud of his spiritual development. It would shape him into a decent, God-fearing man one day, they told him.

"I loved the Lord and I liked to hear what they said about Him in church. He was something special to me. I believed what the priest said about Jesus. I thought it would be great to be like Him. I wanted to follow Him. That's how I wanted to live. That way I could be a decent guy. You know, help people and all that.

Jesse focused on being an architect or mortician because those jobs "paid good money." But he soon came under an evil influence. A grandfather, a hoodlum, became his mentor and role model. He was released from prison when Jesse was 13 and soon exerted his influence on him.

"He was a real man. He was quiet and had good manners. He got into a big shoot-out one time. His partner got shot and my grandpa jumped right in the middle of the gun battle. He picked up his partner, threw him over his shoulder and kept firing back as he got the guy out. Just like in the movies. That's what he got known for. His bravery. He was my idea of a man. He wasn't afraid of anybody or anything. He was just a solid guy. My kind of man. I had to be like him."

Jesse soon emulated his idol, acting out his own gangster fantasies. He developed the street jargon of a hood and swaggered about the streets and school. He received the attention he craved.

"The kids in school made fun of me. I wore pegged trousers and had my hair slicked back. I smoked cigarettes. I didn't really like them, but they made me look older and tougher. I was a smart-aleck, too, wising off all the time. They called me the 'Little Hood'. I didn't care. I liked it. That's what I wanted to be."

The Ultimate Test

As Jesse turned away from Jesus, crime became his savior. His emerging, untested Christian faith clashed with the harsh realities of human nature and the real world. The church and his parents had taught him forgiveness was a basic tenet of the Christian faith, but it didn't fit into his new life.

He and several friends were going rabbit hunting after classes. He stored a pellet gun in his school locker. One of his friends squealed on him to school officials, who summoned police. They lectured him and confiscated the pellet gun. He was expelled the next day.

Jesse never returned to school. That day he learned to hate snitches, not forgive them. His religious faith, put to its first test, failed him. What he had been taught about God and Jesus now seemed meaningless, even hypocritical. They had forsaken him.

"The priests would always tell you that you had to forgive people and turn the other cheek, just like Jesus. The Golden Rule and all that nonsense. But they wouldn't forgive me and I didn't even do anything bad. I figured to hell with them. Who needed them anyhow?"

Jesse would educate himself on the mean streets and acquire talents necessary to attain the good life, just like his grandfather. It was how to survive in his new world.

By then Jesse's home life was deteriorating. His parents quarreled frequently, often in their children's presence. Time and idleness weighed heavily on his mind, now the devil's playground. He had flirted with venturing into the exciting pastime of crime, but he lacked courage to do it himself.

"I thought it would be great fun and I could use the money. I wanted to be a big-time gangster like I'd see in the movies. Like my grandpa. I couldn't wait. But I didn't know how to pull it off."

A trusted friend took him on his debut into crime. It was spontaneous and the results were predictable. They were sitting on Jesse's front porch discussing how to burglarize a house. There was only one way to learn. They broke the rear windows of two nearby houses and crawled inside.

It wasn't on the scale of the notorious Brinks Robbery in 1950. The take was less than $100 in currency and coins. Jesse threw away his share, fearing the money could be traced to him. His friend was a blabbermouth and bragged about their score. He was arrested and came in on his partner. Once again, a friend had betrayed Jesse. He vowed never to commit such treason.

Jesse received attention, but not how he craved. His father grounded him for a month and ordered him to change his ways. The suburbs weren't a safe harbor for his son after all. He said he hoped the Juvenile Court would send him to reform school to teach him a lesson. Jesse considered that betrayal by his father. Was there anyone he could trust?

One night, Jesse wanted to talk to his mother about what was happening, to confide in her his fears and hopes. It was 2 o'clock in the morning and she was late returning home from the dance studio where she worked as an instructor. An expensive car was parked in front. His mother and a man were inside. He knew what they were doing. His father was working that night, but he got off early and came home. He severely beat the man while she fled down the street.

Jesse brooded, confused and overwhelmed with uncertainty about his and the family's future. He again felt betrayed and abandoned. Two police officers came to the house that afternoon.

"If you're going to take my dad to jail I won't let you talk to him," he told the officers.

He slammed shut the door. He had protected his father. He told him to let the officers in. They took him into custody. His mother had obtained a court order committing him to a state mental institution for observation because of his violent behavior. She also filed for divorce.

Jesse wept uncontrollably when he heard that. His mother tried to console him, but he wouldn't listen to her. She was the cause of the family's problems. He would have nothing more to do with her. He stayed in his room for two days and came out only to eat his meals. His father was released a week later.

The Juvenile Court judge placed Jesse on probation for the burglaries. He warned him if he got into trouble again or continued associating with his old friends his probation would be revoked and he would be sent to reform school.

Jesse's probation was an opportunity for revenge. How better to show his defiance and punish his parents for rejecting him than by being busted again? He now was rushing headlong into crime at the age of 14.

Not long after the judge put Jesse on probation he saw a souped-up sports car parked near downtown. "Miscarriage" was painted in yellow on both doors. Jesse thought it was an appropriate description of himself.

"It was the kind of car every kid dreamed about. I hung around, drooling and thinking about what to do. One day the keys were in the ignition. I didn't have to think any more. It was mine."

Jesse didn't have much experience driving and he was too young for a license. He assumed police would arrest him quickly. It was what he wanted. But they didn't and he drove the car undetected for almost a week, parking it down the street from his house. One afternoon, he picked up a girl for a ride into St. Louis. Police gave chase as he sped west on a freeway at 90 miles an hour until he was stopped at a roadblock. The thrill of the chase inspired him.

He pleaded guilty to a federal charge of driving a stolen car across a state line and was sentenced to three years in a federal juvenile correctional institution. He was released to his father's custody. Parole was no less confining than prison. If his father was strict before he now was harsh.

"He told me I wasn't anything but a punk and that I was no good. I told him he and mom made me that way. He didn't accept that. He just hit me and knocked me down. He hollered at me and kicked me. He always used to tell me about forgiving people, but he didn't forgive his own son."

Jesse eventually believed his rebellion was counter-productive. He decided to try to straighten out his life. He worked as a laborer, a cook, a landscaper and an automobile body mechanic. Hard work was a temporary substitute for hostility, but there was little that held his interest for long. Getting money, lots of it, became more compelling.

What little faith in God remained in Jesse was abandoned. He no longer needed Him. He was his own master with his own standard of conduct, answerable only to himself. Another Jesse Stoneking, the violent one, was born.

A Gangster To The Rescue

Jesse met Carolee, a petite, shy blond his own age, two years after his parole and they married several months later. He finally found someone who would love and care for him and not abandon him as his parents had. They rented a shabby two-room apartment in East St. Louis.

Jesse bought his first car, a 1958 Chevrolet for $1,050 with $100 down from Jake, a used car lot owner and a lower echelon East Side hoodlum. He drove it a few blocks and the engine threw a rod. He was furious. "I couldn't even afford to have it towed away. I jumped on Jake about it, but he just threatened to crack me if I bothered him anymore about it and I didn't pay the car off."

Jake had a generous streak. Or so he pretended. Jesse soon found himself in a game of chicanery disguised as compassion - starve him to break his resistance and then feed him to gain his trust and gratitude. He was to be a puppet with Jake pulling the strings.

Jake needed a handyman and Jesse could work off the $950 he owed on the car. But it wasn't profitable for Jesse. He worked 12 hours a day, six days a week. After the car payment was deducted he took home $25 a week, barely enough to buy groceries.

Jake made Jesse an irresistible offer. He and Carolee could live with him in his house rent-free if she was his housekeeper. Jesse eagerly accepted the proposal, but there was a hidden motive he wouldn't know for years.

Jake also was a pimp and that made Jesse vulnerable because he also was a philanderer. "I had this young girl I was seeing on the side. One day Jake says to me, 'You could make some bucks with her. Let me send her to Centralia. There's a whorehouse there. We'll get her making you four, five hundred a week'. I told him it sounded great. I didn't think of myself as a pimp like Jake was. It was just a chance to make some quick bucks. I wouldn't be doing anything illegal."

She earned Jesse $800 in just two weeks. She described some of the sexual techniques she used. He was offended and beat her. "Being a pimp wasn't for me. Man, I just couldn't handle that. I got out of that real quick."

Jake's next course in crime was thievery. Jesse was neither a reluctant student nor a slow learner. Jake assured him he had a bright future in crime. "He taught me how to go out on scores. It was fast money. I was poor and I was seeing all those high rollers around in Cadillacs with broads and money and I wanted some of it."

Among the high rollers who came to Jake's lot were Art Berne, who took over the East Side Outfit when Frank "Buster" Wortman died in August 1968, and his 300-pound lieutenant, Don Ellington. Jesse was impressed and Ellington took a liking to him. By 1970, Jesse realized he was a pawn in Jake's miniature criminal empire and he walked away.

"I wised up. I was the one going out on the scores and taking all the risks and he was making all the money. He was giving me fifteen percent of what I stole. Big deal! You could go to any fence and get twenty-five percent. I decided that from then on I would be a loner."

Jesse ardently pursued his new endeavors with Ellington his tutor. Jewelry and gems caught his interest. He read books and talked with jewelers and professional thieves. He became a proficient gemologist and it wasn't long before he was known as a hard, but fair bargainer.

Fencing was a matter of expediency, although profit was the principal motivation. He could make as much money selling hot goods with less risk than stealing them. It wasn't long before he was a polished, career criminal and one of the biggest fences on the East Side, gaining him recognition in the underworld. Money was freedom and it became the rationale for everything he did. Over time, he fenced more than $5 million worth of stolen goods, giving him a profit of at least $500,000.

To many, Jesse seemed brooding, even a loser. That was how he wanted to appear and he worked hard to promote it.

Silence was a resource of strength and intimidation, concealing what he was contemplating. While others talked and blew their cool, Jesse observed and analyzed, permitting him to peer into a man's mind and identify his vulnerabilities. Jesse's head, not his heart, dictated his decisions and actions. His mind was trigger-fast, capable of quickly analyzing and reacting to any threatening situation while his adversary debated what to do.

He trained his tongue to be a powerful weapon. He wasn't articulate, but rarely was he ambiguous unless it served a purpose. An opponent could be humiliated and tongue-lashed into submission. Or he could be velvet-tongued and condescending, subtly manipulative if he was working a scam or trying to get inside someone's mind.

He was a student of human nature, a prerequisite for a successful con artist. He quickly recognized human frailties, particularly greed, fear, lust and indecision. When those traits showed up on his radar screen, they alerted his basic criminal instincts and he went to work. He essentially had to be a cobra – strike and get back in hiding before anyone knew what happened.

"To rip a guy off when he thinks you're his friend and doing him a favor without him knowing it takes brains. You don't have a gun to rely on. You only got yourself and your brain."

Jesse's talents and personality weren't unnoticed by Ellington. Nor was Jesse oblivious of Ellington's professionalism and his connections. Each could benefit the other. Ellington introduced him to Berne, short and rotund with a perpetual smile and a gruff voice, who was known in mob circles as the "fat cat" for his profits. The East Side mob boss was inaccessible to young, unconnected street punks, but Jesse now was associated through Ellington.

Berne recognized him as an innovative thief and a good money-maker. He was impressed by his obvious obedience, respect and loyalty, rare qualities in young, upstart hoodlums. He gave him a few jobs, mostly arsons. Jesse never knew the reasons for the torch jobs or who put out the contracts and he didn't ask.

Berne inducted Jesse into his outfit a year later when Ellington sponsored him. "Don says, 'Art, why don't you bring Jesse in'? And Art says, 'As far as I'm concerned, he's in. I just haven't told him yet'. It wasn't like in the Mafia where you have to go through those silly rituals."

Maternal Conflict

One woman, even a wife, wasn't sufficient for Jesse. His testosterone flowed at full speed and he craved love - physical and emo-

22

tional and lots of it - from whomever, whenever and wherever he could find it. Girlfriends and prostitutes helped satisfy his ravenous sensual needs that nurtured his vanity.

As his stature in the underworld increased and his sensuality flourished, his marital life wilted. Arguments with Carolee were frequent and bitter. He was devoting more time to crime than to her. She was possessive about her man and resented taking second place in his life. She occasionally suggested he model himself after Jake, but he laughed. He didn't place any significance in that, but he would years later.

It was during a brief separation he met Dorothy, a cute 17-year-old who aroused his eroticism. He immediately fell in love with her and nominated her his consort. He didn't know one-night stands, a few hours of pleasure with a young woman, would result in a commitment and strife for decades.

Dorothy told him two months later she was pregnant. She demanded a wedding ring and marriage vows. A Christian who attended church regularly, she wasn't about to have a child out of wedlock. But bigamy wasn't on Jesse's long list of acceptable crimes. There was no financial profit. He finally admitted he was married. She accepted it conditionally, demanding he give her and their child family status equal to his wife. There was no room for negotiation.

Jesse also hadn't disclosed his true occupation to her. He told her he was an automobile mechanic, but his growing mob reputation soon blew that cover. "She asked me if I was in the Mafia. I asked her where she heard that. She said someone told her. Then she says, 'I hear when you guys get in the Mafia you can never get out'. I told her to mind her own damned business. No way was I in the Mafia. I wasn't lying about that, but I finally told her the truth. She didn't get too mad."

Jesse could handle Dorothy's pregnancy, but then Carolee announced she, too, was expecting. The logistics of maintaining two families without each knowing of the other bewildered him at first. But he was a man of honor and he would take care of both. Obligations were obligations.

Jesse rented a house for Dorothy, bought new furniture and paid all of her expenses. Supporting two families was no small burden. He had to hustle more and walk a thinner line. Justifying his absence from Carolee to spend time with Dorothy required more shrewdness. One mistake, one clue to his infidelity would bring a firestorm from Carolee.

Carolee's baby was due two weeks before Dorothy's and Jesse foresaw no complications. Time was on his side. But on the night of August 11, 1973, the heavy hand of fate struck.

He called Carolee about 10 p. m. and she was feeling fine. No problem there. He went to see Dorothy. She was in labor and he took her to the hospital. They were greeted in the obstetrics ward by a matronly, heavyset nurse whose disgust at their lack of marital status was obvious.

Dorothy wouldn't deliver until tomorrow. Jesse returned home. Carolee was waiting for him, her suitcase by the door. She also was having labor pains. His impending doom now was obvious. He was about to be caught in the crossfire of two opposing armies with him the common enemy.

A wheelchair was at the entrance to the hospital's obstetrics ward and he pushed Carolee toward the admitting desk. The same nurse who helped Dorothy came out of a doorway. He almost ran into her with the wheelchair.

"Who's this?" the nurse asked angrily.

"My wife," Jesse replied cautiously.

"What's she doing here?"

Jesse was annoyed. "What's it look like? She having a baby."

"Her, too?" the nurse asked, incredulously.

Carolee looked up at him, confused. "What's she mean, Jesse?" He was at a loss for words. Carolee turned to the nurse. "What did you mean, 'Her, too'?"

Jesse glared at the nurse. "Well, I guess I got him confused with someone else," the nurse finally said. She turned to him. "Mr. Stoneking, you're going to have to talk to the administrator about this," she whispered. "This is going to be a problem."

Carolee overheard her and was even more confused. "What's wrong, Jesse? What's she talking about?"

"Something about the hospital bill," he assured her. "I'll take care of it in the morning."

The nurse wheeled Carolee into a room and closed the door. When the nurse returned he tried to explain to her. She interrupted him, the look in her eyes wilting. "Young man, I'm not going to tell her anything. But I want to tell you something. You better get your life straightened out. You should be ashamed. Don't you have any respect?"

There was nothing Jesse could say. She told him Carolee also wouldn't deliver for some time. He went home, confident that by noon the next day when he returned at least one of the expectant mothers would have had her baby.

But neither Dorothy nor Carolee gave birth by late morning. The nurses were different, but they knew about Jesse. "They couldn't wait to get a look at this Stoneking guy, the big stud. They started giggling. One nurse said, 'It's him. Here he comes'. Another nurse said, 'It's a shame. I hope he gets what he's got coming'."

Three rooms separated the two women. Jesse visited each briefly and then left. It was too traumatic, too dangerous, for him to linger. He told both women he would keep in touch with the hospital.

Dorothy delivered her baby boy early that afternoon. An hour later, Carolee gave birth to her baby, also a son. Jesse visited each mother twice that day. It was the least he could do, but it required all the agility of body and mind he could muster not to create a war zone.

"I'd just go see Dorothy, then run over to the other room to see Carolee. Sneak here, sneak there. The nurses kept telling them to walk a little. Dorothy would want to take a walk in the hallway and I'd say I was too tired. Carolee would say, 'Don't you want to take a walk and see your son'? I'd tell her I already saw him once today. He won't change that much in an hour. There was no way I was going to go out in that hallway with either one of those broads."

Taking them home was another major problem. Jesse told Dorothy he would be out of town and had arranged for a cab to pick her up exactly at 11 a. m. He would take Carolee home at noon. But fate administered the coup de grace about 8 a. m. Nurses told him what happened.

Both women walked out of their rooms about the same time and went to the nursery. They sat next to each other while feeding their babies. They talked and Dorothy said her husband was Jesse Stoneking. Carolee flipped out. She said her husband was Jesse Stoneking.

" Can't be. You're crazy," Dorothy shouted. "He's my husband. This is his son."

They looked at the bracelet on each baby's arm. The last names were the same. They hollered at each other. Then their rage turned to Jesse, each cursing him.

"Well, I got one hell of a battle going with both of them when they got home. Dorothy's more hurt than anything and Carolee, she's just plain ticked off. I had to tell Carolee the truth. I said it was her fault. If she hadn't separated from me that time I wouldn't have been so lonely and I wouldn't have had to turn to another woman. I told Dorothy there was no way I'd leave my other family, but I would take care of her. I finally got it all settled."

Jesse accepted his dual obligations. Both families would want for nothing in the way of food, clothes, entertainment and toys. What his children would lack was knowledge of the Lord. They didn't need to know about that, he explained.

After he told me about the dual births, I asked him, not accusingly, how he reconciled back then living in a state of adultery. He didn't have a choice, he said. The situation warranted it. What else could he have done? I didn't pursue it further.

CHAPTER THREE

Both Sides Of The Law

J esse was ready to kill. Not one man, but two. He wouldn't be committing a crime. It would be an honorable, legally justified response to the criminal offense he was witnessing.

He was standing guard on a boxcar in the sprawling rail yards late at night when a van pulled up. Two men got out and pried open the door of the freight car with a crowbar. They began unloading cases of cigarettes.

They were breaking the law, but that wasn't what infuriated Jesse. They were encroaching on his exclusive turf - his principality - and that was an offense punishable by death. That score belonged to him and Don Ellington, who was on his way.

They surely were armed and killing them would be lawful. He had carte blanche as a police officer to defend himself when threatened by criminals. That would be how he would exonerate himself in his report. They had tried to shoot him. If they were unarmed, he had a throw-away gun he would say they aimed at him.

Jesse slowly drove the squad car with its headlights out closer to the thieves, staying in the shadows of the boxcars. He still was partially concealed, but he wasn't close enough to shoot them. Another 50 feet and they would be within range. He took his .45 semi-automatic service revolver from its holster and put it on the seat within reach.

Then he realized he couldn't kill them unless they actually posed a threat. He would have to cancel the score and it was too valuable to do that. It would bring too much attention to him, cause too many questions to be asked. He would have to call for assistance immediately and the revolver would be confiscated for examination. He couldn't just leave bodies cluttering the rail yard.

It was time to do his duty and enforce the law, this time for his own benefit. He switched on the flashing lights and was on them in seconds.

Their arrest was negotiable. "Listen, officer, there's enough for all of us," one of the men said politely. "We'll cut you in for half. That's fair enough. Right?"

They couldn't bargain with him. He rammed the revolver's barrel in the man's chest. "You think I'm a crook?" he snickered. He beat the man's head with the side of the pistol. Blood gushed from the wounds and he slumped to the ground nearly unconscious. Beating a man who tried to bribe an officer was excusable. That would be in his report along with his statement the man tried to attack him.

"You shouldn't resist a police officer," Jesse growled. "That's against the law. So is trying to bribe a cop."

He handcuffed them, took them to the station and booked them on a federal charge of stealing from an interstate shipment. Justice was served. He would write his report later. He had more important, profitable business first.

Jesse returned to the rail yards and stood guard while Ellington and a friend loaded the remaining cases of cigarettes into a panel truck. They left those the thieves had taken in their van. His report would say he caught the subjects as they made their final trip and were cleaning out the boxcar.

Jesse would collect three times – his wages as a police officer, his share of the score and a reward from the railroad company for interrupting a theft. It was a profitable night.

It wasn't a sense of civic duty or a dedication to law and order that induced Jesse to become a police officer in 1973 at a monthly salary of $375. It was a permit for Ellington and him to steal. Besides, how else could a hoodlum legally carry a gun? In just three months they stole $2 million worth of merchandise.

National City was a collection of inexpensive residences, warehouses and the stockyards across the Mississippi River from St. Louis' north side. It was between the northern city limits of East St. Louis and Brooklyn, an oasis of sin for years in the metropolitan area. The sprawling East Side rail yards with their valuable cargoes in the boxcars were what attracted Jesse.

He had told a police sergeant he knew he went straight after his youthful skirmishes with the law. The officer covered up his arrest record. Three days later, wearing an ill-fitting uniform, a tarnished badge and the revolver, Jesse swore to uphold the laws of Illinois and of the municipality. He was committed to protecting lives of innocent citizens, but not the railroad property.

Jesse volunteered for the late night watch, claiming it was an expression of his gratitude for the job. His real motivation was the early morning hours were the best time to steal. His scheme was sophisticated in its simplicity with railroad detectives his unknowing accomplices.

"They would tell me that there was a certain boxcar out in the yards that had to be watched because there was something valuable in it and it would be there for only a couple of hours, or maybe just that night. They'd ask me if I'd guard it. Sure, I'd be glad to. I'd get hold of Don and we were on our way. I was the lookout in my police car. I could listen to the railroad detectives on their radios and I knew where they were all the time.

"Don would take the seals off and a couple of his guys would unload the car. Then, he'd put the seals back in place and solder them to the doors so no one would know they had been opened. The railroad detectives wouldn't inspect them because they would look like they hadn't been touched."

The empty boxcars wouldn't be discovered until they were at their destination, perhaps a thousand miles away. Where the theft occurred would be unknown. Jesse's activity report would state he observed nothing unusual the night of the theft.

Judge And Jury

It was an attempt to enforce his personal laws that ended Jesse's career as a police officer and his lucrative source of income. The department received a tip a man was dealing narcotics to youngsters. Those dope dealers were the lowest form of life, a catalyst for Jesse's rage. He volunteered to investigate.

Investigation to Jesse wasn't a time consuming, complex effort gathering prosecutorial evidence and building a case. He was the cop, prosecutor, judge, jury and executioner. The chain of evidence began and ended with him. Lean on the guy and run him out of town. Even execute him, if necessary. Why bother trying to catch him dirty? Case closed. Expediency in justice.

Jesse briefly watched the suspect and then arrested him. "He had a bad personality problem. He just wouldn't cooperate. He stared at me and then he started hollering things at me. I kept telling him I didn't want to hurt him and to shut up, but he didn't."

The man wasn't respectful. "I don't like you and what are you gonna do about it?" he hollered at Jesse.

"Well, I'll tell you what I'm gonna do. I'll just beat your (expletive) head in."

The man laughed. "You ain't tough enough."

That did it. Jesse beat him severely about the head until he was nearly unconscious.

"What kind of policeman are you?" the man yelled.

"Well, I'm the kind of cop that hates dopers, especially ones who sell to kids. You're lucky if you leave here alive."

The suspect, whose name Jesse never knew, asked to make a long distance telephone call to Washington, D. C. Jesse laughed. "Who you going to call? The president?"

Jesse listened to the man's call. It was to a federal narcotics agent. The man wasn't a dope dealer. He was an undercover agent infiltrating a dope ring.

"I felt kind of bad. He was just doing his job, but so was I. His people from St. Louis came to get him. The head guy asked me what happened. I said, 'You guys should have politer agents. They ain't got respect for police officers'. I just went home. I got fired the next day. I knew it was coming, but I didn't deserve it."

A Refined Hood

Jesse gradually refined his lifestyle, developing underworld class few hoods displayed - stylish clothes, flashy adornments and his attitudes and demeanor. His temper had been incendiary, but now he managed to control it. That distinguished him from hoods who showed their wrath to prove their manhood and invincibility.

Berne took notice and was impressed. He made him his driver and bodyguard, a responsibility granted few others so new in the outfit. Jesse now was a man of honor, a wise guy who walked with the elite, secret fraternity of men both feared and held in awe. It had been a foregone conclusion he would advance rapidly. He was that kind of guy.

There was another reason consecration by the mob was important for Jesse. It was a substitute family and Berne was a pseudo father who gave him the recognition and respect he never got at home. He now had the identity he craved so much. Organized crime replaced Christianity as his faith.

Jesse didn't consider himself responsible for what he became. His parents were. "I still hadn't forgotten what my mom and dad did to me when I was a kid. They kicked me out. I couldn't ever get that out of my mind."

A Friend In Deed

Jesse had second thoughts about being a loner. He needed a close friend, someone beside Ellington he could trust and in whom he could confide. He found that in Mark Stram, nine years younger and just out of the Army. He aspired to be a big-time crook and Jesse could be his tutor.

They soon became partners. "I'd send him and his buddy out on a lot of scores, showed them how to do them, kind of like Jake did with me. He proved he had a lot of guts and developed into a first-class thief. And he was loyal, too. That's really what I liked about him."

Common sense, anticipation and intuition were necessary to success and, more importantly, to survival, Jesse instructed him. Take unnecessary risks and the odds of getting caught - and killed - increased. Expect the worst to happen on a score and then plan for it. Consider every contingency and leave nothing to chance. Obey that unexplained feeling that something is wrong.

Get to know as much as possible about the victim, he advised. A proud man can be impulsive and dangerous. A braggart is a fool. Tell one person about a score and the entire world will know it. "The joint is full of guys who talked their way inside" was his favorite admonition.

Jesse became his angel. One Friday night, Stram and a friend were arrested for a house burglary. The loot was found in their car. The following Monday was Labor Day and they would have to spend at least three days in jail before a preliminary hearing when bond was set.

Jesse by then had political clout. He gained some of it just by being a member of Berne's outfit, but he acquired much of it by doing favors for people, especially lawyers who had a lot to offer in return. Quality jewelry, even though stolen, at bargain prices could return huge dividends beyond cash.

Jesse called a lawyer known as "the fixer" who had bought hot jewelry from him. He was a close friend of a Circuit Court judge who scheduled the bond hearing for the next day. The judge ordered Stram and his friend released on $1,000 cash bond each, an unusually low amount. Jesse posted the bonds. Outside the courthouse, he gave the lawyer another $500, which he assumed would go to the judge.

The trial was scheduled for October. The judge called the case, but the arresting officers were absent. Someone conveniently had forgotten to notify them. The case was promptly dismissed. It cost Jesse another $1,500, money well spent. He had bought Stram's loyalty. It was what he had to do as his boss.

CHAPTER FOUR

First Kill - A Rite Of Passage

A standing ovation and handshakes greeted the popular, fiery Pat Hickey that night in January 1976 as he finished addressing the crowd of Pipefitters' Local 562 members and walked down the center aisle of the auditorium.

His life was promising, just as he wanted for the union members. But that wasn't what the mob sought. It wanted him dead in the next few minutes. And it would be Jesse's first kill, his long-awaited rite of passage in the underworld, his ordination as a full-fledged hoodlum.

As Hickey walked through the doorway to the parking lot outside, Jesse and Ellington got up from the rear row and followed him. Their timing had to be perfect, their departure not suspicious.

Hickey started his car as they got to their late model, dark blue Chevrolet sedan with a stolen Illinois license plate. Ellington handed the keys to Jesse. He was about to "make his bones," but he'd rather be the triggerman than the wheel man. It wasn't Ellington's first hit and it was his decision. He had planned it.

Hickey's car approached the gate and he waved at the armed guard. He turned into the street as Jesse backed out of the parking space.

Ellington shifted in his seat. "Art says we can't let Hickey get on that plane. We gotta crack him." He looked at Jesse and grinned. "This is your first one. You think you can handle it?"

"What do you think?" Jesse said confidently.

Ellington slapped him on the shoulder in a gesture of good will. "Art wouldn't have brought you in on it if he didn't think so."

It was what Jesse wanted to hear. He had to seal his allegiance to Berne and the outfit with this piece of work. Not with words soon forgotten, but with blood etched into the memory. Hickey's blood.

Hickey's car was about 100 yards ahead in the outside lane. Traffic was light and Jesse quickly closed the distance. Ellington reached under the driver's seat for an untraceable .38 Smith and Wesson. A friend who worked at a steel mill would dispose of it, he assured Jesse.

He chuckled. "It'll be part of a steel girder somewhere. We'll take him when he gets to the main road. He'll have to stop or slow down there before he turns right. Get alongside him like you're making a left turn. I need a clear shot. It'll be easy."

Jesse pulled closer to Hickey. Ellington turned off the interior lights and then rolled down his window. The frigid air slapped Jesse's skin and he realized he was perspiring. The adrenaline raced through his body. It was a pleasant rush. He had wondered if there would be euphoria or fear as he helped end a life. Now he knew.

"I have to stay cool," Jesse thought. "Just like Don. I wondered about Hickey. Did he have any kids? Any grandchildren? Not that it mattered. The outfit always has a reason. You just do what you have to do. Do it and get it over with."

Ellington steeled himself for the kill. "Now!" he shouted.

Hickey slowed for the intersection and the cross-traffic. Jesse pulled closer. The front of their car now was at the rear bumper of Hickey's. He could see Hickey's silhouette behind the wheel.

He eased the car forward until it was even with Hickey's. He glanced to the right. Hickey, now five feet away, was clearly illuminated by the street lights. He was unaware of death alongside him.

Ellington cocked the pistol and raised it. He swung it to the right.

"Aw, hell, get out of here, Jesse!" he screamed.

"Huh?" Jesse asked, surprised.

"Just get the hell out of here. It's a bad scene," Ellington said.

"What the hell was wrong?" Jesse asked. So close and they let him escape.

"He saw me!"

"So what? You were gonna crack him anyhow."

"So what? What if I had missed him or only wounded him? We'd have one hell of a beef going," Ellington said angrily.

Jesse didn't believe him. He drove in silence back across the Mississippi River. Ellington panicked at the last, crucial instant and chickened out. That didn't make sense. He was a hitter, a professional. Pulling off a kill together would have sealed their commitment to each other. But how could Jesse put his trust with such a coward?

He wondered how Berne would react. They had to answer to him. There was little doubt of the boss' impending fury.

Phantom On The Payroll

Hickey's insurgency made him Berne's enemy. A popular state representative and influential Democratic Party figure, he was president of Local 562 with headquarters in north St. Louis County. He refused to knuckle under to Berne, who with the approval of the Chicago Syndicate put a stranglehold on the union. Hickey made waves and Berne wanted to make money. That put them on a collision course.

Hickey was popular with the membership as a stand-up guy who was dedicated to improving the lot of the working man, not the mob. He could be trusted. He even was elected president over Berne's hand-picked candidate.

Berne feared his fiefdom was being jeopardized by the anarchist. Using his own influence, he was hired as the union's security consultant. Security was what the mob boss made it – his own protection and welfare.

Berne was paid $500 a week – a quarter of a million dollars over the previous 10 years – and was given a credit card and gasoline for his car. He was a phantom on the union's payroll. He did no work and only showed up at the union office to collect his paycheck and sign papers.

"That job's strictly under the table, ain't it?" Jesse once asked Berne. "Just a title and a paycheck?"

"That's right," Berne responded.

He said his secretary covered for him by preparing records showing he had performed numerous duties when he had not.

"I sign the papers, but I don't know what she's giving me," Berne explained.

Berne was convinced Hickey was a government snitch and why he was going to Washington, D. C., the night of the scheduled hit. Berne couldn't allow that. He feared Hickey was igniting a grassfire that would become a conflagration he couldn't extinguish and would consume him.

Jesse hadn't seen Hickey and shortly before the hit Berne pointed him out. "Art told me, 'There's that lousy no good (expletive). He's gotta go'. I knew what he meant. He didn't have to tell me. I'd see Hickey once more. When I killed him."

Jesse and Ellington reported to Berne the next day. He, too, questioned Ellington's explanation, his anger obvious in his eyes. Later, he told Jesse: "I should have sent you alone in the first place instead of that jerk Don." He would let Hickey's execution rest for awhile in case he actually had seen Ellington.

A Questionable Friendship

After the Hickey hit went bad, Jesse's close relationship with Ellington became tenuous. Murder was serious business and Jesse wouldn't have tried to hit Hickey that way.

"I wouldn't have been rushed into it by Art. I would have told him, 'Hey Art, I'm the one doing it and it's got to be my way'. I would have watched Hickey for awhile, see where he went and what he did. Then at the right place and time I'd whack him. No way would I have gone into that meeting. That'll get the cops looking right at you. If I was Art, I'd have Don cracked even if I had to pull the trigger myself. Don was a coward, all talk. No guts."

Murder was for free in Berne's outfit, an obligation his minions accepted. The Hickey hit would have been for retaliation and to protect the boss, something that had to be done.

Berne said nothing more about Hickey. Jesse assumed he somehow had worked it out. He got to know Hickey casually over the next several years. He called him the "walking dead man." When

I interviewed Hickey 10 years later he said he had no idea how close death came to him, but he wasn't surprised.

Making his first kill and earning his rite of passage remained an aphrodisiac, a compelling motivation for Jesse. It was a commitment to himself he was anxious to fulfill. One day he would have another opportunity to experience the awesome power of taking a life. In the underworld, assigning a hit is the ultimate trust by the general and accomplishing it a symbol of respect by the soldier.

"They don't just tell anybody to hit someone. It doesn't work that way. They got to know you and you got to be one of them. You really don't have a choice when they tell you to crack that guy. If you don't, they'll come after you. They'll think you were weak and weren't man enough to be in the outfit."

Jesse cared little who died by his gun. His attitude about taking lives was a reason he became known in the underworld as the Stone killer. "I really didn't want to know him except to kill him. There's something bad about knowing the guy you're going to clip. But there has to be a good reason for hitting somebody. The outfit doesn't crack somebody for no reason at all. Yeah, that's the way you become a man. By cracking people."

I was stunned initially as he described the hit on Hickey and his cavalier attitude about murder. I had no doubt he was truthful. He surely wouldn't fabricate something like that. That raised a more ominous question. How many murders had he actually committed? I suspected there were others. His nickname suggested that, but I assumed he wouldn't discuss them. The statute of limitations might have expired on attempted murder, but it never did on actual homicide.

Rise To Power

The secondary level of leadership in Berne's outfit was in disarray. Several hoods were facing prison sentences. Ellington fell into disfavor with Berne over the Hickey fiasco. Berne summoned Jesse to a bowling alley in Fairview Heights, Illinois, where he hung out.

He shook Jesse's hand and grinned. "You're my new right-hand man, Jesse."

Jesse was elated. "I appreciate that, Art."

"Chicago approved it, you know. You just keep on with what you got going. That's your business. But you're the guy I'm gonna depend on. You'll be my personal representative. Just be there when I need you."

Jesse had arrived. At the tender age of 31, he now was one of the few elite, a man of honor. He would bask in the prestige and power that came with being Berne's underboss. That gave him protection. He now had access to the ultimate seat of power, speaking and acting with the Chicago Syndicate's authority. He was its number two man ruling southern Illinois.

Berne gave Jesse the recognition he craved and denied him by his parents. "I still hadn't forgotten what my mom and dad did to me when I was a kid. I couldn't get it out of my mind. I guess Art's outfit was like a family to me and he was my father. He was my God, too. Not the one that let me down."

Jesse vowed never to disappoint Berne or betray him. He would repay him many times over. His loyalty didn't deter him from coveting Berne's leadership position in the underworld. He was growing old and had health problems. He would die or step down before long and Jesse would be his logical successor to the ultimate throne of power.

Berne publicly confirmed Jesse's position. They were at a wedding reception in St. Louis. Most of the elite of the St. Louis' area's three organized crime factions were there. It was Jesse's debut into underworld high society.

"Art introduced me to all of them. He said, 'I want you to meet my new right-hand man. I want it understood that if anything happens to me, he'll take over on the East Side'. They were glad to hear that. They made me feel real welcome."

Jesse later grew close to Anthony "Tony G" Giordano, the Mafia don, and became his servant with Berne's approval. He often escorted him and ran errands for him.

Giordano's influence was extensive. He had blood ties to the Joe Zerilli Family in Detroit and controlled the Smaldone Family in Denver, some said with the blessing of the "Commission" in New York. Nick Civella, boss of Kansas City La Cosa Nostra, had a close working relationship with him as did the upper echelon of the Chicago Outfit.

Early in his crime career, Giordano was part of a ring smuggling heroin from Italy to St. Louis and Detroit, then distributed throughout America. He knew Charles "Lucky" Luciano, who presided over the operation. Giordano was arrested more than 50 times over 40 years on charges ranging from carrying concealed weapons and robbery to income tax evasion and counterfeiting tax stamps. He was sentenced to prison in 1974 for conspiring to acquire hidden ownership of a Las Vegas casino.

The relationship Jesse developed with Giordano was propitious for the upstart hood's career. The underworld was quick to take notice. Anyone the don allowed that close to him had to be someone special.

Through Giordano, Jesse also came close to John Vitale, then the influential Mafia consigliere. Early in the 1940s, Vitale was arrested after authorities found a large amount of heroin in a tavern he owned in downtown St. Louis. Federal agents said Vitale and his associates bought pure heroin for $250 an ounce, diluted it and sold it for $2,500.

CHAPTER FIVE

The Big Heist

D eath was closing in on the Missouri Highway Patrol officer. Jesse had to kill him to protect himself and the $2 million in stolen gems and jewelry he was transporting.

It was a few minutes before 9 o'clock on a Saturday night in January 1978 and Jesse was anxious to get away from Republic, a small town in southwestern Missouri. He and Stram had been there only a short time and their presence had to remain unknown. He had just helped pull off the biggest score of his career.

The rural, two-lane highway outside of town seemed safe enough. Few police officers would be patrolling the area. Jesse stayed within the speed limit and was vigilant. His eyes alternated between the rear view mirror and the road ahead as they always did when fleeing a score. He had to be aware of approaching danger.

A pair of headlights suddenly appeared in the mirror. They were on bright and the car seemed to be traveling faster than the speed limit. Probably teen-agers drag racing, Jesse assumed. Red and blue lights began flashing. A siren pierced the silent night. It was a police car!

Jesse knew trying to outrun the squad car would be futile. He was in unfamiliar territory and wouldn't know where to go. He slowed and pulled to the side of the road. The cop obviously was chasing him. The victims of the robbery apparently had freed themselves quicker than expected. By recovering the fortune and arresting Jesse and Stram, the cop would be a hero in a small town. He might get promoted or receive a reward.

"We got problems, Mark," Jesse said anxiously. "Something went wrong. The cops found out about us somehow. You guys cut the phone wires, didn't you? " Mark assured him they had. "We gotta do what we gotta do, Mark. Don't worry, buddy. I'll take him down. We'll be okay."

Jesse grabbed the semi-automatic pistol from his belt and chambered a round. He rolled down the window. He rested his right hand with the pistol on his lap, his left hand on the steering wheel. His finger tensed on the trigger, his mind concentrating on killing.

The officer probably would approach with his pistol in one hand and a flashlight in the other. He would order Jesse and Stram to raise their hands to their heads and get out of the car. Depending on where and how the officer stood, Jesse would fire as he raised his right hand or he would throw open the door to knock him off balance and then kill him.

The officer probably had radioed for assistance. Other cops would be arriving and be on the prowl over a wide area. How the officer got the make of the car and its license plate number didn't matter. That he did was his death warrant. Jesse was ready to kill.

The headlights blinked to dim and the siren went silent as the squad car swung to the other lane and sped by. It was a Missouri Highway Patrol car. Jesse breathed deeply. They were safe. He didn't have to kill a police officer.

But another threat no less deadly awaited Jesse. He wasn't aware who actually owned the jewelry they stole and that hits soon would be put out on the thieves.

Sultan Of Sin

Bob Neal Carson, an unlikely gangster, called Jesse a few days earlier. He appeared to be a good old boy, the country cousin whose infectious, impish grin charmed – and disarmed – friend and foe alike. Gangly with unruly hair and a typical Ozark drawl, he seemed nothing more than the used car dealer and motel owner he was on the surface.

But he was a ruthless racketeer, once the sultan of sin in the rural, central Missouri Ozarks. The town of Saint Robert and the surrounding area about 125 miles southwest of St. Louis near the Army's Fort Leonard Wood were the Sodom and Gomorrah of the Midwest.

It had been the largest red light district in the Midwest, if not the country. Numerous bawdy houses, gambling dens, drug trafficking and official corruption flourished. More than 400 prostitutes worked the houses and the streets. Violence inspired by competing gangs resided on the streets. Carson was said to receive $12,000 a month from one house of prostitution.

Carson ran a hapless collection of wannabe hit men, enforcers and pimps who were the laughing stock of the Missouri under-world. They were their own worst enemy, the gang that couldn't shoot straight. Carson was the kingpin until the federal government, aroused by the violence and my investigative stories, closed it down in the early 1970s as Berne's outfit was preparing to make its entree.

Carson, aware of Jesse's reputation as an adept thief and strong-arm guy, had a score worth a fortune. Jesse and Stram met with him near Saint Robert the next day. A jewelry wholesaler had set up shop temporarily in a vacant store in Lebanon, a small town about 40 miles away. He had at least a million dollars worth of jewelry and gems for sale.

"I mean, fellows, this guy's begging for us to come and take it," Carson said. But they had to move quickly. It was Tuesday and the sale ended on Saturday.

Jesse cased the store. The merchandise was worth much far more than $1 million. The salesman was to move the jewelry from the store after the close of business at 5 p. m Saturday. He gave Jesse his business card with his name and an address and telephone number in Lebanon.

"This guy's got a ring with a big diamond and little ones on his finger," Jesse told Carson. "We got to get that one. It'll be worth at least twenty grand."

Carson wanted to take him down the next day, arguing the longer they waited the more jewelry would be sold. Jesse insisted they needed to do more research and thoroughly plan a heist that big.

He and Stram returned to the East Side and bought a used car, paying for it with cash and registering it in a fictitious name at a non-existent address. Carson did the same. The "crow cars" would be used in their surveillance of the jeweler and in the robbery. Carson now had a partner, a young man named Hans.

The wholesaler's routine didn't vary the next two days. He closed the store at 9 p. m. and drove his black Lincoln to a house at the edge of town, which Jesse assumed was his home. The house number was the same as on the business card.

They would hit the jeweler on Saturday night in the sanctity of his home. It would be less risky than taking him down in the store. Stram and Hans would go in while Jesse and Carson were the back-ups.

There were only two police cars in town. Shortly before 5 p.m. Hans slashed the left tires of police chief's cruiser parked in front of his house. The other police car was in front of City Hall. Hans also punctured two of its tires.

At 5:15 p. m., the wholesaler began carrying boxes of the merchandise from the store to his Lincoln. Jesse and Stram watched him in the waning light from one end of the block. Carson and Hans were at the other end. There was no way he could escape the trap they set for him. It was near zero and they had to endure the bitter cold. Idling engines gave off gray exhaust that would draw attention to them and they shut them off.

After the salesman loaded the car, he drove off toward the house a few minutes away. Jesse trailed half a block behind and Carson followed. The Lincoln turned into the subdivision and the two tail cars drove by.

Jesse went to an outside telephone booth at a convenience store a few blocks away. He had to gain the salesman's confidence so they could get the drop on him in the house with the least risk of violence. They assumed he would be armed because of the value of his merchandise.

Jesse dialed the telephone number and a woman answered. "Could I please speak to the gentleman who's running the jewelry sale?" he asked politely.

"Oh, that's my father. Just a minute."

"Yes sir, how are you this evening?" the salesman asked

"Just fine."

"What can I do for you?"

"I don't know if you remember me or not. I was in your store a couple of days ago. I'd like to buy the ring I looked at."

"Did you give me your name?"

Jesse had given him a false name. "Yes I did. George Andrews."

There was a moment of silence on the other end. "Oh, yeah, I remember you. A nice, polite guy. Which of the rings are you interested in?"

"The white gold one with the five diamonds in it."

"Sure, I remember that one. A real beauty."

Jesse relaxed. "How much did you say you wanted for it?"

The wholesaler thought for a moment. "A thousand."

Jesse didn't want to appear too eager. "Would you take nine hundred?"

The jeweler thought. "Well, okay, it's worth more but nine hundred it is."

Jesse was halfway there. "When can I pick up the ring?"

"Can you bring the money here? I'll leave the ring with my daughter."

Jesse was confused. This was unexpected. "Where's she live at?"

The jeweler chuckled. "Where you're calling to. The address I gave you."

"Oh, yeah. Do you have the ring with you?"

The wholesaler said he did. Jesse would be there shortly.

"Whenever you want to pick it up is okay," the man offered. "My daughter will be here all night. I'm leaving right now to go home."

Jesse was alarmed. "Home? I thought you lived there."

"Oh, no, I live in Republic. I'm just staying with my daughter during the sale. I was using her store."

"Well, you tell her I'll pick it up in an hour or so." He hadn't foreseen this. He should have gotten the Lincoln's license plate registration from a friend in law enforcement.

He and Carson agreed to follow him. They could force his car off the road and take it with the jewelry inside. That would be dangerous and they would lose the crucial element of surprise. A shootout might result. Jesse wanted that only as a last resort. It would be best to do it in his home. They were unfamiliar with Republic and they would be pulling it off blind.

Republic, a small town, was about 12 miles southwest of Springfield, a city on Interstate 44. They had walkie-talkies for an emergency, but hadn't used them during the surveillance for fear of being monitored. They needed to be in constant communication with each other while in strange territory at night.

Carson drove in front of the jeweler when on the interstate. Jesse stayed a discreet distance behind. He moved closer when they neared an exit in case the jeweler left the interstate. Because they didn't know where he lived, it was essential they not lose him.

The Battle Plan

It was almost 7 o'clock when they got to Republic. The jeweler drove to a ranch house and parked in the attached garage. Jesse quickly surveyed the house. He and Carson went a few miles into the countryside, where Jesse would brief them.

Jesse was a general preparing his troops for a decisive battle. Stram and Hans would force their way inside the house, he said. They were to steal the Lincoln if the jewelry still was inside, as he assumed it would be. As always, timing and precision were crucial. They must be in and out in five minutes or less. Each minute beyond elevated the risk of being caught in a violent confrontation. Concentrate on getting the jewelry and don't be distracted, he told them.

Their demeanor – coldly professional and confident – would be as menacing as their guns. They must be threatening, but not using violence unless it was necessary. He and whoever else was in the house had to be intimidated, making them more compliant and less likely to resist. They were not to speak. Voices were identifiable. Silence could be threatening.

The tutoring was more for Hans' benefit. He was an unknown factor. Jesse only had Carson's word and that wasn't good enough for this score.

A church was across the street and down a short distance from the house. Services were underway and many cars were on the lot. Carson parked in a dark corner with a clear view of the house.

Hans and Stram paused at the front porch. Each pulled a wool ski cap from his pocket and slipped it over his face. Hans drew his pistol as Stram punched the doorbell and then pulled out his revolver.

As the doorknob turned Stram hunched his shoulders and threw his weight against the door. A young girl, no more than 14, screamed and reeled backward. Stram shoved her onto a couch in the living room.

The salesman was talking on the telephone in the kitchen. Stram was on him before he could react, jabbing the pistol against his right temple. He replaced the receiver in the cradle and cut the cord. He patted down the salesman, but there was no weapon.

Hans found the other telephone in a bedroom and cut its cord. The keys to the Lincoln were on a kitchen counter and he went to the garage. The jewelry still was in the car. He returned and nodded to Stram.

The salesman gasped as Stram twisted his right wrist sharply until it went limp. The ring Jesse described was on the index finger of the right hand. Stram yanked on it. The jeweler curled the finger and it wouldn't come off. He tried again. It stayed in place.

Stram pointed his gun at the man's face and then at the ring, indicating he should remove it. The salesman shook his head. Hans flipped open a switchblade knife, gesturing at the finger. Stram grabbed the ring again and twisted it violently. The man shrieked in pain. The finger cracked as it broke. The ring came loose and Stram dropped it into his pocket.

The salesman's wife came up from the basement. She stifled a scream. Stram motioned with his gun to the living room. He herded them both inside where the young girl sat petrified.

"What do you want?" the salesman asked. Stram said nothing. "The money is in my pocket. Just don't do anything to us. We're just ..." He stopped appealing when Stram put the pistol to his head.

Hans motioned for all three to lie on the floor as Stram took lengths of rope and a roll of duct tape from his coat pocket. He quickly bound their wrists behind them and their legs. Then he sealed their mouths. They would be able to free themselves, but by then they would be long gone.

As the girl was being bound, she no longer could contain her fear. She screamed and then sobbed. Stram saw the anger in Hans' eyes and he shook his head. Hans ignored him and kicked her several times in the head. As he cocked his right fist, Stram grabbed him and put his pistol to his forehead. Hans backed off.

After securing them, Stram searched the man's pockets and found a wad of $10,000 in bills. They were fast coming up on their deadline. Stram and Hans went to the garage. Hans opened the garage door as Stram got behind the wheel. They drove off and Carson pulled in behind.

Stram's and Hans' excitement was spontaneous as they shouted and laughed. They had made the big score. Jesse and Carson were reserved. Much still could go wrong. They would stop worrying six months from now when they hadn't been questioned or arrested. They quickly loaded the boxes and display cases into Jesse's car. The Lincoln was left behind. They were to meet at Carson's motel and divide the loot.

It was after the Highway Patrol car passed them that Stram told Jesse about what Hans did to the girl. Jesse was furious. When they got to Carson's motel, he grabbed Hans by the shoulders and hurled him against the wall. He yanked the automatic from his waistband, rammed the barrel into the center of his chest and cocked it. Stram stopped him from killing him

"You worthless piece of crap!" Jesse snarled.

Hans cringed further against the wall. "What the hell's wrong with you?" he asked, his voice quivering.

"You don't hurt kids!"

"I didn't hurt her," Hans protested weakly.

"What kind of man are you, anyhow? Kicking a young girl when she's down on on the floor."

"Aw, it didn't ..."

Jesse plunged his fist into Hans' stomach. Hans doubled over. Jesse hit him hard in the face with the barrel of the gun. Hans sagged to the floor, nearly unconscious. Blood streamed from the jagged cut on the upper right cheek and the broken nose. Carson watched with amused interest.

"I never want to see him again, Bob. If I do, I'll kill him."

They unpacked the loot. There were hundreds of jewelry items, including antique watches and trays of gems. Some of the diamonds were five carats or more. Jesse knew they probably were worth more than $2 million. They split it as evenly as possible. Jesse sold his share almost for its value of $500,000. He traded one diamond ring for a new Cadillac Eldorado.

The Unknown Victim

Carson called Jesse and told him local newspapers reported the robbery. The salesman said the merchandise was uninsured because he couldn't afford the premiums. But the jewelry and gems were underwritten by a different, unknown guarantor.

Tony Giordano called Jesse a week later and wanted to meet with him. When Jesse saw him he could tell he was upset. "You hear anything about that big jewel heist down near Springfield?" Giordano's voice was accusing.

Jesse was going to tell him about it and give him a half-carat diamond from the loot as a symbol of his gratitude and respect. He grinned and then chuckled. "What do you think? I'm ..."

Giordano interrupted him before he could admit his involvement. "This jeweler got taken off by a couple of guys. Two million in jewels. Maybe more." His stare was wilting. Jesse didn't respond. "Well, that stuff belonged to the family in Kansas City. He was selling it for them."

Jesse was shocked. They had robbed the Mafia! Then he laughed to himself. It was just thieves stealing from thieves. He knew what their response would be and Giordano confirmed it.

"They've put out hits on the guys who pulled it off. Those jerks are dead."

Jesse stayed composed. He almost had signed his own death warrant. "Yeah, I heard about it. Not that the family owned the stuff. Who were the guys?"

"They don't know yet. They will. It won't take long."

"How'd they hear about it?"

"Just the word out on the street. That's all. They said it was a real professional job." He leaned toward Jesse, staring coldly in his eyes.

"The kind you'd pull off. That's what they said. They're looking at you pretty hard."

Jesse was being trapped. Giordano's loyalty first was to the Kansas City family and not to him. He stared back at Giordano. "Thanks for the compliment, Tony. No way was I involved in it." He laughed. "I wish I was in on a score that big."

"I hear you weren't seen around town for a couple of days."

Jesse controlled his panic. He had anticipated this and had an alibi. "I was down in New Orleans. A guy I know down there wanted me to help him pull of a big heist. Only it got screwed up."

"You got proof?"

"You know you don't leave any evidence around when you do a score. I didn't tell anyone about it."

Giordano studied him for a minute, then grinned. "I don't doubt you, Jesse." He stood and patted him on the back. When Jesse stood up, he hugged him in the Mafia tradition. "You're my man, Jesse. No doubt."

Jesse called Carson and told him what Giordano had said. He ordered him to make sure Hans kept his big mouth shut, as he did Stram

Lap Of Luxury

Jesse had few peers when it came to stealing whether by burglary, robbery or swindling. His scores weren't all that audacious and dramatic and he didn't want them to be. That brought too much heat and he didn't want to stand out in the crowd as many hoodlums did. He had to stay off the radar screen.

He preferred working by himself or with only one or two accomplices at most. The more who knew about a score, the less control he had, greater the risk of discovery. And the more people who were involved increased the chances of one becoming a snitch. Tempting rewards often were offered in big scores. Money loosened lips and dissolved loyalty.

The school drop-out made at least $2 million in several years, little of it legally. That allowed him sit in the lap of luxury. He had to be a big earner to support his two families and to satisfy his obsession for opulence. He lacked nothing and he displayed his wealth for all to see, indulging in excesses because the world owed him that.

Gaudy diamond and gold jewelry adorned his fingers and wrists and hung from his neck. One ring he wore had almost four and a half ounces of gold in the mounting and 15 carats of flawless diamonds.

Much of the food he consumed was fit for a king and was eaten in lavish, expensive restaurants patronized by the wealthy and the prestigious, where presence indicated prominence. Dinner tabs for him and friends of $800 to $1,000 and $200 tips were common.

New, expensive cars were a passion with him, status symbols in his world. He bought numerous new Cadillacs, Lincolns and Corvettes a year. "I was a new car fanatic. I'd buy one, sell it, buy another. I'd buy two at a time. I couldn't stop. Sometimes, my house looked like I was a new car dealer."

Jesse had no debts, paying for everything with cash, as he did for the two $100,000 houses he provided for both families. Charge accounts and loans created a paper trail that could lead to his unreported income, luring the Internal Revenue Service and eventually leading to prison.

Cash, lots of it, was of primary importance. There rarely was less than $200,000 in large bills stashed in a strongbox under the kitchen floor of his and Carolee's house. It was his emergency fund. A big time fence and hood needs instant access to funds. His pockets always bulged with a roll of several thousand dollars.

The pursuit of opulence and self-pleasure were blinding obsessions. There was little else worthwhile chasing in life. It was an opiate and once he tasted affluence he became addicted to it, seeking more and better. Would he one day go from prince to pauper? Not in his lifetime. He had erected an insurmountable wall between himself and God to protect his wealth and his vanity.

CHAPTER SIX

Escorting Death

Death was pulling up outside the motel room in Charlotte, North Carolina, and Jesse knew why. It wasn't because of the simple real estate deal that brought him there. It was a big drug deal gone bad and he was caught in the middle of it.

Several vehicles screeched to a halt. Doors opened and slammed shut followed by too many footsteps to count. A woman's voice, heavy with a deep southern drawl, barked commands.

It began six weeks after the jewelry score when Bob Neal Carson asked Jesse to escort Jack Mayhew to Charlotte to help him collect $175,000 on a real estate transaction. He was having trouble being paid and he needed muscle. All Jesse had to do was project his tough, menacing self. If he had to bash a skull, so what? Jesse wasn't in the mob to be loved, only feared and to make money, Carson said.

Jesse would be paid $25,000 to be Mayhew's bodyguard – the easiest and most legal money he ever had earned.

Jesse asked Carson why he didn't escort Mayhew if it was so easy and profitable. He said he didn't need the money so soon after the heist. Besides, he was indebted to Jesse for setting up the robbery. There was a certain honor about him. Like when he leaned on Hans for hurting the young girl.

Carson introduced Jesse to Mayhew, a small aircraft pilot. Scrawny, weighing all of 120 pounds and standing five feet, five inches tall, he wore dark-rimmed glasses and appeared meek as a mouse. He could have been a kindergarten teacher, but Jesse knew appearances can conceal a treacherous man.

Mayhew said the man who owed him the money would cause little trouble. All he needed was someone whose mere presence was threatening to induce the man to pay up and Jesse filled that need.

"You just want me to sit around looking tough, huh?" Jesse chortled.

"That shouldn't be too hard for you to do," Mayhew answered. "If there's any trouble, I don't doubt that you can handle it. I'll just say you're my partner and we want our money or else."

"If he says screw you, then what?"

"We'll just do what we have to. Rough him up or whatever. That won't be necessary."

During the flight to Charlotte, Jesse's intuition disturbed him. Why would Mayhew pay so much money just to collect a debt? Why not just file suit? Something didn't add up. "Here I was getting myself involved in something I didn't know anything about. I didn't even bring my forty-five along. I left my guardian angel behind."

They took a cab from the Charlotte airport to a motel where Mayhew had reserved a room. The man who owed him the money was to meet him there shortly. Jesse's uneasiness worsened when they got there.

"Something's not right here, Mayhew," Jesse said. "This isn't exactly a property deal, is it?" His stare at Mayhew was withering.

Mayhew's face reflected his concern. "No, it isn't exactly a property deal. You know, like land or a building."

"What do you mean, Mayhew?" Jesse asked threateningly.

Mayhew hesitated. "Well, you see, I made a flight for these people and they haven't paid me yet. There was an accident."

"What kind of flight?" Jesse demanded. He had a suspicion.

"It's no big deal. Don't worry about it."

"I worry about anything that involves me," Jesse said testily. "Now, quit jacking me around." He was in Mayhew's face, his voice ominous, his fist clenched in front of him. "You tell me right now what's going on or I'll walk out of here and leave you to yourself."

Jesse touched a raw nerve. An instant look of panic swept across Mayhew's face and clouded his eyes. "You can't do that. They'll ..."

Before Mayhew could finish Jesse grabbed him by the coat lapels. "It's dope, ain't it? You're a (expletive) dope runner!"

Death Comes Knocking

While Mayhew searched for an answer, Jesse heard the vehicles pull up outside. Then, a knock on the door. Mayhew froze in fear. Jesse cautiously opened the door. A shrewish woman in her 50s, wearing glasses and with short graying hair, brusquely pushed her way inside. Three husky men, two with revolvers in their belts, the other with an automatic rifle, followed her. Two other armed men were outside the door.

She glared at Mayhew. He laughed feebly. "Hey, Tish, how are you? You're right on time."

The woman ignored him. She scowled at Jesse. One of the men slowly swung his rifle toward him. "Who's that (expletive)?" she asked angrily, pointing at Jesse.

"A friend of mine from St. Louis, Tish. He's okay." Mayhew's fear was obvious.

"Yeah. How do I know he isn't the heat or a shooter?"

She nodded to one of the men with a pistol. He went to Jesse, patted him down, and then Mayhew, but found no guns or recorders.

"I tell you, Tish, he just came along for the ride," Mayhew insisted.

She fumed. "You rotten, no good (expletive)! You're a dead man. You know that? That's why we're here."

Mayhew searched for words. "It was an accident, Tish. It couldn't be helped."

"Accident my ass! You lying (expletive). You think they give those planes away? It cost me a lot and it was the first flight. And you ditched it in the ocean. And loaded yet! You put me in the trick bag for a lot of money. I had to pay the people in Jamaica. They don't care about mistakes!"

Mayhew pleaded. "But, Tish, the radio ..."

Tish went to him, her face inches from his. "I don't care about the radio! None of you are getting out of here alive. There's no way I can let you live. It doesn't work that way."

Jesse was trapped in the middle of an international drug smuggling operation about to turn deadly. "I got put right in the trick bag. I'd be lying if I said I wasn't, but I wasn't about to show it. I'm thinking I was a dead man. I might as well just try to jump out the window. But I knew that wouldn't work. The odds were totally against me with all those guns. I had to do something and quick."

Jesse remembered the small pocketknife in his trouser pocket. It wasn't much, but it was the only weapon he had. He lunged toward Tish, removing the knife from his pocket and opening it. He grabbed her, spun her around in front of him. One arm was around her waist. He held the knife in the other hand and put the blade to her throat near the carotid artery.

It happened so quickly the bodyguards didn't see it coming. They stared awkwardly at him, then leveled their weapons in his direction. The man with the rifle inched forward. He scowled at Jesse, his finger tensing on the trigger.

'You don't want to do that," Jesse said. "You want her to die?"

He cut the skin of her neck near the artery, not deeply, but enough so blood flowed out and down her neck. Momentary horror swept across her face and she sighed. It had the desired effect. The bodyguards lowered their guns. Tish struggled helplessly and gasped for breath. Jesse now had control, as tenuous as it was.

"Let me tell you something, lady," he said, his voice calm but commanding. "We're both getting out of here alive. If you try to stop us you're not getting out of here alive."

"Listen, this guy screws up like he did and now he comes down here and wants to get paid his hundred and seventy-five grand. After he loses a plane and a load of grass and coke. All because of his stupidity! Well, he's not getting paid and he can't live."

"I can't let you do that. That's why I'm down here with him. To protect him. And I'm not going back without my money from him, either."

Tish sighed deeply. "Let's talk about it."

"There ain't nothing to talk about. There's no way I'm gonna trust you."

She told bodyguards to wait outside. Jesse freed her and secured the door. She reached for her shoulder purse, but he grabbed it and opened it. A .25 Beretta automatic was inside, as he suspected. It had a full clip with a shell in the chamber.

He put the knife back in his pocket, holding the revolver steadily. He gave her the purse and she took out a handkerchief, putting it to the cut on her neck.

"Who are you?" she asked, her voice quivering.

"You know anybody from St. Louis?"

"Yeah, some people who are connected."

"Ever heard of Art Berne?" She said she had. "I'm Jesse Stoneking. I'm one of his."

She was cautiously impressed. "Why should I believe you?" Jesse shrugged his shoulders indifferently. "You mind if I check you out?"

"Do what you gotta do."

She took an address book from her purse, paged through it and scribbled a telephone number on a piece of paper. She unlocked the door and called one of the bodyguards. Jesse kept the Beretta aimed at her head.

"Teddy, call this number," she told the bodyguard. "Ask for John Vitale and tell him you're calling for me. If he doesn't believe you or doesn't remember my name, tell him I said to ask him about that night twenty years ago in this bar in Chicago when he got drunk and tipped the barmaid a hundred dollars." She laughed. "And then wanted to get in my panties. Then ask him if he's ever heard of a Jesse Stoneking. Tell John to describe him."

Vitale was a close friend of Berne's and would vouch for Jesse. The tension eased and they chatted for awhile. Jesse still kept the Beretta trained on her.

Jesse suggested Mayhew be allowed to leave and she agreed. He called a taxicab and was gone in a few minutes. Jesse assumed she would settle up with him later. "I figured I might as well save his life even though he had lied to me. It's what I had agreed to do. I knew enough about these dopers that they probably wouldn't let him live very long. Frankly, I didn't care what happened to him after he got out of here. He was on his own then. It was me I had to worry about."

The bodyguard returned a short time later and whispered in Tish's ear. "You're okay. John says you're as good as platinum." She chuckled coarsely. "He said you're not to be messed with or we'll have big problems."

Sitting On A Gold Mine

Tish now confided in him as if he was a trusted confidant. She ran one of the biggest drug smuggling operations in the country, using eight pilots, including Mayhew. They were in various motels around town waiting to get the $175,000 per flight she paid them. The money would be arriving soon, which was why she had an entourage of armed guards.

Jesse knew he was sitting on a gold mine. "I'm thinking, seven pilots at a hundred and seventy-five grand each. That's a million and a quarter. That would be one hell of a score. Grab the money and run. Maybe I'd make it past her army."

Tish saw advantages in Jesse. "I like you, Jesse. You're a good man. Tough and cool as hell. You got a good head on your shoulders. Why don't you come and work for me? A hundred and fifty thousand a year. Guaranteed. You can get your own deals going on the side. You'll make half a million, a million a year, easy."

"Sorry. I gotta pass on that," Jesse answered. "You people are too dangerous. Too radical. I don't want that."

"Nobody with me gets hurt. I guarantee that."

"I've heard that before. There's a lot of broken promises on the road to the cemetery. Thanks, but no thanks."

She put a hand on his shoulder and caressed it. She looked him in the eyes, smiling warmly. "Maybe you and me, we can get something going." She giggled. "A little fun and games. You know, relax each other."

He kept his thoughts to himself. "Can you imagine that broken down old broad wanting me to jump in bed with her? Man, I ain't ever been that hard up and never will be. She was probably trying to set me up. How'd you like to be married to a woman like her? You'd have to say, no ma'am, yes ma'am, kiss her butt all over the place or she'd crack you. I had more important things on my mind.

Getting my hands on that cash that was about to be coming through the door."

"Sorry, I gotta pass on that, too," Jesse said.

Tish didn't give up. "Let me do you a favor, then. There's this doctor in Fort Lauderdale who owes me half a million and he won't pay up. I want him hit. It's worth a hundred thousand to me to see him dead. You get the money up front." She handed him a piece of paper. "Here's his name and address. Just go there and do what has to be done."

"Look, no hard feelings, but I just don't deal with you people. You're too treacherous. You'll kill anybody for nothing. Someday, you're liable to crack me. I just don't trust your kind of people. Nothing personal."

Tish smiled understandingly. "It goes with the business. What can I say? I admire you, though. You tell it like it is. You don't pull any punches. Straight from the shoulder."

Just then there was a knock on the door. Tish let in another young man. He put two leather suitcases on the bed and left. She opened each and inspected the stacks of large denomination bills.

"There's a million and two-hundred and fifty in there I got to give to my pilots. Except Mayhew," she said. "Ever seen so much money at one time?"

Temptation overwhelmed Jesse. "I said to myself, 'Okay, Jesse, grab that money and run like hell'. Maybe just one of the suitcases. I won't be greedy. I still got the Beretta. I could shoot her in the head, shoot the other guys as I run out. Really surprise them. Grab one of the cars and I'm outta there with all that money."

Jesse was ready to try it when Tish looked suspiciously at him, as if reading his mind. She parted the drapes and pointed outside. "Look over there in case you got any crazy ideas."

Jesse looked out the window. Two police cars with two officers in each were at both entrances to the motel. She rapped on the window and motioned. The bodyguard who had brought the suitcases took them out. Jesse watched as he put them in a white van.

Jesse now knew his score was over before it started. "I saw them cops and I thought, 'Well, Jesse, there goes your money'. I sure wish I had some guns with me. I'd take all that money and live happily ever after. I'm an outlaw. That's what I worked for. To get a score that big."

"I own this town," Tish said. "I get what I want here. Those cops work for me."

Jesse chuckled. "I guess you don't have to worry about anybody taking your money, do you? You're kind of robbery proof."

"Anybody gets within twenty feet of that van is dead."

She asked what kind of payment Mayhew had promised him. He told her.

"You'll get it. I'll come up to St. Louis personally and give it to you."

Jesse was dubious. "Who's this broad kidding? I ain't never going to see her again much less my money. I didn't really care at that point. I just lost a million bucks and I should care about twenty-five grand? All I wanted to do was get the hell out of there."

He gave her his telephone number, then unloaded the Beretta and handed it to her.

She wasn't kidding him about making good the $25,000 Mayhew owed him. She flew to St. Louis four days later in her personal jet. Two of her bodyguards accompanied her. She gave him a neatly wrapped package and a suitcase.

"There's your money," she said. "And there're eighty thousand quaaludes in the suitcase. There're worth two dollars each. Give them to Mayhew and pay him off for me. I never want to see the (expletive) again."

Jesse half-heartedly attempted to locate Mayhew, but he couldn't find him. Carson didn't know where he was. He had disappeared. Jesse wondered if Tish had killed him and the offer to reimburse him merely was an alibi. He probably was hiding out somewhere. Jesse didn't care.

Jesse abhorred dope more than ever now, but he had Mark sell the quaaludes and they split the proceeds. It would be adequate compensation for the trouble Mayhew had caused him.

Carson insisted he hadn't known the true reason for Mayhew's trip to Charlotte. Jesse believed him until he learned from a friendly police officer that the federal government had issued a report describing him as an international drug trafficker working out of

Charlotte. The information could have come from only one source. The agents probably leaned on Carson and to save his own hide he made up the story about Jesse.

"What can you say? It wasn't the first time I'd been snitched on and it probably wouldn't be the last. The world was full of those creeps."

CHAPTER SEVEN

The Word On The Street

By the fall of 1978, Don Ellington was viewed by many in the underworld as a walking corpse. It only was a matter of time before he took up residence in a grave.

Ellington, whose dedication to the outfit once was etched in blood and guts, was in open rebellion. He no longer was subservient to the boss and was loyal only to himself.

Berne was an old, ineffective, bungling boss who was letting the outfit fall apart, Ellington ranted. Berne was greedy, like with the handbook operation owned by the Chicago Syndicate and run by him. Other outfit guys shared the profits, but not him. If he ran the outfit everyone would get a piece of the action. Being the boss was what he wanted.

Jesse at first didn't take Ellington's mutiny seriously. He was blowing off steam. Guys did that all the time. Jesse couldn't fault him for saying Berne was stingy. He personally knew that. As Ellington's rebellion increased, Jesse decided to tell Berne. It was an obligation.

Berne took it calmly. "I don't know about Don," he said. "What's gotten into the guy, anyhow?"

Jesse shook his head. "The guy's going crazy, I guess."

"Keep an eye on him. You never know what he's up to. Maybe you should have a little talk with him, Jesse. Put him straight." He snickered. "Have a prayer meeting with him. He needs to apologize to me and get back on track."

Jesse talked to Ellington that night at Cahokia Downs Race Track where he was a bartender, a job Berne got for him. Also by the boss's grace, Ellington was business agent of the Bartenders' Union local.

"Art's hearing some bad things about you, old buddy," Jesse said.

"(Expletive) Art Berne! He ain't nothing but an old man. The outfit needs a new boss. You know that."

Jesse was surprised at his hostility. "Maybe you ought to keep your mouth shut, Don. You know how Art is. He don't like anybody talking about him, especially his own men." Ellington shrugged his shoulders. Jesse hadn't gotten through to him. "You know, if you got a bitch against him, go talk to him. Straighten it out. He'll listen to you."

Ellington fumed. "You can't talk to him. He ain't gonna do nothing anyhow. You and I been together for a long time. We been partners. What you say we get rid of the old man. I don't mean whack him, or anything. Get our own outfit going. Take his outfit over."

Jesse's anger increased. "I don't want to hear that, Don. You gone nuts or something?"

Ellington changed the subject. His wife was threatening to leave him and he craved female companionship. "You know a nice young gal I can take out for dinner and maybe go dancing? No sex, just a good time. You know what I mean."

Jesse laughed to himself. Ellington, almost bald, was a slob. Standing 5 feet. 10 inches tall and weighing 350 pounds, he was vulgar in appearance and demeanor. Would he want to expose a woman he knew to him? But he wondered if his marital problems were causing him to bad-mouth Berne? Maybe lining him up with a date was a way to gain a little control over him.

"Yeah, there's this girl I bang once in awhile. Her name's Kathy. She's a hooker off and on. A hell of a good looking broad. Like a movie star. I'll see what I can do for you." He didn't tell him Kathy also was a friend of Berne.

"Tell her nothing serious, just fun," Ellington insisted.

Jesse gave Kathy a hundred dollars. She knew about Ellington and wasn't enthusiastic about being seen with him. Jesse promised her there would be no sex, just a good dinner and talk. The date was set for Friday night.

Kathy called Jesse Saturday morning. She was in the hospital and wanted to see him. He was shocked when he saw her. Her left arm was broken and her face was swollen with numerous cuts and bruises. Both eyes were black. She wept uncontrollably.

She said Ellington took her to dinner and then to a cocktail lounge. After two drinks, he wanted to show her something upstairs. He took her to a bedroom and ordered her to undress. He raged when she refused. He beat her and raped her. She was unconscious after that and didn't know what had happened.

Jesse's anger detonated. His mind demanded revenge. Ellington again betrayed him, this time personally. He had forgotten Ellington was convicted of rape in 1954, but that didn't matter.

"The first thing I thought was finding him and killing him with my bare hands. I wouldn't say a word. There wouldn't be anything to talk about. I'd just beat him until there was nothing left of him. Maybe cut his balls off and shove them in his mouth. I mean it. That's what the Mafia does when you betray them."

Jesse eventually cooled down. Berne should handle it. It also was an offense against him personally. He called Berne and told him about Kathy. There was a long silence on Berne's end. When he spoke his voice was icy.

"Bring him in, Jesse. At the bowling alley. I'll be there by four this afternoon."

The telephone went dead.

Jesse went by Ellington's house. His late model Cadillac was parked in the driveway. He called him outside.

"What's up, Jesse?" Ellington asked, feigning pleasure. He obviously knew why Jesse was there.

"We gotta go see Art," Jesse said. "He's got a job for us."

"Screw him," Ellington muttered.

"He wants to talk to us now."

"What about?"

Jesse needed to deceive him to avoid a violent confrontation in the front yard.

"Like I said, he's got a job for us."

Ellington tensed. "Well, I ain't gonna talk to him."

Jesse sighed. "You ain't got a choice, Don." He pulled his angel from the small of his back and rammed it into Ellington's huge gut.

Ellington laughed weakly. "You wanna frisk me?"

"You better not be heavy going to see Art," Jesse growled.

Ellington agreed to go with Jesse. Berne was waiting for them at a table in a corner of the almost deserted restaurant. His impish smile was replaced by a scowl. Ellington reached out to shake his hand. Berne waved it off.

"Sit down," Berne ordered gruffly. Ellington sat across from him. Jesse stood behind him, his hands on his hip near his gun. "I'm worried about your attitude, Don," Berne said, his voice razor sharp, his anger unconcealed.

"What attitude?" Ellington asked weakly.

Berne leaned forward, his hands folded in front of him, his eyes penetrating Ellington's. "You're saying a lot of bad things about me and the outfit. I want an explanation."

Ellington snarled. "Go (expletive) yourself, Art. All of you. I never got a dime out of any of you people. Who needs you?"

Jesse shook his head at Ellington's blatant defiance. Berne's face turned red. His lips quivered and his chest heaved. He stood, his hands resting on the table, his paunchy body trembling in anger. "Get him out of here, Jesse! I don't wanna ever see him again. Never! Understand?"

The meeting lasted only a few minutes. Berne hadn't even accused him of the rape. He didn't have to. That inequity was no worse than what Ellington had just committed, personally offending the boss to his face.

Jesse knew the message Berne's words conveyed. They were a kill order. Ellington's last rites. Jesse had a good idea who would be given the contract.

Ellington was silent for a long time, deep in his own thoughts as Jesse drove him home. His silence gave Jesse a sense of satisfaction. Ellington obviously was contemplating his fate.

"I guess I really messed up, didn't I?" Ellington finally said.

Jesse didn't answer him. Silence was intended to intimidate him.

"Art's gonna hit me, isn't he, Jesse?" Ellington asked.

Jesse still didn't answer.

"Look, Jesse, you and I been around the block a lot of times. Remember that deal in National City?" He tried to force a laugh. "We made big bucks out of you being a cop. Anyhow, you're still my best friend."

Jesse remained silent, his face threateningly unemotional.

"Can't you talk to Art?" Ellington pleaded. Jesse's ominous silence continued. "I guess this is it, huh?

Ellington was sniveling like a child. Jesse restrained his hatred. "Things'll work out, Don. They always do, don't they, buddy? Art's just blowing a lot of smoke. Just keep your big fat mouth shut and let it die down. Look, we're still good friends, Don."

Revenge In Full

Jesse was concerned Ellington might try to hit Berne. He warned him to be careful. Jesse wasn't concerned about his own safety. After all, they still were buddies. Or so Ellington thought.

If Ellington feared the ultimate punishment for his unforgivable act of rebellion against Berne, he didn't show it. His invectives continued unabated.

Ellington lived eight more days. He breathed his last about 8:30 p. m. on October 22, 1978. Four slugs from a .38 tore apart his head and face as he sat in his Cadillac off Route TT near U. S. Highway 61 in Jefferson County in the southern extremities of metropolitan St. Louis. He was far from his territory on the East Side.

It was dark and nearby residents heard what they believed were shots. They saw a car speed away, but couldn't identify it. The engine of Ellington's Cadillac was on fire and police pulled him from behind the wheel. His foot was lodged against the accelerator causing the engine to idle fast and overheat.

Investigators assumed Ellington was killed by someone he knew, probably a trusted friend. His wife told them he left at 7 p. m. for a meeting. He never went anywhere without his .38 revolver in a paper bag on the floor of the car. It wasn't there. She said he seemed frightened of something of late, but she didn't know why.

Police learned Jesse owned a clubhouse on a lake 10 miles from the murder scene. They searched the grounds the next morning. Hundreds of shell casings were found in the back yard, apparently from target practice, but none were .38 caliber. No weapons were on the lake bottom.

There was an abundance of possible motives for the Ellington hit – a struggle for control of prostitution, an underworld rivalry, a score gone bad and, foremost, Ellington's insubordination. Jesse was at the top of the list of possible killers. It was surmised he was involved or at least had knowledge. Investigators descended on the underworld, but no one admitted knowing anything or really cared.

Jesse and Berne went to Ellington's wake and funeral, paying their proper respect. Their absence would arouse more suspicion. Each sent a large spray of flowers. Many underworld dignitaries also were there.

Jesse was arrested the next day. Police surrounded his home in O'Fallon and he was led outside with his hands cuffed behind him. Neighbors watched from their windows. It was a terrible indignity. His son, then only three years old, witnessed his arrest. Jesse related what happened.

"He's crying and screaming. 'Daddy, where are you going? You coming back'? I told him I'd be right back, that it was all a mistake. I'm mad as hell at those cops. There wasn't any reason to bring an army to arrest me and embarrass my family like that. Who did they think I was, anyway? Jesse James, the outlaw? They should have known that outfit guys don't shoot it out with the cops."

Jesse was released without charges. His stature in the underworld reached a new height. Those in the know were aware of Ellington's defiance of Berne and his execution was expected. The wise guys had it right. Unless it was because of some personal conflict, Ellington wouldn't have been cracked without Berne's approval. If Berne approved it, Jesse surely knew about it and probably did it.

The FBI attention focused on Jesse. Its agents, too, were convinced he at least had knowledge of the hit, if not involvement. It was becoming evident he wasn't just an insignificant street punk, a common thief. It was time to look more closely at him. The invisibility with which he surrounded himself was evaporating.

"He Was Cracked By One Guy"

After Jesse told me of Ellington's rebellion years later, I asked him if Berne gave him the contract. He didn't answer me, as I assumed he wouldn't. I asked who he thought killed him. I didn't expect him to open up about that, either. Murder is a deep, dark secret. If you did it, prison or death row awaits you if you don't keep your mouth shut. If you know about it, then your life span depends on how quiet you remain.

Jesse didn't pause before responding. A slight smile curled his lips. "The word on the street was that Ellington was set up and that he was cracked by one guy. He thought the guy was his friend, but he wasn't his friend anymore. He hated him. You rape and beat up a girl like that and you ain't got any friends. All you got is enemies.

"Anyhow, the word on the street was that Ellington wanted to do an insurance job on his Cadillac. Hell, that was one of my rackets. The word on the street was the guy he thought was his friend followed him down there and they were supposed to meet the contact who was going to get rid of the car. Only there was no guy there to take the car. He was just set up that way. That's what the word on the street was. You can believe it."

That was the word on the street, but it was a word authorities hadn't heard. Ellington had been silenced, just as Berne wanted.

Jesse had just confessed a murder to me! I was stunned. He did so obliquely, but nevertheless it was an admission. I had no doubt. He didn't hesitate or search for the right words. He spoke them spontaneously and not as if they were rehearsed. It was too detailed and too coincidental with what he had told me about Ellington's behavior, especially beating and raping Kathy.

I assumed telling me was a symbol of his trust of me and his commitment never to lie. But that created much indecision for me.

Did he do it on his own or did he carry out a contract from Berne? He had admitted that was what Berne wanted during the confrontation with Ellington.

Regardless, it was premeditated murder. His FBI control agents later said he hadn't told them what he did me. I had exclusive information.

Was I obligated to give the information to appropriate authorities? He hadn't pledged me to confidentiality. I wasn't bound by any legal or any moral standard to keep silent about a confession, as was a minister or an attorney.

Source confidentiality was a fundamental, absolute maxim of investigative journalism for me, but did it extend to covering up murder? I had been threatened with contempt of court several times, once with dismissal from my job, for refusing to identify sources whose careers hung in the balance. But this was different. They weren't guilty of any offenses except talking to me and disclosing confidential information for legitimate reasons. They hadn't taken a life.

I was familiar enough with the justice system to know what he told me by itself probably couldn't be used to prosecute him. It likely would be considered hearsay evidence with little supporting corroboration except for Ellington's misbehavior. A friend familiar with legal procedures confirmed that.

I finally decided I should publish what he told me and see what resulted. I believed it was a professional obligation and I hadn't been pledged to confidentiality. If law enforcement was interested officers would come knocking on my door. I was on disability retirement from the Post-Dispatch and I included his assessment of the Ellington murder in a magazine article about him. I never heard from a police officer.

What Jesse told me about Hickey, Ellington and his attitude about taking human lives aroused more confusion in me. Why was I feeling empathy for such a cruel, coldly insensitive man? How many notches were on his gun? How many graves were there because of him? How many tears were shed because of his guns? It was too horrendous to contemplate. Did I really want to know?

My relationship with Jesse now came into question. Should I immediately end it and erect a barrier between us, especially since

I no longer was a working journalist? Throw him out of my life? But would walking away from him be proper and honorable? What effect might it have on him? We had become friends professionally and personally and I assumed he was relying on me to a degree.

An even more puzzling, frightening question flashed through my mind. Was the killer instinct addictive and still lurking in him? It might be asleep now, but would it be awakened one day by his anger or frustration? Would someone die? Would it be directed at me for some perceived act of betrayal?

The True Answers

I went to the only true source of advice I knew to find answers. The Bible doesn't hesitate condemning those who take lives, even those who attempt to, such as in the Hickey hit. There are many such passages, not the least the Ten Commandments. John spoke of killing in his First Epistle:

> "Everyone who hates his brother is a murderer; and you know that no murderer has eternal life abiding in him." (3: 15)

In Leviticus, God is quite outspoken about it:

> "And if a man takes the life of any human being, he shall surely be put to death. And if a man injures his neighbor, just as he has done, so shall it be done to him; fracture for fracture, eye for eye, tooth for tooth, just as he injured a man, so shall it be inflicted on him. Thus the one who kills an animal shall make it good, but the one who kills a man shall be put to death." (24: 17, 19, 19-21)

There was another aspect of the issue. Was I sitting in judgment of Jesse? I had assumed it was justifiable condemning someone who had killed, who even confessed it.

Jesus advises in Luke we must do the opposite:

"Be merciful, just as your Father is merciful. And do not judge and you will not be judged; and do not condemn, and you will not be condemned; pardon and you will be pardoned." (6: 36-37)

Paul told the Romans judgment of a man can be a stumbling block for him.

"But you, why do you judge your brother? Or, you again, why do you regard your brother with contempt? For we shall all stand before the judgment seat of God. So then each one of us shall give account of himself to God. Therefore, let us not judge one another anymore, but rather determine this – not to put an obstacle or a stumbling block in a brother's way." (14: 10, 12-13)

Forgiveness is spelled out clearly in the Lord's Prayer. After Jesus recited it, He proclaimed:

"For if you forgive men for their transgressions, your Heavenly Father will also forgive you. But if you do not forgive men, then your Father will not forgive your transgressions." (Matthew 6: 14-15)

The Bible reflects an equally important aspect. Faith in Jesus Christ and confessing our sins to Him will bring us forgiveness, an essence of the Christian faith. God also tells us in 2 Chronicles a repentant Jesse would be forgiven by Him, even for his homicides.

"And My people who are called by My name humble themselves and pray, and seek My face and turn away from their wicked ways, then I will hear from heaven, will forgive their sin, and will heal their land." (7: 14)

The Bible unquestionably told me to forgive the sinner, but not the sin, that I shouldn't turn my back on Jesse. I should forgive him just as God would. He hadn't sinned against me personally. There were too many stumbling blocks already in his life. Besides, what he did was back when he was the hoodlum he no longer was. He was a totally different man now, turning himself around and reaching out for God.

Nevertheless, I was concerned about what was ahead for him. He said he had lived by the sword and he surely would die by the sword because the Bible told him so. He said Jesus assured him in Matthew about that.

"Then Jesus said to them, 'Put your sword back into its place, for all those who take up the sword shall perish by the sword'." (26: 52)

Was this an omen? Would Jesse one day reap what he had sown by how he had sown it? With the sword? As the Bible says, it depended on his atonement. I knew he was seeking that.

I knew he was reaching out to me to fill a need. He told me he had no true friends because he couldn't find anyone he trusted enough. I assumed he trusted me and that was an honor.

I often detected what I believed was humility and contrition, sometimes in the tone of his voice, his words and in his eyes. It was as if he was saying he was sorry for the evil he had done and desperately wanted to make it right.

Re-establishing his loyalty was a priority with him, he said. He had betrayed friends and associates, even those who were evil, and that still bothered him. He admitted he had danced with the devil to some pretty lively tunes and now the evil one was demanding his due tenfold. I said if he turned to the Lord for strength he would be able to resist paying Satan his extortionate demands.

He conceded he was struggling with his inner-self about what he once was. I told him God tells us in the Bible we must not live in the past, although we should learn from our mistakes and sins so as not to repeat them. We must live for today. God has given us that and He already has tomorrow planned for us.

Tears came to the eyes of this once brutal, murderous man who before had shed none for anyone. I hoped they were tears of humility and not of conscience. Then he really opened up to me. He desperately wanted to restore the faith in God he had as a youngster, but wasn't sure how he could. He knew he needed the resolve only God can provide.

He asked me how a man like himself could be forgiven by God. I assumed there were other horrendous crimes, probably murders, he chose to remain silent about, but which God knew. I assured him, as he had learned as a child, forgiveness is granted him through God's grace in Jesus Christ.

I told him there are Bible passages about forgiveness of sin with no consideration given to the severity of them. One of my favorites is in Colossians:

"And when you were dead in your transgressions and the uncircumcision of your flesh, He made you alive together with Him, having forgiven us all our transgressions." (2: 13)

I hoped Jesse would become an inspiration for all who knew him, including me. What better one could a person have than a brutal, vicious hoodlum known as the "Stone Killer" who had seen the light of salvation and now wanted to live a beneficial life instead of a destructive one?

Don't let me down, Jesse, I thought. And don't ever let yourself and God down!

Most of the uncertainties I had about Jesse now were settled. But Jesse had more to tell me, greater sins and evil to unload. And greater reason to believe in God, but also to abandon Him.

CHAPTER EIGHT

The Merciful Killer

R ichie Martinez deserved to die and Jesse was to be the executioner. One didn't live to a ripe old age after swindling the boss and then threatening to kill him.

Berne ordered Jesse to bring Martinez's life to an end. As his lieutenant and enforcer, that was what Jesse was there for, what the "Stone Killer" did best. Especially since the Ellington hit.

It began with Harvey Caputo, a cop gone bad. He had been an asset for the outfit, then commanded by Frank "Buster" Wortman, because of his knowledge of impending gambling raids and other police actions. His law enforcement career ended when his association with the outfit became known. So did his benefit for the mob. All he could provide was speculation.

Berne, Wortman's successor, kept the gangling Caputo, who looked more like a country preacher, at arm's length. Once a cop, always a cop, he told Jesse. You just can't ever trust them.

By the late 1970s, Caputo saw narcotics as the key to his future. He started small in marijuana, striving to build an empire by reinvesting his profits. Now, he was ready to deal cocaine, where the big money was. He went to Jesse to find a contact.

Jesse knew few dope dealers and trusted none of them. He didn't even want to be acquainted with them. He was friendly with Martinez, a professional burglar who was a casual dope dealer. Jesse introduced him to Caputo and they agreed to start off small and invest $25,000 each. Martinez promised they could double, even triple, their investment in a short time.

Jesse told Berne about the arrangement. He had a right to know. He wasn't about to get involved in drug trafficking either, but he demanded a piece of the action because it would be in his territory and with his knowledge. Jesse told Caputo and Martinez that Berne was to be given 10 percent of their profits. Jesse wouldn't accept any money from drug dealing, although he, too, would be entitled.

Martinez went south with Caputo's $25,000 to purchase cocaine. A week, then two, passed and there was no word from him. Caputo suspected Martinez had ripped him off and he wanted to put a contract out on him. Jesse cautioned patience. Besides, he said, since Berne was involved he would have to approve the hit.

When Martinez returned to the East Side, he didn't have the cocaine or the money. He spent it all having a good time.

"What do you mean, you ain't got it?" Jesse asked threateningly.

"I didn't buy it, that's why," Martinez answered defiantly.

"You give the money back to Harvey?" Jesse demanded, knowing the answer.

"I ain't got enough to do that."

Jesse exploded. "What the hell did you do with it?"

Martinez was indifferent. "It's like this, Jesse. You know how inflation is. Things are so high, I spent it."

"Spent it? On what?"

"Food. Booze and broads. A little coke. You know, the good times."

"What about hour head, Richie? What are you gonna do about that? Harvey ain't no dummy. You don't know how he is. He'll hit you in the head."

Martinez laughed. "If you think he's going to try to crack me, let's you and me go hit him first."

"You gotta be crazy, Richie. Out of your mind."

Caputo had resigned himself to what Martinez had done. He and Jesse went to see Berne. He wasn't in a forgiving mood. After Caputo left, Berne told Jesse what to do. "These punks got to have some respect, you know. We got to make an example of him. Just take him out."

Ironically, there was a compassionate side to Jesse. He neither was a robot who killed blindly on command, nor was he a casual hitter who took lives for little reason other than the thrill of it. The cause had to be legitimate and demanding. Killing Martinez wasn't and Jesse wouldn't carry it out, even in defiance of Berne.

Jesse warned Martinez that Berne put a hit out on him. Martinez wasn't concerned. "That dummy can't get by with something like this. Who in the hell does he think he is, anyhow?"

"He's the boss. That's who he is," Jesse responded. "You're in a world of big trouble, Richie. If I don't hit you somebody else will."

Martinez was even more arrogant. "Screw Art Berne! We'll crack him, too."

"It don't work that way. Maybe if you gave the money back to Harvey."

"I ain't got that kind of money and no way of getting it."

"You only got one choice, Richie. I'm giving you a pass. You get out of town and don't come back for a long, long time. Maybe never. I'll take care of it. You don't and you're a dead man. If Harvey doesn't crack you, I'll whack you. That's a promise."

Martinez accepted Jesse's amnesty. Berne laughed when Jesse told him he had taken care of the matter. "You crack him, Jesse?"

"You don't want to know, Art."

"Yeah, I do," Berne insisted.

"Put it this way. He ain't around no more and you ain't going to see him. He's gone forever."

Berne was satisfied. "You sure take care of things, don't you? You're my man I can trust. It cost you anything?"

Jesse grinned. "Don't worry about it, Art. It's taken care of. I do what I'm told to do."

Jesse's compassion was a dangerous character flaw that could shatter his cold killer image on which he depended so much. If it ever was known, he would become just another two-bit, loud-mouthed, spineless hood with nothing to back up his words. His threats would terrorize and succumb few. He could become vulnerable, challenged by every punk who came along. His life expectancy no doubt would decrease dramatically.

He rationalized about saving Martinez. "Richie was just a thief with a big mouth. No big gangster. He didn't hurt anybody. Art didn't lose any of his own money. And Harvey, all he lost was money he made from dope. I ain't going to kill a guy for ripping them off like that. Just like Tommy Callanan."

Callanan was a business agent for Pipefitters Local 562. Both legs were amputated when a bomb demolished his car in 1973. He now was confined to a wheelchair. Mafia underboss Joe Cammarata, a pipe fitter, blamed Callanan when he found a bomb in his pick-up truck. He put a contract out to Berne because of his control of the local. Berne gave it to Jesse, but he couldn't carry it out.

"Me and Mark watched the guy for a couple of days. It was pitiful, seeing him in that wheelchair. One night we followed him and his bodyguard to this restaurant. I go up to him and introduce myself. He knew who I was. I told him, 'Tommy, watch your back'. That's all I said. He got the message.

"There was no way I was going to hit a guy like that in a wheelchair. I figured he suffered enough already. I just went back and told Art that there was no way to get close enough to him, which was kind of true with that bodyguard around him all the time. Art didn't much care.

"I knew that if Art ever found out I had lied to him and had disobeyed him about something like cracking a guy, I'd be lucky if he only kicked me out. He'd probably have me whacked. I'd have deserved it. It was just something you didn't do in the outfit. Nobody would have trusted me anymore. And when a boss doesn't trust one of his men he ain't got much use for him."

The Art Of The Scam

Caputo accepted his loss as a cost of doing business, but he didn't abandon his aspiration to become a major cocaine dealer. This time he wasn't going to start off so small. He had $150,000 to invest, not all of it his. He needed a partner and again went to Jesse, who might be a compassionate killer, but he wasn't merciful when it came to swindling Caputo.

Berne gave his blessing to the scam. He would receive his usual 10 percent cut, this time at least $15,000.

Jesse introduced Caputo to a friend who used the cover name of Mancuso. "He was one of the best con artists I ever knew. He used to be a cocaine dealer, so he knew the game. They agreed that each would put up a hundred and fifty thousand. He said with that much money they could double their investment and come out of the deal with at least three hundred grand clear each."

Mancuso gave Caputo a small bag of cocaine and suggested having it treated to prove its purity. He said it almost was pure and came from the same shipment from which he would get their share. Caputo tasted it. It was good stuff, he said.

Mancuso said his contact was in Mobile, Alabama. He drove there and rented a third floor motel room near downtown with a clear view of the street in front. Two days later he called Caputo and said he had made the connection. He told him to bring his money. Caputo would drive to Mobile. He didn't want to carry such a large amount of cash on a flight and return with the cocaine.

Mancuso gave him the number of a pay phone in the lobby and instructed him to call at 2 o'clock the next afternoon. Caputo wanted to know where he was staying, but he wouldn't tell him. It wasn't time yet for him to know.

Steve, a friend who would pose as a dealer, came to his room at 2 o'clock the next afternoon. He had a camera bag crammed with plastic bags of baking soda. Steve had worked several scams with Mancuso, who gave him $5,000 for his work.

Caputo called Mancuso at 3:10 p. m. Timing and intrigue were crucial. Mancuso instructed him to drive to a small shopping center six blocks from the motel and park there. He told him where to find a public telephone and to call him at the same number. Mancuso figured it would take Caputo about 20 minutes to get to the shopping mall.

When Caputo called from the shopping center, Mancuso asked him the name of the shop directly in front of him. He needed to be sure Caputo was where he was supposed to be. Caputo complied.

Mancuso gave him the name of his motel and room number and told him to walk there. He should knock three times, wait five seconds and then knock twice. If the door wasn't opened it meant there was trouble. He should leave immediately and try two hours later. Caputo was impressed with the security measures.

Mancuso could observe him approaching the motel and see if he was being followed. He had walked the distance from the mall to the motel three times at different paces, timing himself. It should take Caputo no more than 15 minutes.

When Mancuso saw Caputo two blocks away he went to the lobby telephone and called 9-1-1. His voice was excited as he said there was a man in the lobby brandishing a pistol and threatening to shoot. He returned to his room. Caputo now was a block away. He carried a black briefcase. Police sirens wailed as Caputo walked out of Mancuso's view near the front of the motel.

As Caputo waited for the elevator, three police officers with riot guns and pistols drawn rushed into the lobby. He panicked, believing he was being arrested. He ran up the stairs to Mancuso's room and knocked as instructed. Mancuso opened the door halfway. Steve stood beside him with the camera bag.

"The cops are down there!" Caputo said breathlessly. "Let me in."

A look of astonishment came to Mancuso's face. "No way. I can't be found here. I'm wanted for parole violation in Alabama." He gestured to Steve. "And he sure as hell can't be caught here."

Mancuso grabbed the briefcase and inspected the money. Steve opened the camera bag, showed Caputo the contents, zipped it shut and handed it to him. Caputo wanted to inspect the cocaine, but Mancuso said there wasn't time.

"It's as good as you can get," Mancuso said. "You have my word. Just go down there like nothing's wrong and I'll see you back on the East Side tomorrow." He slammed the door in Caputo's face.

Mancuso knew by then the police would learn from the desk clerk and others in the lobby there was no crisis. Caputo was safe, although he probably would be concerned and not take time to inspect the fake cocaine. Steve soon left and Mancuso checked out five minutes later. He didn't want to be there in case Caputo discovered the fake cocaine prematurely.

The Hard Sell

Mancuso was back in St. Louis the next morning. Jesse's role in the scam was to begin. They took Berne's $15,000 off the top and split the balance, allowing Mancuso $10,000 for his expenses and Steve's fee. Caputo called Jesse that evening and related what happened in Mobile. Jesse told him to stash the cocaine for a month until the heat died down. Caputo was impatient because he had two buyers lined up, a doctor and a lawyer. He said he tried to call Mancuso, but was unable to reach him.

Caputo called Jesse three days later, his voice threatening, his anger obvious. Jesse assumed he had discovered the cocaine was fake. He told Caputo to meet him that night in a motel in Fairview Heights, just east of East St. Louis. Jesse once helped the desk clerk out of a jam. Stram got there half an hour early. He told the clerk a meeting might get a little heated. The clerk promised to ignore it.

Stram was Jesse's back-up. He played a pinball machine near the meeting place. Caputo was sitting on a couch, a briefcase beside him, when Jesse got there. The locks were closed and Jesse knew a gun was inside. Two young men obviously his bodyguards were sitting off to one side. They tried to appear tough and watched every move Jesse made.

Jesse went to Caputo and opened his coat up enough to expose his angel in his belt. The silencer on the gun was intended to suggest Jesse might be planning to kill him. Then Jesse opened the lid of the briefcase and saw the revolver. He closed it and spun the two combinations on the locks. There now was no way Caputo could get his gun in time.

"What's up, Harvey?" Jesse asked, faking lack of concern.

Caputo scowled. "Where's my money?"

Jesse remained cool. "What money?"

"I said where is it?"

Now, Jesse showed anger. "You don't talk to me like that. You got something on your mind?"

"I got ripped off on that deal."

"Those your guys over there?" Jesse asked, looking in the direction of the two young men. Stram was watching the exchange, ready to come to Jesse's aid. Caputo shrugged his shoulders. "You think I don't know they're with you?" Jesse said, still feigning anger. "You think I'm some kind of hoosier?"

"Calm down, Jesse," Caputo said defensively.

"Calm down, my ass. Now, tell me how you got ripped off."

Caputo said a friend tested the cocaine and discovered it was baking soda. He tried to find Mancuso, but couldn't.

"Why you telling me about it? It was your deal. Not mine."

"Yeah, but you lined it up and I'm out a hundred and fifty," Caputo protested, but less threatening.

"I didn't line anything up. Let's go in the restroom and talk this over," Jesse said. It wasn't an invitation. It was an order.

Caputo shook his head at his two bodyguards. Jesse followed him to the restroom, but not too closely. He was a dangerous man, unpredictable.

"You think maybe I had something to do with this?" Jesse asked, his voice now calm and disarming.

"Well, no, but ..."

Caputo was off guard as Jesse shoved him hard against the far wall. He jammed his revolver against his throat and cocked it. His hand was steady. "Now listen, Harvey, and listen good. You got ripped off. That's your problem. Understand? You go see Mancuso, not me."

"You got it wrong, Jesse," Caputo said, his voice faltering in fear. "I'm not blaming you."

Jesse pulled the gun from Caputo's neck and waved it threateningly in his face. "Don't make that mistake again." He didn't have to tell him what would happen if he did.

Jesse left the restroom. He glanced at the two bodyguards as he walked past them. They were impassive. Stram fell in behind him, a sinister smile on his face. Caputo would cause no more trouble. Or so Jesse thought.

"So what does Harvey do? He goes crying to Art. I already told Art what had happened. Harvey says, 'You gotta do something about this crazy Stoneking. He's a mad man'. Art just shook his head. He told him, 'You mess with Jesse anymore and you're a dead man. You don't know who you're dealing with'."

CHAPTER NINE

A Reason To Die

J ohn Paul "Sonny" Spica was a rising star in the St. Louis Mafia, but he was wedged between two relentless forces of death. It was a question of when, how and by whom he would die. And that put a target on Jesse's back, causing him to plot a massacre.

One of the juggernauts aligned against Spica was the Kansas City Mafia, which was demanding his execution for his betrayal. He had aided a dissident gang in promoting death and insurrection.

The other was a renegade St. Louis cabal poised to kill him in its march to power in organized crime. It was the autumn of 1979, a year after the Ellington hit, and Spica was following in his footsteps. He, too, was a loudmouth rocking the boat. He also was making death threats.

Spica was no stranger to contract murder. He was sentenced to life imprisonment in 1963 for killing a St. Louis County woman's husband for $3,000, but was paroled in 1973. His closest friend in prison was Carl Spero, a young, aggressive, Kansas City gangster. That relationship would put the noose around Spica's neck.

Another friend of Spica's in prison was James Earl Ray, the assassin of Dr. Martin Luther King Jr. The U. S. House Committee on Assassinations in 1978 reported evidence indicated Spica brokered the contract on King. It said a Spica relative in St. Louis was believed to have received an offer of $70,000 for King's murder. Spica admitted knowing Ray, but denied the allegation.

After Spica was paroled, Tony Giordano began grooming him. He eventually would be "made" – formally inducted into the Mafia as a "man of honor." One day he even might attain the status of "capo." Jesse and Spica became friends. He was likable with a good personality, although impetuous at times.

Spica also was making his bones as an aggressive earner and a loyalist. To Giordano, he was more than a soldier. He made him a partner in a vending machine company he owned in Fairmont City on the East Side and his driver and bodyguard.

Spica committed unpardonable disloyalty in 1979. Spero and his brothers were locked in deadly combat with the Kansas City Mafia family of Nick Civella. Eight men were killed in two years. In May, 1978, Civella's men ambushed the Speros. One brother, Michael, a Teamsters' Union official, was killed and another, Joseph, was wounded. Carl was partially paralyzed.

Carl Spero had to respond. At his request, Spica gave him a case of dynamite for bombs to take out Civella's soldiers. What wasn't known was Civella had a mole inside Spero's gang. Civella called Giordano, with whom he had a close working and fraternal relationship. Giordano was responsible for the errant Spica and Civella demanded he be sacrificed on the altar of La Cosa Nostra discipline.

Jesse overheard the confrontation. "Civella said, 'You got a man we want. Either you take care of him or send him to us.' But Tony wouldn't do it. Tony gave him his word that Sonny wouldn't do anything else. Then Civella agreed that they would leave Spica alone. Civella told Tony, 'If he ever comes in my territory again, we'll whack him'."

Jesse was present on November 7, 1979, when Giordano assured Spica the crisis had passed and nothing would happen to him. He was safe. Jesse wasn't sure Civella had extinguished the fires of revenge. Words, even promises, can be meaningless when getting even is involved.

Spica apparently unwittingly contributed to Carl Spero's death a few months later. On June 20, 1980, he was killed when a bomb he was carrying accidentally detonated. His body was mutilated beyond recognition. Twenty-five of 40 rental storage units nearby were destroyed. It was believed the bomb was intended for a Civella operative and was made from the same dynamite from Spica.

Death From Another Side

Spica apparently wasn't aware of the deadly conspiracy beginning to swirl around him. His unbridled passion to climb the ladder of success and his big mouth clouded his vision. As a result he stepped on the wrong toes.

The other force aligning against him was no less lethal than the Civella Family. It had a propensity for settling disputes with bombs, bullets and mayhem – kill now and ask questions later. One didn't threaten Ray Flynn and expect to live for long.

Flynn, a member of Berne's outfit, was a ruthless labor racketeer in St. Louis. His arrest record didn't reflect his proclivity for violence. He had accumulated only seven arrests for burglary, robbery and arson in 25 years. He never went to trial on any of those charges. Instead he pleaded guilty to two of them, was sentenced to prison on one and put on probation for the other.

The St. Louis underworld was a triumvirate of the Syrian Outfit on St. Louis' south side bossed by the venerable James "Horseshoe Jimmy" Michaels Sr., who had considerable political clout; Berne's East Side Outfit; and the Mafia, which was one step above the others on the mob's ladder of influence.

A renegade gang headed by John Paul "Paulie" Leisure operated on the sidelines, openly defiant of the contemporary mob dictate of making money, not waves and bodies. The Sicilians viewed his outfit as "Hollywood gangsters."

Détente had been negotiated years earlier. There was little obvious strife, although conflict always lurked beneath the surface of tranquility. In the name of peace, each outfit respected the other's autonomy and turf, although the Mafia wielded the most authority with the Chicago Syndicate having ultimate influence in major issues.

Construction unions were a major power base and a source of lucre for the three factions which had a stranglehold on some of them. Unions provided gangsters on the payrolls as officers with facades of legitimacy and reportable incomes. During the 1970s, at least 30 hoodlums and associates held offices in a number of unions on both sides of the Mississippi River.

Sweetheart contracts were negotiated with some employers. Strikes often brought contractors facing deadlines for work completion scurrying with cash in hands, seeking quick solutions. Thugs in the guise of union leaders shook down builders in return for granting concessions to use non-union workers or to pay wages below prevailing union scales.

Welfare funds were raided with phony insurance claims. Jobs on construction projects were leverage to get members indebted to the mob and to vote favorably in elections of officers. Featherbedding was tolerated because it was the cost of doing business.

St. Louis' three Laborers' Union locals were profitable for the mob. Giordano oversaw them and they were divided among the three underworld outfits. Berne, in addition to the Pipefitters Union, controlled Local 42. Local 53 was under the Mafia's jurisdiction and was ruled by Joe Tocco, a cousin of Giordano's. Local 110 was the realm of the Lebanese-Syrian gang overseen by the Michaels.

In the autumn of 1979, Giordano, with Michaels' approval, brought his nephew, Matthew "Mike" Trupiano, into Local 110 as president. With Giordano's influence with Mafia families around the country, Trupiano was appointed an International Laborers' Union representative. Whether Trupiano or other hoodlums who held union office ever got calluses on their hands with manual labor, or even picked up a shovel, is doubtful.

Trupiano was heir apparent to the throne of power in the St. Louis Mafia. Giordano, suffering from incurable lung cancer, was grooming him for leadership. As a young man, he was exiled from Detroit to St. Louis under the care of his uncle after having an affair with a mobster's wife, a capital offense under Mafia justice.

Trupiano, an improbable mob boss, didn't fit the "Godfather" image. Unlike his uncle, he inspired little respect and much derision. Strict discipline was not part of his governance. Although he was large in physical stature, it wasn't the decisive, tough guy likeness of a ruthless crime lord he projected. A bungler, he was prone to whining rather than acting when things didn't go his way.

The underworld was tranquil until September 1979 when Thomas Jefferson "T. J." Harvill, business manager of Local 42 and a crony of Berne's, died of natural causes. It was the position of ultimate power in the local. Flynn, then only a business agent, and Berne lobbied the Chicago mob for the lucrative job. Flynn was appointed to the position with Giordano's approval on October 4. The position paid $3,000 a month in salary and $350 for expenses.

Giordano made a counter-move a week later at a meeting at the Banana House, a distributorship on Produce Row on St. Louis' near north side, often a gathering place for gangsters. Trupiano and other Mafia members attended. Jesse, Berne and Flynn were there as was Myrl Taylor, business manager of the Eastern Missouri District Laborers' Council. Giordano brought Spica. The Syrians were conspicuously absent.

Giordano said he wanted to more fairly realign underworld presence in the three Laborers' locals. It was a poorly camouflaged Mafia move to gain more power. Spica would become a business agent in Local 42, a position of influence and a catalyst for his second dilemma. Giordano announced he also was putting Jesse in Local 53 as a business agent.

No one much cared about the appointments except Flynn, who was disrespectful of all mob authority except his own. No way would he share power in Local 42 with anyone but his people and Spica wasn't one. His opposition to Giordano's interference was undisguised. Berne argued Giordano's decision must be unchallenged because he is the boss. Giordano, his anger boiling, insisted his decisions were final. All agreed except Flynn.

Jesse accepted the appointment as a gesture of Giordano's gratitude, but he knew it was part of his effort to increase the Mafia's dominance. The position paid a nominal salary of $320 a week, less than half of Spica's pay, with no expenses, but he wouldn't have to do any work. He would resign six months later.

A few days later, Jesse, Berne, Giordano, Giammanco and Spica were at the vending machine company in Fairmont City.

"You know, that Ray Flynn, he ain't no mover," Spica said. "I'm a mover. We're gonna make some money in that union. I'll just wait about six months and then I'll hit him and we'll take over."

Gordano said nothing and shrugged his shoulder. Jesse assumed he already had sanctioned the hit. Spica's fate had just been sealed.

Spica's words puzzled Jesse. "Sonny must be crazy. If you're gonna clip a guy like Ray Flynn the last person you want to tell in advance is Art. He'll go right to Ray. It's like committing suicide. Well, Art goes back and tells Ray and Ray hits the ceiling. Ray says he's going to crack Spica first and Art said to go on, to let him know if he needed any help."

Flynn eventually cooled off and decided to try diplomacy and arm-twisting to solve the problem peacefully before resorting to the gun.

Jesse witnessed what happened next. "It wasn't long after that when Art and I met with Tony. He asked Tony to tell Sonny to stop threatening to kill Ray. Well, Tony, he's insulted. He hollers at Art and tells him never to threaten Sonny like that again. Later, Art just shakes his head and says, 'I don't know what'll happen now'. I had an idea."

The Professional Hit Man

Spica didn't believe in a conspiracy of silence. He discussed his intention to take out Flynn several times in Jesse's presence. He also told Paulie Leisure, who lurked in the background ready to take advantage of such a volatile situation.

Leisure, a Syrian, headed the splinter group of cutthroat gangsters, including his brother, Anthony, assistant business manager of Local 110, and a cousin, David, not known for his intelligence. Leisure didn't want just a piece of the action, but most if not all. When the time was right he would begin his move by consolidating control of the Laborers' Union locals as a power base. There was nothing Leisure wouldn't do to rule the underworld, even climbing over dead bodies.

It was generally believed in intelligence circles if Leisure succeeded his outfit would be reminiscent of the Capone gang in

Chicago, well organized, omnipotent and cold-blooded. Organized crime in St. Louis would take on a dangerous character it hadn't known for a long time and the body count would be high.

Paulie Leisure had appealed to Joey Aiuppa for recognition of his outfit, but the Chicago boss turned him down and told him to take it up with Michaels. The Leisures weren't about to negotiate with Michaels because he stood in the way of their planned march to power. They were thinking about eliminating him, anyhow. Paulie Leisure already was calling himself the "number one Syrian."

Once Giordano's bodyguard, Paulie Leisure now despised the Sicilians, especially the lumbering Trupiano, whom he considered weak and ineffective. He derisively referred to him as "square head." He suspected the Mafia was moving to take over all three Laborers' locals. Spica confirmed his suspicion.

Flynn was ruthless, but Leisure also was deadly. His hands were bloodier and there were more notches on his gun than any St. Louis mobster in many years. Intelligence agents considered him a professional hit man, a broker of murder, who had taken at least 14 murder contracts throughout the country. He also was thought to have killed perhaps a dozen men in the St. Louis area.

The rumors of Leisure being an assassin were factual, as far as I was concerned. I had proof of that.

Leisure and I were awaiting a flight to St. Louis from Chicago's O'Hare International Airport. He went to a restroom, leaving his carry-on luggage and briefcase in the waiting area. That was curious. Who would leave them unattended? I doubted he was that careless. Was it intentional?

I checked the identification tags, which I assumed was what he might have wanted. They bore the name, address and telephone number of a man from Youngstown, Ohio. The city in northeastern Ohio was noted for its gangland killings. Had Leisure wanted my attention diverted from him? He apparently recognized me or believed I was a law enforcement agent.

I sat across from him during the brief flight. He opened the briefcase. No papers, folders or books were inside, only a pack of cigarettes. I wondered if he was returning from a hit somewhere. I followed him after we landed. He hurried through the airport and boarded a hotel commuter bus. I didn't. I wasn't that brave. It apparently also was part of his cover.

I determined no man with that name lived in Youngstown and such an address and telephone number didn't exist. Intelligence sources agreed he probably was returning from a hit and the phony name and address were his cover. There were no murders in Youngstown then. I doubted he would have used that identity if he did a hit there.

Alliance Of Death

Leisure obviously recognized Spica's threat to kill Flynn as a means of advancing his own goals. He offered Flynn his assistance in thwarting Spica. That meant killing him. It would be a propitious alliance greatly enhancing his power structure. Flynn would be a valuable asset and a powerful weapon. Together, they would be a challenging force against the Sicilians.

Leisure needed to profile Spica, know his lifestyle, his likes and dislikes, the little quirks in his personality. He had to develop a relationship with him and gain his trust. He socialized with Spica and his girlfriend. He confided what he said was confidential information, but which was false. He called Spica for spontaneous meetings intended to prepare him to be lured to his death without arousing suspicion.

Leisure had a more pragmatic reason. "You gotta keep your friends close and your enemies closer," he told his close associate, Fred Prater, who later became an informant.

It was decided to kill Spica with a bomb. Flynn was an expert bomb maker and installer. A 1977 Cadillac identical to Spica's was borrowed from a friendly car salesman who kept no written records of such transactions. Flynn practiced wiring the bomb containing 12 sticks of dynamite to the brake lights and the taillights. The hit now was imminent.

Late at night November 6, 1979, Anthony Leisure and Flynn went to Spica's apartment building on a quiet residential street in the western suburb of Richmond Heights. His Cadillac was parked as usual on the street in front. There was too much activity in the neighborhood to install it. They were successful the next night. Spica had a few more hours to live.

At 8 o'clock the next morning, November 8, Spica paid the ultimate price when he stepped on the brake pedal. The instantaneous blast was horrendous. Part of his body was inside the car, part outside, and his legs were severed. He was alive when the first neighbors arrived, but he died in a few minutes.

The passenger door was blown 30 yards and debris, including one of his shoes, was hurled 75 to 100 yards. Windows rattled and dishes shook in buildings two blocks away. Fortunately, there were no passersby on foot or in cars or the death toll would have been higher.

It was the day after Giordano assured Spica the crisis with the Kansas City family was over and he was safe.

An hour after the bombing, Giordano called Paulie Leisure and told him what had happened. He knew of his friendship with Spica. "Oh, my God, I wonder who could have done that," Leisure told Giordano, feigning shock and anger. When he hung up, he gleefully said to Prater, "The guys got it done. The kid's dead."

Giordano initially believed Civella reneged on his promise and ordered Spica hit. But he soon learned Flynn and the Leisures were responsible. He summoned Berne and Jesse to a "sit down" at a restaurant in Fairmont City later that morning.

As they sat at a table, a casually dressed man entered and chose a booth within hearing distance. He began reading a newspaper. Police was written all over him. They went to a table on the porch at the rear of the restaurant.

Giordano stared menacingly at Berne. "Okay, Art, I don't want no bull. Which one of your people can handle a bomb?"

Berne was agitated. "I don't know, Tony. What do you mean?"

"Which of your guys is capable of bombing Sonny Spica?" he demanded, his voice rising.

"Louie Shoulders was, but he's dead. Bosco Owens could, but he's in prison."

Giordano's anger flared. "Don't screw with me, Art! We've been around too long. What about Ray Flynn?"

"Maybe. I don't know, Tony."

Giordano pounded his fist on the table. "I know, Art! It was Flynn who did it. I got the word."

Berne was in a corner. "Why would he want to crack your guy?"

"You know why, Art. He didn't want Sonny in Forty-Two."

"Sure, he was pissed off, but not that much, Tony," Berne said, not convincingly.

"He's your man, Art. You're responsible for him. You know that."

Berne had to placate the seething Giordano. "If he did it, and I mean if, I don't know anything about it. It's not my responsibility. I was as surprised and upset as you were."

"Let me tell you something about Flynn, Art. He don't show respect to anybody, especially us. He forgets who we are and that ain't right. He knows I got cancer and I ain't gonna be around too long. So, what's he doing? He's getting ready to try to take over everything with them Leisures. Including your outfit! Believe me."

Berne was perplexed. "That's crap, Tony. He's just a hot-headed Irishman, that's all."

Giordano's anger exploded. "You blind, or something, Art? Can't you see what's happening. Flynn's screwing with them crazy Leisures. I'm telling you they're out to take over everything. They'll start a war that nobody can stop. And you and Jesse are gonna get caught in the middle. They're not gonna give you two a pass. They'll come after you because you're in their way."

Berne was silent, staring into the distance. Giordano let his words sink in before he spoke again. "I gotta tell you, Art, Flynn's gonna get hit. He's gotta go. I just hope he did it on his own." He pointed a finger at Berne. "Anyone else who was in with him on this is gonna get hit, too."

Berne was shaken. "I can't stop you, Tony. You got to do what you think is right."

The Spica hit was of little concern to Jesse. He saw little danger in it for himself. "Flynn had every right to kill Spica," he thought. "He had threatened him and he wasn't one to make empty threats. And Tony had every right to retaliate against Flynn. It was something they had to settle. I didn't want any part of it."

Berne and Jesse conveyed Giordano's threat to Flynn. "I don't want any problems like this," Berne said. "You got a beef with Jesse, you get it settled or you're gonna have trouble with me. Jesse's my man and he's protected."

"You got it wrong, Art," Flynn countered. "I ain't got any problems with Jesse."

"You better not have. Don't go thinking Jesse's got anything to do with whatever Tony's up to over there cause he doesn't."

Flynn shrugged it off. Berne knew Giordano wouldn't rest until Flynn was dead. He told Jesse he was considering disassociating himself from him.

"I'm gonna be like that guy, what's his name?" Berne said.

"What guy?"

"You know, the guy in the Bible. He flies an airplane."

Jesse laughed. "There weren't any airplanes back then, Art."

"Pontiac, or whatever his name was."

"You mean Pontius Pilate?"

"Yeah, that guy. I'll just say, 'Okay, where's the soap? I wanna wash my hands of him'. Ray ain't got me with my arm around him no more. Once he's on his own, he ain't got no protection. When that's taken away from him, he's dead."

Jesse at first assumed that was the end of the conflict with Flynn. But was he misreading him? Would Flynn give up that easily? Even Giordano warned him Flynn might make a preemptive strike against him.

"Watch out for that guy, Jesse," Giordano said. "Don't trust him. You know he and them Leisures are tight. He might think that since you're close to me I'd give you a hit on him and want to crack you first."

Paranoia ran deep in the underworld after Spica's murder. Flynn was not as unconcerned as he pretended and he went nowhere without one or two armed bodyguards. Mob leaders wondered what else the unpredictable Flynn and the Leisures had planned. Giordano and other ranking hoodlums installed remote starters in their cars. Berne didn't go to that expense and trouble. He had his wife start his car each morning. Even Jesse checked his car before starting it, as he would later in life.

An Enemy Surfaces

Jesse noticed Flynn was displaying more animosity toward him after the Spica hit. They hadn't been close before, but since he joined forces with the Leisures he seemed even colder. Jesse wasn't too alarmed at first. Flynn was just being himself.

"He didn't like me and I didn't like him. His guys didn't like me either. They were jealous of me because I was solid. I didn't have to go to them for anything. I didn't need their connections. I had my own things going. Flynn wanted to be the power. After he went with the Leisures, it was get rid of the guys that were dangerous. And I was dangerous. So, knock me out of the picture."

Not long after Spica was killed, the Leisures made a move on Jesse. He and Berne went to a funeral. Many hoodlums, including Paulie and Anthony Leisure, were there. Anthony took Jesse aside to talk privately.

"Why don't you come over here with us?"

"Well, Anthony, I don't want to do that. I can't do that."

"You'll make more money with us. I can guarantee that. Big bucks."

"Money's got nothing to do with it. I'm loyal to Art and I'll stay with him."

"Okay, you're on your own then, Jesse."

"I've always been on my own, Anthony."

Leisure shrugged his shoulders. "It's your call, Jesse."

Jesse knew it was a disguised threat. "Until then, I didn't suspect I was being focused on to be cracked by them. But after Anthony said that, I knew they were trying to set me up. Get me off guard and get closer to me to kill me."

It wasn't long before Jesse knew for sure he was in the Leisures' and Flynn's gun sights. Three of Jesse's trusted friends told him J. D. Michels, one of Flynn's cronies, was asking questions about him - where Jesse hung out, where his homes were, where he ate dinner and other personal matters. They were concerned. Jesse knew Michels, once Flynn's bodyguard, was dangerous. He pleaded guilty in 1972 to second degree murder in the killing of two persons in a bar.

Diplomacy to Jesse meant head-on confrontation, taking the initiative to gain the advantage before matters got out of hand. Jesse found Michels in a tavern. He didn't have to order him outside. His angel in his waistband spoke for him.

"I hear you been looking for me, J. D.," Jesse said sternly.

Michels was cocky. "Not me, Jesse."

"No? How come you been asking questions about me?"

"I said I wasn't."

Jesse stepped closer. "Three people don't lie. You got a beef with me?

Michels' arrogance faded. "Nope. Why should I have?"

"That's what I'm asking you. I just want to make you aware that I know you've been asking around about me. If I hear any more of that you and I are going to have big trouble. Understand?"

Jesse detected a slight trace of fear in Michels' eyes. "What do you mean by that?" Michels asked defensively.

"Just in case you got something on your mind, friend."

The confrontation with Michels might be over, but Jesse knew it wasn't with Flynn and his henchmen. He began toying with the idea of killing them all.

CHAPTE TEN

Set-Up For Murder

J esse was concerned the night of December 15, 1979, as he had
dinner by himself in the fashionable Nantucket Cove in St. Louis'
West End. The seafood was excellent, although expensive. Not that
it mattered. The price of personal pleasure never was a concern

He wanted no companionship, no frivolity, only quiet time to
sort out matters. He had stood up successfully to Michels, but the
confrontation brought him to near burn-out. Was that incident an
omen about his life?

His mental resources were draining, making him vulnerable and
creating uncertainty. He had to restore his cognitive power. He must
be able to anticipate what might await him, but recently there was
too much fog of ambiguity blurring his forward vision.

On the surface, at least, it appeared no immediate threat was
looming, although in his world it often was disguised. He had heard
no words of discontent. Flynn was keeping a low profile. That there
had been no revenge over the Spica hit was surprising – and encouraging. Nor were there any rumbles from the Leisures. But Jesse
knew silence sometimes concealed impending tragedy.

As Jesse lingered over a cognac and coffee, an argument erupted
at a nearby table. An Air Force colonel who had dinner with his wife
and two children wanted to pay his $140 bill with a check because
he didn't have enough cash and he didn't use credit cards. The

waiter and manager were adamant that checks were not accepted. The colonel was embarrassed and Jesse could see tears in his wife's eyes. He went to them.

"This gentleman's an officer in the Air Force,' Jesse told the manager. "He's not going to stiff you. You don't need to embarrass him and his family like that."

"Mind your own business," the manager said sarcastically.

"My business right now is this officer and his family," Jesse responded

The manager backed off. Jesse gave the waiter a hundred and seventy dollars in cash. The colonel was astonished at the charity of this stranger. He offered Jesse a check, but he refused. The officer would know his name and he didn't want that. He told him to give the money to charity.

It was a day of benevolence for Jesse. That afternoon he saw a ragged, unshaven man aimlessly wandering the streets, poking around in trash cans. He obviously was homeless or an alcoholic, a nobody who had nothing and no one in his miserable life but his unproductive self. He could be that man if it wasn't for his good fortune and himself.

He handed him five $20 bills. He didn't want to insult him and he told him they had fallen from his pocket. The man accepted them with trembling hands and thankful eyes. Jesse hoped he would use it for essentials and not for booze or dope.

Bushwhacked

Jesse's beeper sounded as he drove to the East Side. Giordano gave it to him when he took him on as a trouble-shooter for his East Side vending company. Giordano offered to pay him, but he refused. He was repaying Giordano's trust in him. So far, he had received only two calls in six weeks.

He called the company's answering service. A cigarette machine in a tavern in a blue collar suburb was out of order. The caller had asked if Jesse was on duty. It was almost 10 o'clock when he got there. He frequented the bar and it was known he took service calls for Giordano's vending company. Barney, the bartender, waved at him.

Jesse checked the vending machine. It was working. Barney hadn't called about it. A red flag went up for Jesse. "What's going on here, Barney?"

"Don't ask me," Barney said, laughing. "Maybe you made a mistake."

"I don't make mistakes," Jesse said gruffly. "Somebody called."

Barney shrugged his shoulders. Jesse sat at the end of the bar and ordered a scotch and water. He drank it quickly and ordered another. "My gut told me something was wrong. Barney wouldn't lie to me. We were friends. I wanted to think it was just a prank. A drunk playing games and asking for me. That didn't make much sense, either. Something told me to get out of there. But I didn't have anything better to do. Maybe I'd find out something if I just hung around."

Jesse's suspicions increased several notches when a man he knew only as Troy came to him. He was wiry with a crew cut and spoke with a southern accent. Jesse had heard he was a police informant.

"Stoneking, I hear you don't like me," he said, his voice patently threatening.

Jesse faced him. "That's right. I hate stool pigeons."

"I don't know why you feel that way. I'm not a rat snitch."

"I don't even want to talk to you, Troy. Just get out of here."

Troy turned conciliatory. "Look, Jesse, let's just forget about it. I know where there's a couple of nice broads in a motel not far from here. We can get it for nothing. They owe me. Let's go get laid."

Jesse wouldn't have accepted the offer even if they were friends. He wasn't that careless or horny. "You didn't hear what I said. Get the hell away from me."

Troy left. A few minutes later a prostitute he knew sat next to him. She was excited. "Jesse, you've got to get out of here," she whispered. "They're out to get you."

"What are you talking about?" Jesse was only mildly curious.

"They're going to shoot you. I heard Troy and them talking about it down the street."

"Who? Why?" he asked.

She didn't answer him and left. Jesse assumed she was high and he wasn't concerned. Just then he saw in the mirror behind the bar the image of Wayne Harris, a young punk, approaching him. Someone muttered, "Not now." Harris went to the other end of the bar and joined Jimmy Hollen, a thief.

Jesse also didn't consider that a serious threat. "Troy was just a hoosier smarting off. That's all. Nobody's gonna try to crack me in a room full of witnesses. Maybe when I left. Then I remembered I left my angel in my car. I probably wouldn't need it, anyhow. I was going to leave in a few minutes."

Barney approached him. "You got to get out of here, Jesse. Now! I just heard Harris and Hollen talking. They're out to cause you trouble. Tonight!"

"To hell with 'em, Barney. I ain't done nothing to them. They're a couple of pussies, anyhow." The scotch in him was talking.

A few minutes later, Harris and Hollen came up to Jesse. "What do you want?"he asked without turning around.

"Just wondering what you've been up to." Harris put his hand on Jesse's shoulder in a friendly gesture. "I'm kind of down on my luck and need a job. Can you do me any good, Jesse? Get me in the union?"

Jesse gave him one of his Local 53 business cards. "I'll see what I can do for you. Give me a call in a few days." He had no intention of helping him.

"Look, I know about this good score," Harris said. "Worth maybe forty, fifty grand. Let's go some place where it's not so noisy and talk about it. I gotta get on it right away."

"Later!" Jesse said gruffly.

"I can do you some good," Harris said and left.

Barney went to a storeroom in the back and Jesse followed him. It was time to leave. He wasn't thinking clearly. The liquor had dulled his senses. He asked Barney to give him the pistol he knew was under his white bar apron. Barney refused.

Jesse grabbed the pistol, checked to make sure it was loaded and put it in his own waistband under his jacket. Barney shook his head in disgust and returned to the bar. Jesse made his way into the tavern. He had to walk near Harris and Hollen.

"Hey, Stoneking, I think you're a two-bit punk. A worthless piece of junk," Harris whispered as Jesse passed.

Jesse spun around. "What'd you say?"

"You think that piece you're carrying is gonna do you any good?" A sarcastic smile twisted Harris' face.

Harris reached to his belt under his coat for his gun. Jesse grabbed his wrist with one hand, shoving it upward just as he pulled the trigger. The slug tore into the ceiling.

Jesse drew Barney's pistol and fired twice. Both rounds slammed into Harris' chest. He was dead before his body sagged to the floor. Customers screamed and ran for the door.

Jesse crouched instinctively and turned to his right. Hollen drew his pistol. Then two explosions and the searing impact as both slugs ripped into Jesse's lower right chest. The impact hurled him backward onto the floor. He fired the pistol until it was empty.

Hollen slumped to the floor, mortally wounded.

Pain slashed through Jesse's abdomen as he backed out the front door. He threw Barney's gun into a trash receptacle and then crashed into a six-foot-high chain link fence. He grabbed a four-foot length of two-by-four on the ground, the only weapon he now had. He heard the front door of the tavern being bolted from inside.

A pleasant sleepiness, a strange euphoria, swept over him. He wanted to lie there forever. Sirens approaching in the distance spurred his mind a little. His body commanded him to stay where he was, but he couldn't. He tried to sit up. The pain forced him back down.

He had to get out of there. He would be arrested for murder even though he had killed in self-defense. He staggered to the street, not knowing where he was going or what he would do. He felt of his chest inside his shirt. His hand was covered with blood. He soon would be unconscious and bleed to death. He couldn't accept that sentence.

A garage alongside a house came into his blurred vision. He staggered to it. A car was inside with boxes and junk. He could go no farther. He eased himself down. Fatigue overcame him again. It didn't matter. He could die there and not out in the street.

An ambulance and a police car sped by, their sirens shrieking, their blue and red flashing lights piercing the darkness. His mind screamed at him to flee. Ignore the pain. You want to die here?

Jesse stood and lurched toward the house. He knocked on the door. Through the haze he saw an attractive woman open it cautiously.

"Do you have a phone, ma'm?" he asked, his words barely audible. The woman gasped and stepped back. "Is your husband here?" Jesse felt himself slipping into unconsciousness, his legs threatening to give way.

"No, he isn't," she answered

He tried to utter an apology, but he could speak no more. He turned to walk from the porch, but fell to his knees, gripping his abdomen.

"Aren't you Jesse Stoneking?" she asked.

He remembered her. She was a waitress in a restaurant where he and his friends often dined.

"I've been shot," he muttered. Dizziness overcame him as he tried to stand. He slumped back to the porch floor.

She said she would call an ambulance, but he didn't want that. She drove him to the hospital. He was unconscious as he was wheeled into the emergency room. Surgeons operated four hours removing the bullets and repairing internal damage. No vital organs were struck, but he had lost a large amount of blood. One of the doctors later told him he would have soon bled to death had he not gotten to the hospital when he did.

When he partially regained consciousness the next morning, two men were in his room. "One of them said he was a cop. I told them to get the hell out of my room. They were the last people I wanted to talk to. Mark came to see me. He had a piece with him for me and he put it in the drawer in the table next to the bed. The phone was ringing off the hook. Guys wanting to know if a gang war was starting. A couple asked Mark if there was anyone I wanted hit in retaliation."

Giordano brought Jesse a new expensive leather coat. The one he wore the night of the shooting was ruined. Giordano was concerned and was convinced he had been set up. Jesse didn't disagree.

"These are bad times, Jesse," Giordano told him. "You watch yourself until we find out what this is all about."

A Deadly Visitor

Jesse was sedated and almost unconscious the next afternoon when he saw the distorted image of a woman standing in the doorway. She moved closer.

He propped himself up. "Dorothy? Carolee?" he asked, his voice barely audible. He shook his head and the blur cleared a little. The woman was pointing a pistol at him. Then the metallic click as it was cocked.

"You should be dead, Stoneking," the woman screeched.

"Who are you?" he asked, his voice faltering.

A shadow appeared behind her. It was Stram. One of his hands locked around her wrist, the other wrenched the pistol free. Without saying a word, he escorted her from the hospital. He drove her to a deserted area in an industrial complex, made her lie on the ground and put her own pistol to the back of her head.

He demanded her name and why she wanted to kill Jesse. Without emotion, she said her name was Jeanette and was a friend of Hollen and Harris. She only wanted to finish what they had been paid to do. She didn't know who hired them, but she said it was some hoodlum. He took her wallet from her coat pocket and looked at her driver's license for her address.

Stram left her there. He would take care of her later if Jesse wanted it done. Jesse told him it would serve no purpose. She wasn't the target of his revenge. Friends and outfit members now guarded him around the clock. Only nurses, doctors and those whom they or Jesse knew were allowed in the room.

It took Jesse several days to sort out what happened and rationalize the motive behind the shoot-out. He initially believed Harris and Hollen wanted to make a name for themselves by cracking Berne's right-hand man, but that didn't add up.

"They were punks and would always be. There was no way they could make it into the outfit even if they did hit me. They'd be walking dead men. I realized they tried to get me outside and whack me. When that didn't work, they tried to get me in a situation where they could kill me in self-defense in front of witnesses. But they weren't smart enough to make that work, either.

"Someone else had to put them up to it and give them a hit on me. Why else would someone ask if I was on duty? I knew that when Mark said the woman told him about a hoodlum paying them to do it. Flynn had to be behind it. He and Michels. I didn't have much doubt. When I found out for sure I'd go after them. They wouldn't be alive for long."

A Mirror Of Himself

Jesse confided in me years later that while recuperating he did something he had refused to do most of his adult life. His close brush with death caused him to engage in introspection, trying to unravel his life and assess his future. He searched his soul, looking for some purpose in life other than the underworld and where crime was taking him. The mirror of his soul reflected his sordid life and he didn't like what he saw. It was too truthful, too frightening. Too accusing.

Thoughts of his youthful dedication to Jesus Christ demanded his attention, but he had to put them back into the darkness of his distant memory. It was too enlightening, too incriminating and demanding for his present life. Someday maybe, but not then.

His soul was a grand jury returning indictments against him. Much of his life was an orgy of narcissism and self-sufficiency, a never ending, never satisfying ego trip that drove him further from the truth. The tough-guy image, the "Stone Killer," the mental agility of a criminal mastermind pushed him further down the road of the fast life and the big bucks. The road to hell.

What did it all mean? He wasn't sure anymore. Nothing seemed permanent in his life. Nothing justifiable. His life was becoming a whirlwind.

Paranoia introduced itself to Jesse. Was God warning him to get back on the straight path? Did the shoot-out at the tavern portend the finality of his life, as he had wondered after the Michels' confrontation? Would he one day hear that terrible crack of the pistol held by an unknown enemy or by a treacherous, jealous friend? Or feel that deafening, searing blast of a bomb the instant his body was torn apart? He didn't want to contemplate any of that, but he knew it wasn't just a nightmare.

There were inevitabilities incumbent to his lifestyle. Someday, somewhere he would make a mistake and be arrested. A prison sentence was a certainty. Worse, someone might snitch on him. That was more probable. The dogs of jealousy and ambition always were nipping at the heels of those in power in the underworld.

Common sense briefly implored him to get out of crime while he still could. There was nothing to prevent him from walking away from the outfit. He had taken no oath of lifetime loyalty and servitude on the penalty of death as in the Mafia, although it was expected of outfit guys. He could go straight anytime he chose and just tell Berne he had enough. That simple. But would the bosses accept that? He knew too much. Would his loyalty remain uncorrupted?

All he would want was a quiet, secure life. He could move somewhere far from the East Side and disappear. He had enough money stashed away to live comfortably for awhile. But always he came back to the same inescapable truth.

"I was a hood. That's what I was and that's what I would die being. How could I walk away from that? It was all I knew. I guess I was kind of proud about how far I came, but there wasn't any way I could change and I didn't want to."

Jesse did make a few changes in his lifestyle. Never again would he have as many drinks as he did before the tavern shoot-out. And he would go nowhere without his angel. "You think I had a lot of cars before? I'd drive a couple of different ones every day. A lot of them were cheaper ones. Some days, I'd leave the house in one car, drive to a shopping center parking lot and get into another. There was no way anybody was going to follow me."

Jesse was indicted on two counts of murder and a jury found him guilty. His lawyer, Robert Rice, appealed. The judge granted a new trial when Rice introduced several witnesses who testified Jesse had shot in self-defense. He pleaded guilty to a reduced charge of involuntary manslaughter in Hollen's death and was placed on four years' probation. The murder charge in Harris' death was dismissed.

Jesse wondered why those witnesses suddenly agreed to testify. Rice didn't explain and he didn't ask. He had a good idea. It had cost him $30,000 in fees, but it was a profitable investment. He assumed some of it was used to buy witnesses.

Ignorance Is Protection

And then there were his children. He had kept them insulated from his criminal life. His homes were off limits to underworld associates. Separate telephones were in the master bedrooms of each house. Their unlisted numbers were the only ones he gave his cronies. Carolee, Dorothy and the children were instructed never to answer them.

He never talked about his real life in front of the kids and they were told never to ask. Even Carolee and Dorothy knew little of it, except he was a hoodlum. They really didn't want to know much more. The children still were young and innocent, but inquisitive.

One day he took his daughter to the store with him. "She pops up and asks, 'Daddy, where do we get our money from'? I laughed and said, 'Where do you think'? She didn't know. I said, 'Honey, I'm just a businessman. That's all'. She didn't give it up. 'Where's your office, daddy? How much money do you make'? Finally, I told her to knock it off."

It was why neither Carolee and Dorothy nor the children visited him in the hospital. People rarely are shot like he was without a reason and there would be too many questions asked, too many lies to tell.

"Sometimes, the movies make hoods out to be glamorous. Kids get turned on by that and they want to grow up to be gangsters. It wasn't that way at all and I didn't want my kids thinking like that and believing I was some kind of hot-shot. Some guys would say they were going to teach their kids how to be good burglars or good hoods and how not to get caught. They were crazy. I didn't want my kids to know anything about who and what I was and I didn't want my sons to ever be like me."

Because of his low profile there had been no previous newspaper stories about him. The shield he had built between his children and his nefarious life was penetrated with the shoot-out. Local newspapers identified him as an underworld kingpin. The children now were fully exposed to the real Jesse Stoneking, their father.

After the shootout, Jesse was elevated to sainthood on the streets. Before, he had been respected. Now, he was a revered icon of bravery. He was a man who escaped death's clutches by his own guile and had killed his assassins. A man who had guts. It was how he earned his nickname "Stone Killer." It wasn't what he wanted his children to know.

Berne also recognized those qualities. In the spring of 1980, he promoted Jesse to his lieutenant, the underboss of the outfit. The Chicago Syndicate approved it. "You're the guy I'm gonna depend on," he told Jesse. "You'll be my personal representative. Just be there when I need you."

Jesse now was one of the chosen few. He walked with the prestige and power of the mighty Chicago Syndicate. Southern Illinois was under his and Berne's control. He would bask in the prestige and power that came with being Berne's right arm. He was more untouchable than before. Or so he thought.

"I was Art as far as everyone was concerned. I had a lot of juice. When I walked into a joint, I got the respect Art did. Anywhere I went. Guys would take me out to dinner, hand me gifts sometimes. Once in awhile a guy would give me a piece of his action. They'd tell me they knew one day I'd run the outfit."

Jesse vowed to Berne never to disappoint him. There was no way he would betray the trust placed in him. He would repay Berne many times over.

And now there was no way Jesse could walk away from his life of crime. As far as he was concerned his current lifestyle now was sealed and impenetrable. He might have re-committed himself to the underworld and climbed to near the pinnacle of power, but he soon realized that wouldn't go unchallenged. There was only one way to protect himself. React before he is required to act.

CHAPTER ELEVEN

Night of Terror

It was to be the usual Tuesday night soiree for Ray Flynn and four of his henchmen. Life certainly seemed so rewarding and promising. And they would be safe because they were invincible, a rising power in the mob. No one would dare try to take them out.

The lavish dinner in the popular East Side restaurant filled their bellies. Plentiful booze eased the tensions of the day. The jokes, teasing and raucous laughter added levity to the night.

When it was over, the crew would go to the parking lot where the party would continue for a few minutes with less joviality. Mob business would be discussed where there were no unwanted ears and prying eyes.

But they would have unseen companions. Two pairs of deadly eyes would watch them from a concealed car, as they had before.

In an instant, their blood would flow in the parking lot as death descended on them in a hail of bullets. All at the same time, by a single gun fired by one man.

Jesse Stoneking's revenge would be unleashed, his own life preserved. Those who wanted him dead would inhabit the graveyard instead of him. The assassination attempt at the tavern would be repaid in full with interest.

The night of September 23, 1980, would be one of terror like no other in St. Louis. It would be another Valentine's Day Massacre, this one 51 years later, in the summer and in St. Louis, not Chicago. It would be out in the open and not concealed inside a building, as in Chicago. The killers wouldn't be disguised as police officers. They would be themselves because they would be concealed.

Seven rival gangsters died then in Chicago in history's most savage mob hit. Jesse's would be no less atrocious and just as historic for St. Louis. Sub-machine guns and a shotgun were used in Chicago. He would use just one weapon and he wouldn't need to fire 70 rounds as those hitters did. Fifteen to twenty at the very most. Three or four per man.

Jesse's motive would be the same – eliminate enemies. Al "Scarface" Capone was behind the first massacre. Jesse, no less cold-blooded, would be Capone on this one. He would plan it just as meticulously and pragmatically.

By midsummer, Jesse was hearing Flynn and the Leisures considered him a formidable obstacle in their power grab since he now was Berne's lieutenant. That added urgency to his massacre. Kill now or be killed. "Guys were warning me about them. Tony G. even said it. Nobody ever pulled off anything in St. Louis like I was going to. Five guys at one time. Only no one would ever know who did it."

Flynn remained at the top of Jesse's hit list. Also to be executed were Flynn's brother, Mike, a union official; Bill Politte, a long-time Berne operative who had drifted over to Flynn; Michels; and Cletus Wayne Gaines, a burglar and close associate of Flynn.

Jesse had to keep Berne in the dark about the massacre. He wouldn't approve such an audacious move. He didn't have the guts and he would claim it might wreak havoc in the underworld. Jesse knew it would, but he didn't care.

There were other, consistent rumbles in the underworld. The mob was in conflict, a powder keg with the fuse about to be lit by the Leisures. It only was a matter of time before the whispers and ugly stares erupted into full-scale warfare as the streets resonated with bomb blasts and blood flowed. It was the way organized crime was at times. No negotiations. No concessions. Just bullets, bombs, mayhem and corpses.

Jesse wasn't concerned about such gang warfare. He believed it would provide good cover for his massacre. Others likely would be blamed and the law's eyes diverted from him. When the conflict began depended on Giordano's death. He had terminal lung cancer and his days were numbered. The underworld watched and waited with bated breath, the Leisure gang with itchy trigger fingers. Paulie Leisure didn't want to fire the first shot while Giordano lived and bring down the Mafia's wrath on his gang.

A Hit For Free

Berne was deeply concerned about Flynn's lack of respect for the Sicilians and he told Jesse he had warned him several times, but to no avail. He and Jesse visited the dying Giordano at his house to pay their respect.

Jesse hadn't seen him for some time and he was astounded at how the cancer had ravished him. He was frail and had lost much weight. His hands trembled and his hollow eyes reflected his anguish. His speech faltered and he wheezed.

The conversation soon turned to Flynn. Giordano told Berne "he has to be hit. Why don't you have Jesse crack Flynn?" Berne nodded, but made no such commitment.

He later told Jesse to ignore what Giordano said because he was so sick he didn't know what he was talking about.

Giordano called Jesse in mid-July. It was urgent they meet. He insisted they take a ride because he had something important to talk about and he feared his house was bugged. Giordano put his hand on Jesse's shoulders. "Jesse, I need you to do something for me. It's been eight months now since Flynn and them crazy Leisures whacked Sonny. It's time to pay him back."

"Yeah, Tony, it's time." Jesse knew what was coming.

"I didn't want to do it right away then," Giordano said. "It'd be too obvious. Jesse, now I want you to crack Flynn. You're the only one I can trust anymore." He smiled. "And you got the experience to pull it off."

Giordano stopped to regain his spasmodic breath. "Just Flynn, though. I don't want to cause a whole lot of trouble right now. We'll take care of the Leisures later. Me and Jimmy Michaels, we been talking about that. It'll get done."

Jesse had to accept the hit. It was Giordano's ultimate honor and trust in him.

"I'll take care of you, Jesse. Don't worry about that. You want fifty grand? You got it. I'll make sure the people in Chicago take care of you, too. You could go up there and work for them. You'll be set up for life."

"What's Chicago going to say?"

"Nothing. It's a family matter. I already told them about it and they didn't care. They said it's my business."

"Okay, Tony, I'll do it. But I ain't going to Chicago. Just consider it a favor to you."

"I don't care how you do it. Just get it done."

"I'm not gonna rush into it, Tony. It might take some time. He's probably expecting it. I don't want to make any mistakes. Not on something as big as this."

"That's the way I want it. And don't tell anybody. Not even Art 'cause nobody here knows you're going to do it."

"Don't worry about that."

Jesse took him home. Giordano handed him a big envelope with $50,000 in cash. Jesse turned it down. "I can't take that, Tony. I didn't want your money. I'm doing this for you.

Giordano hugged Jesse, smiling like a kid. His gratitude was unspoken.

Jesse had no misgivings about accepting the hit. It was a commitment not only to Giordano but to himself. His gunshot wounds from the assassination attempt had healed, but its implications still festered. He had no doubt Flynn and Michels were behind it. They missed that time, but they wouldn't stop trying.

Timing was critical, but Jesse couldn't limit the hit to Flynn, as Giordano insisted. Killing just him would alert the others. Taking them all out would be a personal insult to Giordano, an act of disobedience. He would have to wait until he died before doing it. It wouldn't be long. Giordano told him he only had a few months to live.

Jesse didn't think much about the consequences of what he was about to do. "They'll all die in one night. I'll just wipe them all out. Just like that and get it over with. It didn't bother me that these guys were going to die. I knew there'd be a storm coming down not only from the cops but from the rest of Ray's people and the Leisures. But they wouldn't be looking at me. They'd probably think the Italians did it because of Sonny Spica. Let the Leisures take the rap."

The Kill Plan

Jesse perfected his plan for the executions by the end of July. He was as calculating and cold-blooded as ever. He had to be precise. His life depended on it. It was the ultimate challenge and it was exhilarating. He mentally executed his scheme several times a day, looking for flaws, trying to anticipate every conceivable possibility, every contingency, each potential danger. Mark Stram was to be the wheel man, he the shooter.

He obtained three untraceable cars, paying cash for them and registering them in fictitious names at phony addresses in towns distant from the metropolitan area. They were powerful with eight-cylinder engines, dark colored and not gaudy to make it difficult to identify them, especially at night. Two would be used alternately in surveillance of the victims and would disappear in a chop shop when it was over.

A plausible, provable alibi was imperative. He and Stram would make reservations at an expensive motel at the Lake of the Ozarks, a sprawling popular resort area southwest of St. Louis, for three days, including one before and one after the hit. Their presence would be obvious and easily documented. They would use credit cards in their names. Business cards with Jesse's name and his occupation as a jewelry appraiser and salesman were to be handed out.

Money draws attention. They would be big spenders, introducing themselves to local businessmen, maybe even buying a gem from a jeweler, and touring a condominium pretending interest in purchasing it. Bartenders and waitresses would remember them for their large tips and their ostentatious mannerisms. They would flirt with women. Whether they made out didn't matter, as long as their faces were remembered and they as gentlemen.

Stram would drive the hit car and park it at a nearby resort. Together, they would go in Jesse's Lincoln to the motel where they were registered. In mid-afternoon of the massacre, Stram was to pick him up at the motel in the hit car, leaving the Lincoln in plain view, and drive to St. Louis. When it was done they would return to the lake.

Jesse bought his weapons from a trusted underworld source. The serial numbers were removed making them untraceable. It was an awesome arsenal. A 9 mm. semi-automatic revolver and a .12 gauge sawed-off shotgun were for close up. A high-powered 30.06 rifle with a scope would be used at a distance.

A fully automatic M-16 was his weapon of choice. It was fast and more deadly. He would have only a few seconds to take out the five men. He was a marksman, but he practiced firing the weapons.

He was in no hurry to start the necessary surveillance. It would begin in earnest when Giordano died. In the meantime, he and Stram checked out the victims' houses to identify the cars each drove and license plate numbers.

Jesse went to see Giordano the first of August. His physical condition had worsened. He was nothing but skin and bones. He was so weak he couldn't get out of bed and could hardly talk. "You could just smell the death," Jesse recalled

"How's that thing coming, Jesse?" Giordano asked, his voice crackling.

"It's coming, Tony. It just takes time to do it right."

"You sure you can take care of it? You need any help? I can bring in someone from Chicago or Detroit."

"It'll get done. Don't worry about it, Tony. I promised you, didn't I? Jesse Stoneking never goes back on a promise."

Giordano reached out and grabbed his hand, smiling faintly. "I know that," he whispered.

It was the last time he saw Giordano alive. He died on August 29. An FBI agent later said his last words were, "Kill that (expletive) Flynn."

Time To Kill

Not long after Giordano died Jesse and Stram began stalking their prey. Flynn and his crew had dinner at a restaurant in Granite City every Tuesday night. It was a ritual. Jesse and Stram joined them on one occasion as part of the surveillance and bought them a round of drinks.

"I went over and talked to them. They were in a good mood, laughing and cutting up. They were kind of noisy, but nobody was paying them any attention. I went back to the bar and ordered them a round of drinks and then left. Mark asked me why I did that. I told him it was the least I could do for dead men."

They drove from the parking lot. Fifteen minutes later, they parked across the street in the shadows of a building. After half an hour, the five men left the restaurant, standing together in the parking lot for a few minutes talking. They never varied their routine, always leaving by 10:30.

Confident he now was prepared, Jesse decided to make the hit the next Tuesday, September 23.

"It was time to do it. Get it over with. It was no big deal. We'd just wait for them to come out. Mark would drive and I'd open up with the M-16. It'd take only a few seconds. That's all. Five, ten seconds and they'd be dead. Just like in the movies. There was always a chance they wouldn't stand around gabbing and go straight to their cars. If that happened, we'd try the next week. You have to be patient. If you're not, you'll screw up for sure.

"Every so often I'd ask myself, 'Jesse, you know what you're going to do? You're going to whack five guys. Guys you know'. I didn't want to think about that. I'd tell myself, it was either them or me. Take your choice. It was what this game is all about. Anyhow, I'd be carrying out Tony's contract. Only he wouldn't know it."

Jesse told me about his plans for the massacre 20 years later. When he finished he put his hands to his face and sighed deeply. I could tell he was ashamed of himself. His past was harassing him.

"That's the kind of guy I was," he said, his voice choked.

"Was is the proper tense," I responded. "I know Jesse Stoneking isn't like that anymore. That's all part of the past."

"Let me show you how bad I really was. It says so in the Bible in the twelfth chapter of Romans. 'Never take your own revenge, beloved, but leave room for the wrath of God, for it is written, vengeance is mine, I will repay, says the Lord'. So I guess I know what's in store for me because of that. I know I deserve it."

I was impressed that he quoted a Bible passage from memory. That told me much about his reconstruction. He excused himself and went to his car, returning with a Bible. "Guess what. Psalms talks about Jesse Stoneking in the tenth chapter. Here, listen. 'He sits in the lurking places of the villages, in the hiding places he kills the innocent; his eyes stealthily watch for the unfortunate. He says to himself, God has forgotten; He has hidden his face, he will never see it'."

I smiled, not derisively, but compassionately. "Yes, Jesse, God was talking about you. The old you. Not the you today. He talks about all of us in His word. He talks about me a lot."

A New Daughter

Jesse went to see his sister a few days before the massacre. Her friend was there with her three-month-old daughter. He picked up the baby. Her diaper was soaking wet. She had no more diapers because she had no money, she explained. Her husband refused to work and support them.

"I don't know what to do," she sobbed. "My husband's kind of strange if you know what I mean. He really doesn't want to have her. He can't stand it when she cries. Once he even spanked her when she wouldn't be quiet. And she's just a baby. I'm so worried about her. What kind of life she'll have."

She looked at Jesse, her eyes red with grief, tears streaming down her cheeks. "Do you know anybody who might want to give her a good home?"

Jesse was shocked. How could a mother give up a sweet baby like that? "Yeah, I do. I'll take her. Are you sure you want to do this?"

"No. I don't want to, but it's what's best for her."

Jesse picked the baby up again and laughed. "You just lost your daughter. I want to make one thing clear, though. Don't come back and say you've changed your mind. You'll have a battle on your hands."

She promised she wouldn't. She hugged him. "Just promise me you'll give her a good home and lots of love."

"You got it," he said gleefully."

He gave her five thousand dollars and suggested she use part of it to divorce her husband. "Start your life over again. Just don't give a nickel of that to him. If he gives you any trouble, just let me know. I'll take care of it."

Jesse was separated again from Carolee. He and Dorothy legally adopted the girl after the mother signed the appropriate documents. They lied to the judge that they were married and the father's whereabouts were unknown.

Jesse didn't know then, but that joyful event in his life one day would give him another reason to kill.

CHAPTER TWELVE

The Leisure War

Paulie Leisure's kill squads stalked mob chieftain Jimmy Michaels for days, but couldn't get close enough to him until he went to church.

The Michaels hit would be the first clash in what was to be known as the Leisure War that would ignite turmoil in the underworld. It also would grant pardons to Jesse's five massacre victims, but amnesty would be denied him as he became embroiled in deadly mob chicanery.

While Leisure also awaited Tony Giordano's demise during the summer of 1980, he sensed his drive to expropriate leadership of the mob was being threatened by forces aligning against him, particularly Jimmy Michaels and the Sicilians. Leisure's influence was being neutralized in Laborers' Local 110, the power base from which he intended to catapult himself into underworld dominance.

Leisure had to boldly make a preemptive strike to unequivocally establish his supremacy in the underworld. Actions spoke louder than words. While Gordano lingered, he formulated his war strategy.

Under an agreement three years earlier, Anthony Leisure wielded the heaviest hand in the local with authority over hiring and firing. Paulie Leisure installed one of his soldiers, Ronald Broderick, an imposing six-footer who weighed 270 pounds with a propensity for brawling, into the local hierarchy as an organizer. He was Anthony Leisure's muscle.

Now that covenant was falling apart. The Michaels Outfit was usurping more control and was power-sharing with the Mafia by giving it more positions. Trupiano and Giordano's nephew, Vince Giordano, were hired as organizers. Broderick's tenure was about to be ended.

The underworld had to be shown who had the ultimate authority, where the real power was. No longer would Paulie Leisure remain in the shadow of the underworld giants. He would cast his own shadow as he began his campaign to become the high priest, even over the corpses of those who resisted. His killing machine, bolstered by his alliance with Ray Flynn, was ready for battle.

Leisure called a meeting of his outfit in mid-July. Although he ruled his kingdom with an iron fist and a loaded pistol, he was a practitioner of democracy. The members were to vote on a candidate for execution - Trupiano, the elder Michaels or John Massud, an influential Syrian troublemaker in Local 110. It didn't make much difference to Leisure, just as long as one of them died. None would live much longer, anyhow.

Michaels was chosen for extinction. The message his death was intended to convey was unmistakable: Even the high and the mighty would have no neutrality in Leisure's war. The old adage - "Until death do us part"- was about to be implemented.

By the third week of August, Leisure heard Giordano was days away from dying. He still had to wait. To off Michaels now likely would bring an invasion of the armies from Chicago and Detroit. It would be a war Leisure knew he couldn't win. Not yet.

Leisure, the merchant of death, also was a perfectionist. He meticulously planned the Michaels hit in every detail with the same precision as Jesse did for his massacre. Nothing could be left to chance. Not with a high profile murder like this.

Breakfast With Death

Extensive surveillance was to be done with a "work car," a van registered to a "W. W. Karr," a fictitious name at an address in south

St. Louis County. As Leisure and his soldiers went on high alert, the only unresolved question was how Michaels would die. Leisure opted for an ambush. It would be quick and easy.

He made his move a few days after Giordano died on August 29. An attempt by David and Anthony Leisure to assassinate Michaels in his south St. Louis County home failed when it was interrupted by a fierce dog.

Michaels now was to have breakfast with death. He ate most mornings at a south side restaurant, often with a brother, Francis, also an official of Local 110. Both would die. An audacious kill in broad daylight would be proof of the Leisure Outfit's commitment and invincibility.

Leisure assigned the hit to Anthony, Ramo and Broderick. Wearing ski masks and gloves, they were to invade the restaurant through the rear door. The key element would be surprise. Leisure and Ramo were to shoot Michaels with shotguns. Broderick would hold customers at bay with his pistol. He was to shoot anyone who made a suspicious move.

No words were to be spoken. Voices, even muffled by the ski masks, could be identified. They should be in and out in several minutes. Any longer and the initial shock would wear off and they might face resistance. A friendly employee was to unlock the door. As a witness, he had to be killed if he was on the premises.

Using the work car, Leisure, Ramo and Broderick drove past the restaurant at 9:30 in the morning. Both Michaels' cars were parked in front. The two targets usually sat at a table in the rear. They drove to the alley in the back and parked near the door. Broderick tried to open the door, but it was locked. They left.

Both Michaels' cars were parked there the next two mornings, but each time the buildings rear door was locked. They didn't seek an explanation from their friend. Better left unsaid. It just was bad luck.

Leisure decided to bomb Michaels' car as he left St. Raymond's Maronite Church on the city's near south side. David, using a friend's apartment nearby, watched Michaels enter and leave the next Wednesday. Prater was ordered to obtain a bomb. It had to be detonated by remote control rather than by the ignition or the brake pedal. They had to control the location. The parking lot, part of the holy ground of the church, was inviolate. It would be sacrilegious to kill there.

When Prater got the bomb, he and Ramo tested the mechanism several times until they were satisfied it worked and it wouldn't be discharged accidentally. Two days later, a 1979 Chrysler Cordoba identical to Michaels' was stolen. On the dashboard was a sign saying it was owned by a state parole and probation agent. David Leisure practiced installing the bomb on the underside of the vehicle while Anthony timed him.

The Leisures had passed the point of no return and the grim reaper was about to catch up to Michaels.

Time To Kill

At 11:55 a. m. on September 17, 1980, Michaels drove his Cordoba onto the parking lot at St. Raymond's Church. He appeared aristocratic, more an elder statesman than a mobster. Nattily dressed with flowing white hair, mustache and a Roman nose, his gentle disposition set him apart from most hoodlums.

The Wednesday luncheons were popular and the Lebanese cuisine was excellent. Michaels mingled with politicians, some of whom were indebted to him for his influence; government officials, some no less beholden to him; civic and business leaders; and the curious who came to rub elbows with the famous and the notorious.

Despite Michaels' notoriety, to many he was an object of affection and adoration. He was well respected in the Lebanese-Syrian community and the underworld throughout the country. He provided the political clout, locally and in the state, Berne's outfit and the Mafia lacked but needed.

A few minutes later, a van with darkened windows drove onto the church parking lot. Ramo was driving and Anthony Leisure sat next to him, gingerly holding a model airplane remote control. David Leisure and Broderick were in the back seat.

At 12:10 p. m., Loewe parked the tow truck two blocks from the church. He turned on the two-way radio and listened for any messages. Eight blocks to the west, in his towing company office, Paulie

Leisure monitored a police scanner. If he heard any transmissions concerning police activity at or near the church parking lot, he would contact Loewe, who would alert those in the van by walkie-talkie.

Ten minutes later, David Leisure left the van, carrying an attache case containing the bomb. After scanning the area, he crawled underneath Michaels' Cordoba and quickly attached the case to the underside, using rubber straps with hooks on both ends. It took less than a minute.

Michaels and his grandson, James "Beans" Michaels, left the church hall at 3:05 p. m. and chatted for a few minutes by the Cordoba. David Leisure saw it as an opportunity.

"Let's hit 'em now. We can kill both of them," he insisted.

Anthony refused. Killing them at the church would bring intolerable heat. Besides, they had no beef with the grandson.

They followed Jimmy Michaels for several blocks after he left the church. Anthony activated the remote transmitter, but nothing happened. He pressed the button again, but the bomb underneath the Cardoba didn't detonate. They momentarily lost sight of Michaels' car as it merged with heavy southbound traffic on Interstate 55 and headed toward his home.

The cars on the ramp entering the freeway slowed and then stopped. To lose the Cordoba would be disastrous. They couldn't retrieve the bomb once the car was inside his garage. They would have to sit on his house until he left, possibly until tomorrow. That was much too long to put him under surveillance in a residential area. They likely would be detected and the bomb discovered.

They finally entered the interstate and caught up with Michaels. It was 3:20 p. m. when the van closed in from the rear. Leisure activated the remote control again. This time it worked.

A deafening boom and the van shuddered. Then, a plume of orange flame and black smoke erupted from the Cordoba. The car rose three feet and disintegrated. Michaels' body, severed at the waist, was hurled to the pavement like a rag doll 55 feet from the vehicle. The van swerved to avoid it, careening through the smoke. Debris from the shattered car fell over a 200-foot area. Other nearby vehicles screeched to a stop.

"Horseshoe Jimmy" Michaels had died the way he had lived.

In the first few moments, the occupants of the van were silent and awe-struck by the immensity of the explosion and the destruction. Then, realizing they were successful they spontaneously joked and laughed.

Paulie Leisure declared war only 19 days after Giordano had died. He was on his way. He bragged to Broderick, "Now, I'm the top Syrian in town."

It was six days before five other hoodlums were to die in Jesse's massacre.

Debris and oil from the Cordoba splattered the van. They drove it to Illinois where they washed it three times. The windshield wipers were replaced because residue from the explosion could be imbedded in the rubber blades. They daubed after-shave lotion on their faces and in the van's interior to disguise the acrid smoke odor.

A Confessed Hit Man

The day after Michaels was buried, Paulie Leisure was summoned to a meeting with John Vitale, the aging Mafioso who took Giordano's place until Trupiano was groomed to be the don. Leisure was inclined to display his defiance of the Mafia by ignoring the request, but a confrontation with the Sicilians was inevitable and he might as well draw the line in the sand now. Leisure knew Vitale and Michaels were close friends.

Ramo drove him to the downtown Mayfair Hotel owned by Sorkis Webbe Sr., a lawyer, powerful civic and political leader who in reality, but known by few, was a mover and shaker - the Meyer Lansky - in organized crime in St. Louis. He also fronted for the underworld in the Aladdin Hotel and Casino in Las Vegas. Trupiano was at the meeting, but said little.

Vitale was angry over the Michaels hit and blamed Leisure. "I want to tell you something, John," Leisure said calmly, but forcefully. "What happened to him, this is Syrian business. You take care of Italian business and stay out of Syrian business. We'll handle that."

"What is it you want, Paulie? Local 110? Take it, it's yours." Vitale said, his anger subsiding.

"Yeah, we're entitled to Local 110. It was agreed to a long time ago."

"What's coming from you for that?"

"You leave us alone and we'll leave you alone. We won't start anything on our own."

Vitale instructed Trupiano not to interfere with the Leisures in the local.

Leisure later vented his wrath about the Sicilians. "(Expletive) them Dagos. All my troubles and everybody's troubles come from them Dagos. I ain't gonna take no back seat to them. That (expletive) Vitale ain't never gonna see the day he'll dictate to me. I mean, that's the end of the ball game."

Leisure gloated over the most important victory so far in his climb to the top of the mob. He never had talked much about himself to his minions until now. He wasn't aware the FBI was listening to his confirmation that he was a professional hit man.

'I'll tell you one thing … you can take all these people around here, put 'em all together and put everything they did, and this is true … I killed more people than all of 'em put together."

Jesse had met Michaels only several times at social functions and funerals. His hit held no particular significance for him. There would be retaliation sometime, somewhere by somebody. The Leisures surely would find themselves in a war.

The opening shot of the Leisure War didn't provide the cover Jesse hoped for his massacre, but it did for his five victims. There was no way he could pull it off now. Soon after the bombing, most of the underworld's hierarchy was under police surveillance. Flynn was being followed everywhere he went. Other hoods were being randomly stopped and interviewed. The underworld was gripped by paranoia.

"It'd be suicide to try to whack them now," Jesse thought. "Everybody was looking over their shoulders. I was too. I knew it would last for awhile, so I just put it off. I could wait because I knew Ray and his people couldn't do anything to me either with all the heat."

What was wasn't generally known was with the death of Michaels the Leisure Outfit was to get part of his secret interest in the Aladdin Hotel and Casino in Las Vegas. The payoff was to be distributed to various members, as was the $900 given to each earlier from a payment Paulie Leisure received.

CHAPTER THIRTEEN

Surrounded By Treason

A conspiracy began swirling around Jesse soon after the Michaels hit. He was being sold out by a man he deeply respected and trusted, the top ranking, most powerful hoodlum in St. Louis.

Jesse was coming under FBI scrutiny for the first time because Vitale was a snitch. Not only was Jesse still a target of revenge by the Flynn crew, Vitale would try to lure him into another bombing and a murder for retaliation.

Two weeks after the Michaels bombing, Jesse accompanied Stanley "Ski" Kowalski, an old friend and bomb maker from the East Side, to see Paulie Leisure. Jessse didn't sit in on the conversation, but Kowalski later told him Leisure wanted him to make another bomb after bragging how well the remote control device on the Michaels' bomb worked. He was to have been paid $10,000, but Leisure still owed him $5,000.

Two FBI agents visited Jesse a week later and asked if they could come inside his house to talk. He politely refused. There was no way he would talk to them about anything, particularly inside the sanctity of his home. Carolee joined them on the front porch.

"We need a favor, Jesse, and it's worth five thousand dollars to us," one of the agents said.

"Yeah?" Jesse asked.

"We know Ski Kowalski made the remote controlled bomb that killed Jimmy Michaels. He was to get ten thousand for it, but he's only been paid five so far."

Jesse was curious how they knew that. "What makes you think I know anything about that?" he asked contemptuously.

"That's not what we hear." The agent paused for effect. "We need somebody who is close to Kowalski and you are. We'd like to wire you up and have you get him into a conversation about the bomb. It's that simple."

Jesse laughed. "You gotta be kidding."

Carolee giggled. "He wouldn't do it for a million dollars."

"Who do you guys think you are, anyhow?" Jesse sneered. "Coming to my house in front of my wife and asking me to be a lousy snitch?" He told them to leave.

He still was fuming the next day when Vitale called him and asked him to come to his house. He needed a favor. Jesse respected him, not only because he was the interim Mafia boss, but he was a man of honor. Jesse fenced a lot of stolen jewelry to him.

Vitale told Jesse to sit on the couch, but instead he took an easy chair. Vitale insisted he sit on the couch and he complied. They chatted for awhile and then Vitale told him what he needed. "You know, Jimmy and I were real close," he said.

"Yeah, I know, John. It was terrible."

"I can't believe what those crazy Leisures did to Jimmy. Blew him up like that. For no reason at all! A (expletive) shame! An old man like him. He was going to die anyhow from his heart."

Jesse nodded in silent agreement. Vitale paused for a moment, as if searching for the right words. "Let me ask you this. You know your way around. You're a good man. We need a bomb. One with a remote control to set it off."

Jesse was stunned. He said nothing for a moment, trying to assess what Vitale said.

Vitale looked him in the eyes, a slight smile on his lips. "I want you to get it from Ski Kowalski. I want one just like the one he made that they used on Jimmy. You can have him bring it to the Howard Johnson's on Hampton Avenue. We'll pick it up there. I'll give you five thousand for lining it up." Almost as an afterthought, he added, "Of course, we'll pay Ski, too."

An alarm went off inside Jesse. First, the FBI agents and then Vitale wanted him to do the same thing for the same price. "It just didn't make sense. John's got connections all over the place and he could get a bomb anytime he wanted one. Why me? What kind of game was he playing?"

Jesse decided to test Vitale. "I don't know if Kowalski makes bombs, John."

"I know good and well you do," Vitale said matter-of-factly.

"Well, I know this guy in Florida who makes them. Maybe I can get one from him."

Vitale stared at him coldly. "No, I want it from Kowalski. You bring him over here with it. Have him put it in a paper bag."

Jesse said he would think about it. As he drove home, the idea of Vitale being an FBI informant teased him. There was no way he could be a snitch. He was respected around the country, a made guy. But the more he thought the more sense it made. Was Vitale so blinded by his friendship with Michaels that in his obsession for revenge he committed the worst sin of all and became an FBI informant? Jesse knew it was possible.

"If John Vitale knew what the FBI knew, how did he know it? They either had to give it to him or he told them. That I could believe. And then it hit me. John was trying to set me up. He must have thought I was messed up with the Leisures in the bombing. That made me fair game. He could get Ski at the same time. And why did he insist I sit on the couch? Maybe he had one of those hidden cameras and was recording what I said."

Jesse told Berne the next day he suspected Vitale was a snitch and was trying to set up Kowalski and him.

Berne was angered. "You're crazy, Jesse!"

"I'm telling you, Art, Vitale's a snitch for the big eye."

Berne scolded him. "No way, Jesse. You're talking about John Vitale. Not some street punk. You don't know him like I do. He's just an old man who wants to get even for somebody killing his best friend. I don't want to hear any more about John being a snitch."

Jesse wasn't so easily dissuaded. "Why would he offer me five grand to get Ski after the FBI did?"

"I don't know, Jesse."

Jesse persisted. "How come the FBI knew about the five thousand Leisure still owes Ski?"

"Why should I know?"

"Did you tell anyone about that?"

Berne hesitated. He was perplexed. "Well, yeah, I mentioned it to John."

"See, what'd I tell you?" Jesse said triumphantly.

That was how Vitale knew! Berne was the initial snitch. "My boss put me in the trick bag! Good old Art, the bucket mouth," Jesse lamented to himself.

Kowalski suggested making a fake bomb of wood sticks and giving it to Vitale to test him. Jesse liked the idea, but rejected it. If he was sure it only was an FBI sting he would do it, but he was concerned Vitale wanted to lure them across the river to have them hit. He said nothing more about it to Vitale. His silence spoke what he needed to say.

The FBI's interest in Kowalski increased. He lived in a mobile home near Belleville. Agents rented a nearby trailer and kept him under constant surveillance for six weeks. Jesse frequently visited him. Agents were convinced both had something to do with the Michaels bombing or at least had pertinent information. Proving it with enough evidence for prosecution would be next to impossible without an informant on the inside.

Vitale offered that opportunity and he became an FBI snitch. He didn't defect from the Mafia nor was he a paid informant. He just wanted to impose revenge for the murder of his close friend.

An FBI agent described the tentative relationship. Vitale wasn't antagonistic with the agents. He was affable and polite, often joking with them. It was why he was called the "gentleman gangster." He told the agents little except about the Leisures and Jesse. He accepted the agents' request to try to get a bomb from Kowalski and Jesse. The agents' visit to Jesse's house was part of the scheme.

Jesse's background Vitale provided increased the FBI's interest in him. They now knew he wasn't the mediocre gangster they had assumed. Vitale suggested the agents target Jesse. They did and he agreed to help them.

Vitale wasn't immune from FBI scrutiny. He was the object of another FBI investigation. A few days after he met with Jesse, agents executed a search warrant for his person as he returned on a flight from Las Vegas. They confiscated $36,000 in cash, assumed to be skim money from the Aladdin Casino.

Revenge For Revenge

Peace, as tenuous as it was, eventually settled over the underworld. There hadn't been the anticipated retaliation against the Leisures, but the Syrian-Lebanese forces were seeking their pound of flesh. Sadie Faheen, Michaels' sister, contributed $250,000 to a war chest for the killing of all those responsible for his death. Bounties of $50,000 each were placed on Paulie, Anthony and David Leisure. A hit squad was assembled. A war room was set up in a suburban apartment.

Milton R. "Russ" Schepp, chief of police of St. George and a karate expert who was associated with the Michaels family, played a key role. The small municipality abutted the interstate highway where Michaels' car exploded and he was one of the first officers on the scene. He acquired parts for a bomb and assembled them. Periodic surveillances of the Leisures began with two automobiles purchased by Schepp and registered in fictitious names.

While his sworn enemies were plotting his demise, Paulie Leisure's attention was diverted temporarily from them. He learned a professional assassin from Chicago had been contracted to hit him. He had the man's name and description and knew the motel where he was to stay. It wasn't difficult for his operatives to find him. Their boss knew how a professional hitter thought and acted.

It was a deadly mind game Leisure's crew played with him. They ran a tight, bumper-to-bumper surveillance, waking him in the morning and putting him to bed at night. They sat next to him in restaurants and went to restrooms with him. Had he come any-where near Leisure, they would have killed him. He obviously was aware of that. After several days he conceded defeat and returned to Chicago.

Leisure took no great offense at the hit man. He was doing what he would have done. He could have killed him. Nobody would have cared and it would have been justified. Not that there was camaraderie among professional hit men. They were a secret society of faceless men, unknown to each other, who came and went like thieves in the night, stealing not possessions but life.

Leisure praised his crew for protecting him. "I'll say one thing for you bloodhounds. You were on his tail the second he hit town. Them Michaels, we'll eat 'em like hamburgers. You know, we got a power structure. We got an organization. They're just punks. Getting away from us is like trying to walk between the raindrops."

By the spring of 1981, Leisure was regaining power in the Labors' Union. Flynn appointed him an organizer and a member of the Executive Board of Local 42. It was the first fruit of the alliance forged with the elimination of Spica. Installing Leisure in the local was to preserve their interests in Flynn's absence. A federal judge ruled he was ineligible to hold a union office because it had been less than five years since his guilty plea in a 1979 burglary charge.

With Local 42 now secured, Leisure turned his attention to Local 110, the crown jewel of the three labor unions. The purge began with the elimination of two of Michaels' relatives. Only the Italians remained and Leisure would eliminate them in due time. Trupiano so far had obeyed Vitale's mandate and had not interfered.

Blood For Blood

About 7:15 the morning of August 11, 1981, George "Sonny" Faheen, Sadie's son, and Jack Issa, a long-time associate of the Michaels family, parked a block from Paulie Leisure's home in south St. Louis. His Cadillac was in front at the curb as usual. They wouldn't have long to wait. They knew his routine.

Leisure walked out of his front door at 8 a. m., his mother behind him. They chatted briefly in the front yard. He kissed her on the cheek and started for the Cadillac. As he opened the door, she waved to him.

When he inserted the key in the ignition, one of the men watching him punched a button on a remote control. The bomb exploded, ripping out the undercarriage of the Cadillac. A briefcase containing Local 42 documents was found nearby. Leisure miraculously survived.

He was near death when surgeons amputated parts of both legs and repaired serious injuries to his face. His days as a hit man were over. He would be crippled for life. His mother suffered partial hearing loss and minor injuries.

It was six days less than a year after Michaels was hit. It was a long time coming. Revenge - at least in part - had been extracted. Blood spilled for blood. The next day Anthony Leisure and Broderick went to see Vitale. They suspected he was behind it. They later would learn he had approved it. The aging gangster was cordial, but Leisure was terse.

"Who did this to my brother?" Leisure demanded.

"Anthony, one of these days you'll pick up the paper and see it was a family thing," Vitale responded.

Anthony Leisure knew it wasn't just a family affair. He now was sure Vitale had agreed with the Michaels family about the hit. He might even had arranged it.

Paulie Leisure had said as much a few weeks before the bombing. "You can't hurt a guy like me without asking if it's all right. I'm too far up." But he was a renegade and had violated an underworld tenet. He hadn't obtained permission to kill Michaels. No one, not even the crime lords in Chicago, would have approved it.

Flynn urged quick retaliation for the bombing. "Something has to be done about this," he told members of the Leisure Outfit. "I have strong feelings for that guy Paulie. And you have to move fast to get the people responsible."

Invitation To Murder

Two weeks after Leisure was bombed, Vitale again summoned Jesse to his home. He almost refused, but he was curious, yet cautious.

"This is getting bad, Jesse," Vitale said angrily. "No one knows who'll get it next. People are afraid to go out on the streets with all the bombs going off. Nobody's making any money. The heat's all over and people can't move anymore."

"Yeah, I know, John. It's getting out of hand," Jesse agreed.

"You know what's worse, Jesse. Not one of them bums is dead. Not one. And after what they did to Jimmy! They're still walking around."

Jesse laughed. "Not Paulie Leisure."

Vitale snickered. "But he ain't dead."

"He's worse off than dead."

Vitale leaned closer to him, as if confiding some dreadful secret. He had men watching the hospital where Leisure was recuperating, but it was difficult to get near enough to him to take him out. At least two members of Leisure's outfit were outside the hospital at all times, observing who entered. Two armed guards provided security in his room.

"I want Paul Leisure dead, Jesse. So do Jimmy's people. They got fifty grand for someone to take the hit. It won't be easy, but the right man can get it done right there in the hospital."

Jesse didn't answer him. It was difficult concealing his hatred of Vitale.

Vitale stared at him. "The Michaelses think you're the man. I think so, too. They wanted me to ask you to do it. I got the fifty thousand right here. You get it up front right now."

It was a tempting offer. Jesse would be $50,000 richer and one of his mortal enemies would be dead. His "Stone Killer" image would be enhanced. But he couldn't go along with Vitale. He suspected it was a set-up intended to get him killed or arrested for murder.

"John, I don't kill people for money," Jesse said calmly.

Vitale was momentarily disappointed, then he laughed. "I told them you'd probably say that. I didn't think you would."

"No way, John. I don't want to get involved in this mess over here. I want to stay out of it. Like I have been."

Before Vitale could answer, the doorbell rang. Pasquale "Pat" Lopicollo, a huge, gray-haired Mafioso, came in. He was carrying a manila envelope. Jesse knew him and they shook hands.

"I got the package for you," he said, handing the envelope to Vitale, who opened it and took out a stack of large bills. "There are fifty big ones in there. Just like they said."

Vitale thanked him and left, waving to Jesse.

"That came out of Vegas," Vitale said, smiling. "Art gets a piece of it and he'll probably pass some of it to you."

Vitale went to another room and returned with a metal strong box. He took a key from his pocket, opened it and motioned to Stoneking. It was crammed full of large bills.

"What do you see in there, Jesse?" he asked, beaming.

Jesse chuckled. "A million dollars."

"Not quite. Just two-hundred grand."

Jesse knew Vitale was greedy and bragged about his money. He decided soon to take it from him. It also would be a way of paying him back.

Vitale put the box away and returned to the living room. He leaned back in his chair, a confident smile on his face. "I guess you're too busy, anyhow, aren't you? You and your partner, that young fellow. What's his name? Oh, yeah, Mark Stram. Running that chop shop over in Mt. Vernon, dealing in hot cars."

Jesse tried to appear nonchalant, but he couldn't. "How'd you know about that, John?"

Vitale grinned confidently. "Everybody's got a good snitch or two."

"Yeah, there's too many of them around these days." Jesse didn't try to conceal his sarcasm.

Jesse was alarmed at Vitale's knowledge of the chop shop operation. He and Stram set it up a year before and already had made more than a hundred thousand dollars. They were partners with Earl Long, who lived in Mt. Vernon, Illinois, about 75 miles east of downtown St. Louis. Cars stolen in five states were delivered to Long, who dismantled them and sold the parts.

That sealed Jesse's suspicion. "I knew for sure now Vitale was a snitch. No question about it. Only me, Mark and Earl knew it was located in Mt. Vernon. How could he have known? Only one way. The FBI told him." Jesse was right about that.

"Let Me Walk To Kill People"

As he recovered from his injuries, Paulie Leisure reflected on his brush with death. It was an inspiration, as distorted as it was. He told Ramo about a man he befriended in the hospital. They had much in common because his legs also had been amputated.

"I respected this guy because he was really good, a high-spirited guy. What motivated this guy … he was really happy and real good. That's not my reason for wanting to walk again. Mine is even better than his. I pray to God to let me walk to kill people. Now, you know that's wrong. I'm motivated because I want to go out and kill."

Leisure was fatalistic about the bombing. "It's one of the hazards of the (expletive) game. I knew this all my life. You know, by rights, I should've been dead. Ten sticks of (expletive) dynamite! I'm the only one that I know of in the history of the whole country that ever walked away from a car bombing."

The alliance with Flynn had served Leisure well. While he recuperated he wanted to turn over his outfit to Flynn, but he declined, saying Leisure still was capable. It really is a matter of destiny, which was on his side, Leisure mused. "See, one thing, it's your fate. It's marked on your forehead. You're gonna be here 'till it's time to go. It's all written on your forehead the day you're born. And I'm still here, ain't I?"

Jesse now was on Leisure's hit list. "My fate is that I'm gonna run this town. Both sides of the river. I'm gonna be old man Michaels and Giordano wrapped up in one. Guys like that Stoneking and his crew and them Dagos, they're all dead. Vitale, he'll be dead between now and Christmas. You won't see him anymore."

In his tortured mind, Leisure welcomed a confrontation with the Michaels Outfit. "I wish they'd come in here and let's get it over with. It'd do my heart good to blast it out with them. Just give me two forty-fives. I feel like I could still take a couple of slugs and drop them. About six, four or five of them, anyway."

David Leisure had several sources in the St. Louis Metropolitan Police Department who confirmed much of what already was known. The Michaels' family bombed Paulie Leisure. What wasn't known by the Leisures was who was directly involved. The Police Department sources told David who.

Schepp had installed the bomb and Faheen and Issa detonated it. Schepp and Issa fled and couldn't be found. Schepp was in California until August 1983 when he surrendered. David Leisure also was told about the suburban apartment used as the Michaels' war room even before a warrant was executed to search it.

Retaliation had to be swift and deadly. The Leisures needed to unleash all the fury at their disposal. The streets must run with blood of the Michaels clan. Twelve members and associates were put on the kill list. Even those they only suspected or who played peripheral roles were to die. The Michaels' Outfit would only be a memory. A bad one.

David Leisure and Innes Anderson, a repairman for the telephone company, raided a depository of company records in an office building downtown to obtain records of long distance calls to and from the Michaels family involving those in hiding, but they showed little.

Paulie Leisure several times in the past had been to a farm Jimmy Michaels owned near Fredricktown about 100 miles south of St. Louis. It was possible some of the Michaels clan were hiding there. Anthony told Broderick and Flynn to accompany him to the farm. They would shoot and kill whoever was inside.

Broderick drove and when they got near the farm Anthony and Flynn changed into old, worn clothing so they would blend in the rural area. Each armed with a pistol, they walked to the house through a wooded area while Broderick drove up and down a nearby highway. They and Broderick had walkie-talkies to communicate. They searched the house, but no one was inside or staying there. After an hour they called Broderick and told him to pick them up.

As they drove away Flynn suggested several sticks of dynamite be attached to a rope and left dangling down the chimney above the fireplace. When a fire was started the explosives would detonate and the "whole house would blow up," killing all inside, he explained. Broderick opposed it because there might be women and children there. The plan was abandoned when it was learned the Michaels family no longer used the farm.

Leisure's death dealers prowled the streets looking for victims. They needed just one family member to learn the whereabouts of the others. Torture would be the tool.

"If we catch one of those guys we'll have to work on him first," Paulie told David. The victim would be forced to consume laxatives. "Every time he craps we'll whop him with a baseball bat. Maybe red-hot pokers, right? There's nothing wrong with a good blowtorch, too. Make him feel every bit of it." Putting the hands in moving gears of a transmission was an option. Burning cigarettes would be extinguished in the eyes.

"Kill him so easy," David urged. "Make him die slow."

They tried to monitor Sadie Faheen's telephone to learn the locations of those they were seeking, but they couldn't get it done. They also wanted to tap those in the offices of U. S. Attorney Thomas Dittmeier to learn the status of the government's investigation of the outfit, but Anderson said it couldn't be done.

The Leisures learned John Michaels, another grandson of Jimmy Michaels, frequently had lunch at a popular restaurant. They would ambush him from an abandoned house abutting the parking lot at the rear of the restaurant. About noon on September 11, one month after Paulie Leisure was bombed, David and Anthony Leisure, using a stolen white van driven by Loewe, parked in front of the deserted house. They wore ski masks and gloves. Anthony carried a shotgun and David a pistol.

Michaels parked his car on the lot. A friend, Dennis Day, who had no part in Paulie's bombing, accompanied him. As they got out of the car, Anthony opened fire on Michaels with the shotgun. The shot grazed him and he fell to the ground between two cars. Anthony fired at Day. He also was wounded

That Michaels only was injured and not killed angered Paulie Leisure. They hadn't been professional. He scolded them. "One thing, when you do that, you never want to leave there until he's dead. If it ain't right, you pass on it. If I'd only dropped him, I would have gone and hit him again in the head to make sure. I never did like those long distance things."

Prater asked Anthony why he shot Day. "I don't know," he replied coldly. "He was just standing there and I just shot him."

David Leisure, now the outfit's gumshoe, learned Sonny Faheen lived in an apartment in the Mansion House complex downtown near the riverfront, not far from the Civil Courts Building where he was chief clerk. David, Ramo and Frank Termine Jr., a newly recruited Leisure gang member, stalked him for two weeks, using walkie-talkies and two vehicles. Faheen parked his red Volkswagen in the apartment development's garage, often walking to work.

Paulie and Anthony Leisure rejected another ambush. Faheen's car must be bombed. Prater and Broderick argued against it. Innocent people could be injured or killed in the close confines of the garage. The Leisures didn't care. Faheen had to be taken out. Now!

Flynn delivered 10 sticks of dynamite he obtained from Kowalski to David and Anthony Leisure in the afternoon of October 15, 1981. David practiced installing the bomb near the fuel tank of a salvaged Volkswagen.

The next morning, David Leisure, wearing a gray wig, and Loewe drove to the parking garage in separate cars. The bomb was in the trunk of Loewe's car. He parked on another level and Leisure put the bomb in his own vehicle before proceeding to the level where the Volkswagen was located.

Michael Kornhardt, another recently recruited member of the outfit, stayed in Leisure's car as a lookout. Any security guard who wandered onto the scene would be shot.

As Leisure opened the door of the Volkswagen on the driver's side, a plastic coffee cup propped against it fell out. It apparently was a precaution Faheen took to determine if anyone had tampered with his car.

Lesiure unlatched the hood and replaced the cup before closing the door. He attached the bomb to a wire inserted into the ignition. When it detonated, it would ignite the gasoline in the tank, adding to the explosion.

Shortly before noon, Faheen opened the door of the Volkswagen. The coffee cup was in place. It was safe to start the car. He got behind the wheel, inserted the key in the ignition and turned it. He was incinerated instantly.

The explosion reverberated throughout the garage. Acrid smoke swirled throughout the level. Flames scarred the floor and ceiling.

Debris was flung over a wide area, damaging nearby vehicles. Fortunately, no passersby were there.

Partial retribution had been made. It was just two months and five days after Paulie Leisure was bombed.

Leisure and Prater that night watched television news coverage of the bombing. "The Little Man, he gets the job done," Leisure told Prater. It was a nickname he and Anthony often used in reference to David.

Leisure, still recuperating in his home, met with Rich Washington, his bodyguard, and Ramo. They discussed Faheen's death. Leisure had a copy of the police report on the bombing. As usual, the FBI was listening.

He described the bombing from the report. "His cause of death wasn't the dynamite. He was burned to death. They burned him alive. That's exactly what they did. Best thing about it, when he got in the car, he put that seat belt on and locked himself in. He was trapped in there. The gas sprayed and burned him up. His ears and nose were burned off. Both his legs were blown off. When you burn up, that ain't no fun."

Police searched Faheen's apartment and found two loaded semiautomatic pistols. He had placed a toolbox on the floor against the door as he left for the last time. Leisure observed: "Like if he walked in and he didn't feel that toolbox, he would never go in that apartment. He was sharp, I'll say that. But he wasn't sharp enough."

It was the last known act of violence in the Leisure War, although a suspected snitch in the outfit was killed. But it wasn't over for Jesse. Throughout it all, he watched what was happening with growing apprehension. It would have repercussions on his life for a long time.

CHAPTER FOURTEEN

A Day Of Reckoning

It was a year since Jesse aborted his massacre and it was time to resurrect it. A time to finally kill. Everything seemed in his favor and nothing could stop him now.

Time hadn't mellowed his craving for revenge against the Flynn coalition. He was just as committed, but there now was greater urgency – and more opportunity – following the Leisure bombing. The massacre probably would be blamed on the Michaels Outfit as part of its retaliation. Jesse had one concern. Flynn also might see it as an opportunity and make a pre-emptive strike against him.

Because blame likely would be directed elsewhere, Jesse wasn't as meticulous this time in his preparation. Since little surveillance would be required, he bought only one used car with fraudulent registration for the hit. He also didn't have to give himself and Stram an extensive alibi like at the Lake of the Ozarks.

Flynn and his crew still had dinner on Tuesday nights at the same restaurant. Jesse and Stram checked it out and saw they drove the same cars. The five also played cards on Friday nights at the Twin Cities Auto Auction, which the Leisures and Flynn had opened in Jefferson County south of St. Louis. Jesse surveyed the facility and the surrounding area one Friday afternoon and sat in for a few hands that night. It was more opportune than the restaurant.

The massacre would be done there the next Friday night. It wouldn't be difficult. "There were a lot of cars for the auction parked on the lot in front, on the side and in the back. Plenty of places to hide. It was well lighted. I'd just open up on them with the M-16. If I couldn't do it that way, there were woods at the edge of the lot. I could sit in there with the rifle and pick them off."

A Fortune Waiting

While Jesse awaited the execution, he decided to rip off Vitale. The cash he kept in his house was too tempting to resist, even though he knew the danger inherent in doing it so soon after Vitale showed it to him. But it was best to do it before the bloodbath. "So what if he did think it was me? He's not going to file a police report about that money being stolen from him or put a hit out on me? The cops would know he didn't get that cash legitimately. He'd have a hell of a time trying to whack me."

Vitale and his wife went out for dinner most Saturday nights. Jesse and Stram would break in his house shortly after they left. At 7:15 that night, Stram called Vitale's house from a public telephone at a service station a few blocks away. Vitale answered. Disguising his voice, Stram said he had a wrong number. They waited another 30 minutes and drove past the house. It was dark. Stram called again and there was no answer.

They parked a short distance down the street from the house. It would be an easy score since Jesse knew where the strongbox was. They would break in through the back door, grab the cash box and be out in a minute or two.

Just as they were about to do it, Vitale pulled into the driveway of his house, got out and opened the garage door. He and his wife appeared to be arguing. It was probably why they returned early.

"Aw, hell Jesse," Stram said. "I was already counting that money."

"That's the way it goes. What if it was a couple of minutes later and we were inside? We'll get him later."

Traveling Companions

The next Monday as Jesse left home he detected he was being followed by two casually dressed men in a plain sedan. They were professionals the way they tailed him. Fear suddenly reared its ugly head. Was death stalking him again? Had Vitale put a contract out on him? Was Flynn making his move?

He got close enough to see them, but they weren't local hoods. Flynn or the Leisures wouldn't import hired hit men. They had to be the law. It wasn't surprising during these times. It probably was just routine surveillance. They were more an annoyance than a threat and cramped his style. They likely would soon move on to someone else.

Following him were FBI agents Joseph T. "Tom" Fox Jr., a specialist in organized crime, and Terry Bohnemeier, both assigned to the Belleville Field Office. They had targeted the Berne Outfit, but it was Jesse in whom they were most interested, thanks to Vitale.

They had penetrated Jesse's invisibility. He now was viewed as the money man, the mystery operative of the underworld who traveled in the upper echelons of organized crime. But he didn't fit the profile of a high-level hoodlum. He appeared to be squeaky clean, nothing more than a family man. He had no obvious source of legitimate income, which, in itself, was suspicious, and he had no arrest record except as a juvenile.

Fox explained: "On the one hand, we felt he was involved somehow in the Ellington murder. We didn't know for sure why, but we had picked up rumors that Ellington had been rebelling against Berne. Then there was the shoot-out in the tavern. That alone made him a pretty dangerous person."

It was why they began their intense surveillance from the time he left home to his return. They wanted to know him better and catch him dirty at something other than the stolen car ring and the chop shop operation on which a good case was being built. They soon learned his uncanny ability to detect and elude surveillances. He made their professional lives difficult and frustrating.

He pulled off an expressway and stopped his car on the shoulder halfway down the ramp. If they followed and passed him, he backed onto the highway and continued in the direction he had been heading. If they pulled off the roadway and waited behind him, he would drive under the overpass and back on the highway in the opposite direction. They sometimes were left waiting at a red light he purposely ran.

The agents found themselves going the wrong way on one-way streets. Jesse sometimes suddenly made U-turns in the middle of the block, honked his horn, smiled and waved at them as he passed in the opposite direction. He caused traffic jams by driving slow on thoroughfares. They were playing cat and mouse with him, but it was difficult to determine who was the cat and who was the mouse.

They watched Jesse's house in O'Fallon from the parking lot of a bowling alley a block away. They were well concealed and assumed they would be undetected. But it wasn't good enough. Jesse observed them when he left the house and waved to them.

One morning, he brought two cups of coffee and set them on a tree stump nearby. Grinning, he pointed to the cups and then saluted them. His ultimate display of arrogance came the next morning. He drove into the parking lot and pulled alongside them.

"How you guys doing this morning?" he asked politely. They nodded their heads. There wasn't much they could say. "I just got a few errands to run. No big deal. I should be back in a couple of hours. Have fun."

Fox and Bohnemeier were becoming accustomed to his antics, yet annoyed and frustrated. Their surveillance was an exercise in futility. It disclosed little new about him.

Jesse assumed they were playing a game with him to agitate him. They surely had nothing incriminating on him or they would have busted him. "I was just having fun with them, too. I knew it drove them crazy. I really didn't care unless I was going to meet somebody. In a way it gave me kind of protection. I didn't suppose anyone would try to crack me with my guardian angels watching all the time."

Another Reprieve From Slaughter

By Thursday, Jesse realized he again had to postpone the massacre set for the next night. He couldn't kill five men with an audience. He would give the five men a temporary stay of execution for a week or two. There was no way he would call it off permanently.

The surveillance intensified. Instead of one car, now there were two or three with two men in each. He couldn't shake that many cars. A gray van with darkened windows was parked at the end of the block. It was there when he left and when he returned. He assumed it was part of the surveillance. He tried to look inside, but he couldn't see through the shaded windows and the doors were locked. A single-engine airplane hovered over his car some of the time.

"It was like a parade sometimes. The airplane got me to wondering. Was I that important that they used an airplane? There wasn't any way to shake a plane. I wasn't going to pull off a score with that much heat around. They should have known that. I didn't say much over the phone at home, either. They probably had that bugged."

At 10 a. m. on September 16, Jesse left his house for a meeting with Berne. The van wasn't at the end of the block and there were no surveillance cars in sight. He no longer was being watched. The authorities must have become bored without any action. It was time to take care of business and make some money.

As he neared the bowling alley parking lot, four cars appeared out of nowhere and forced his Lincoln to a stop. He didn't see them until it was too late. "The first thing I thought was that I was getting whacked. I reached for the forty-five I usually had under my seat, but I remembered I wasn't carrying it. Then these eight guys, all with their pistols pointed at me and flashing badges, surrounded my car. I knew then it wasn't a hit coming down. I just get out of my car with my hands in the air."

Fox and Bohnemeier identified themselves. Fox searched him while Bohnemeier handcuffed him. Other agents looked through his car. It was over in a few minutes.

"You're under arrest, Jesse Stoneking," Bohnemeier said. "The federal grand jury has indicted you on charges of conspiracy and interstate transportation of stolen vehicles."

"Yeah, sure," Jesse said, not immediately understanding what it meant.

"The chop shop operation in Mt. Vernon."

Fox started to read him his rights, but Jesse shrugged him off. The agents sat him in the back seat of their car.

"This is why there were so many of you guys following me, huh? And in an airplane yet."

"You're an important man, Jesse," Fox said, laughing.

Jesse said nothing. He read the indictment. It was curious it had been returned a week earlier by the grand jury, but they had waited this long before arresting him.

"Why'd you guys wait so long to bust me? It says here that this indictment came out a week ago."

"We were in no hurry," Bohnemeier replied.

"You were probably trying to get something else on me."

Bohnemeier didn't respond. Jesse answered their questions respectfully as they booked him. "Why didn't you take me at my house?" he asked Fox.

"We don't operate that way. We didn't want to embarrass you in front of your family and neighbors."

"You're the first cops I ever saw who are gentlemen. I appreciate that." He was sincere.

"FBI agents aren't such bad guys once you get to know us."

Jesse snickered. "I don't ever wanna know you guys that well."

It was the way Fox and Bohnemeier were. Fox projected the father image. He was unemotionally analytical, soft-spoken and slow to anger. Bohnemeier was the joker, gregarious, sometimes quick tempered and blunt. They treated their prisoners with respect and dignity. They knew Jesse was a proud man concerned about his families. Maybe that would give them a little leverage with him. They nurtured a hope, as faint as it was, he might talk about the bombings.

Fox talked to him in his cell. "Look, Jesse, you're in some heavy crap. You know that." Jesse didn't answer him. "We hear you may be in trouble with the Leisures over in St. Louis."

"I don't know anything about those people," Jesse said defiantly.

"You know as well as we do what they're up to. Maybe you can give us a little information that'll help us put them away for good. Then everyone can breathe easier. You, too. You might even be able to do yourself some good."

Jesse was annoyed. They wanted him to snitch. "You got the wrong guy. I don't know what's going on over there and don't want to. I'll never snitch on anybody."

Fox looked into his eyes, but he found no encouragement, only rejection. The barrier of silence Jesse had built against the law was impenetrable. "Look, Jesse, those Leisures are trying to take over and anybody who gets in their way is on their own. If you don't join up with them ..."

Jesse interrupted him. "You guys think I'm some kind of hoodlum, or something? I'm just a jewelry salesman."

"Sure. And I'm Santa Clause. I'm just telling you like it is. We want to be your friends. You know where to come if you need any help or get into trouble."

Jesse ignored him. He was arraigned the next day. He posted the $25,000 cash bond. He had plenty of time to think that night in jail. Once again, Flynn and the others escaped death. Now he was consumed by thoughts of Vitale. He had gotten his evens. He didn't need to hire a hit man. The FBI agents were his assassins.

"The more I thought about him the more I hated him. He had to know the FBI was going to bust me and he could have warned me about it. He didn't come out and say, 'Hey, you're in a lot of trouble. Watch it'. He didn't say that you're under investigation. 'You're gonna be arrested'. It wouldn't have done much good, but at least he could have been a man about it. It's what I would have done.

"Then I got to thinking why the others, especially Earl Long, hadn't been busted. I guess they were after only me and maybe were trying to turn me into a snitch. That would never happen."

Vitale became the sixth man on Jesse's massacre list.

Rice, who would represent Jesse, met with him the next morning. He learned Jesse's chop shop operation partner Long had ratted on him. Jesse's initial despair turned to rage. His loyalty had been repaid with disloyalty. Seven men now were on his massacre list.

"First Vitale, now Earl Long. I mean, how many snitches were there against me? Was there anybody I could trust anymore? Rice found out that Earl had also faked evidence against me. I was being framed good. I guess I just didn't understand how snitches worked.

"That was all I could think about. Cracking Long. Getting even with him. Vitale could wait. I wasn't just going to shoot Long in the head. I wasn't going to be that easy on him. I'd torture him and make him hurt bad. I dreamed about seeing him laying there, bleeding to death and saying he was sorry.

"I had a right doing that. He was a rat and rats don't have a right to live. Then I realized I would be the first one the 'g' would suspect and that's probably what they wanted. Stoneking on a murder beef. Killing a government witness yet. I could wait, but I wouldn't forget."

There were not-so-subtle hints from the agents a deal might be cut if Jesse talked about his associates and told what he knew about the bombings. It only made his agony worse. He was a stand-up guy. Loyalty was part of his underworld creed. Never could he forsake that.

Jesse pleaded guilty in mid-November. No plea bargaining, no deals, no requests of any kind, just a straight confession. He faced a maximum 10 years in prison, but he wanted to get it over with and do his time. If he went to trial, the prosecution might bring out matters, particularly parts of his life that must remain secret. Some of his people, like Stram, might be implicated and he didn't want that.

Rice warned Jesse he probably would be sentenced to at least three years and ordered to immediately begin serving his sentence.

CHAPTER FIFTEEN

"You're Going To Go Straight"

It was so absurd it was hilarious. Even Jesse laughed, although there was little reason for hilarity that night.

Berne's wife, Loretta, who adored Jesse, was into astrology and was about to become the center of attraction at a bash for outfit guys. The affair was a going-away party for Jesse the night of December 6, the day before he was to be sentenced by U. S. District Judge William Beatty.

Loretta had drawn astrology charts on some of Berne's underworld associates. She had insisted on compiling one on Jesse and he consented just to humor her. What harm was there in that? It was just a big joke. He gave her the pertinent information, including his birth date. Now, at the party, she announced she had finished her charts on him. She had two predictions.

She giggled. "First of all, Jesse's kind of kinky with his women."

The laughter was deafening. Berne was agitated. She was a nuisance and a busybody, he complained.

"Well, it's true, Art," she replied.

"I'm telling you, forget that crap, Loretta."

She ignored him as she usually did. He might control his outfit, but not his wife. "I'm not done yet. Still waters run deep and Jesse's a very, very dangerous person."

Jesse considered it a compliment. Berne glared at her. She continued. "Right now he's in between those waters and they are very deep. Someday, Jesse, you're going to go straight."

The others laughed raucously again. "What the hell's wrong with you, woman?" Berne shouted. "Get out of here with that crap. Jesse's a good outfit guy. He's a lifetime hoodlum."

Jesse grinned. "When I go straight, that'll be the day I die, Loretta."

Loretta had another prediction. "Arthur, someone close to you either has become a snitch or will before very long."

Berne lost it. He shook his head in total disgust. "That woman's gone completely nuts. There ain't nobody in my outfit who's a snitch or gonna be. Stop being a weirdo."

"She's probably talking about Vitale, Art," Jesse said. "A real snitch."

Berne scowled at him. "I told you to stop talking about that, Jesse. Leave it alone."

Jesse was unaware of how accurate Loretta was. Nor did he realize God, too, had a chart. The Lord was increasing His intercession in Jesse's life. The second, more intrusive phase apparently was to begin the next morning as God introduced him to adversity of a different nature, one that would be life altering.

Christmas was two weeks early for both families. Jesse went through the same rituals as previous holidays, but they just weren't the same this year. There was little joy, even when the presents were opened, as gloom permeated each household. The meals were burdensome and unappetizing, the conversations awkward and pretentious. And there were embarrassing questions difficult for Jesse to answer with any credibility, ones that required lies.

After they opened their gifts at Dorothy's house, Jesse's daughter cuddled next to him on the sofa. "Why did Santa Clause come now?" she asked.

He fumbled for an answer. "Because I told him to." He laughed feebly.

"Why? It's not Christmas yet."

The answer eluded him for a moment. It was rare when he didn't have an instant answer in any kind of situation. "Because daddy's got to go away for awhile." It was the closest he dared come to the truth.

"Where are you going?" He couldn't find an answer. There was none. "Are you coming back?"

He picked her up and hugged her. "Of course. That's enough questions."

It was one of the saddest times of his life when he walked away from both families the next morning. "I knew it was hard on them because they couldn't understand what was going on. All they knew was that their daddy was going to leave them. I couldn't look at them when I left. I didn't want them to see me with tears in my eyes."

Unwelcome thoughts, like those after the shoot-out, began pestering Jesse. God was at work. What was most important in his life? Maintaining his status in the underworld or his fatherly dignity with his families? Maybe he should walk away from the mob, but that didn't seem a possibility now. What kind of profitable job could a hoodlum, soon to be a convict, find?

Judge Beatty sentenced Jesse to three years. Fox and Bohnemeier watched as he was led in shackles by marshals from the courtroom like a common criminal, the ultimate indignity. The guilty plea dashed whatever hope they had he would cooperate with them. He could have tried to strike a deal to stay out of prison, but there only was silence from him.

Jesse was taken first to the federal penitentiary in Terre Haute, Indiana, not far from St. Louis. He would be transferred later to another facility. He now considered the sentence only a brief, unpleasant interruption of his life.

"It was no big deal. I could do that much time standing on my head. I'd be out of the joint in no time. I guess you could call it kind of a vacation. Yeah, that's what it would be. A vacation."

The seven victims of his massacre now had three more years to live. Their holiday would end when he again breathed free air. Vitale and Long had priority on his hit list. He wouldn't be able to do all seven at the same time. Nevertheless, he was just as determined as before. In the meantime, he was safe. His enemies couldn't touch him now.

CHAPTER SIXTEEN

A Turning Point

Prison time wasn't the pleasant, inspiring walk in the park Jesse anticipated. Before, he swaggered, but now he shuffled and stumbled. It was hard time with no tomorrows, no promises. Just today and the subjugation and oppressive monotony that came with it.

He had been the drummer to which he marched, but now his parade took him nowhere. The only pavement he pounded was in his cell and in the prison yard. Life was the same every day with the tyrannical prison guards watching every movement and barking nonsensical orders. The swashbuckler was being tamed to be a household pet in the government domicile now his home.

Those marching with Jesse were the same sallow faces that hadn't seen the sunlight of freedom in years. The same limping bodies going nowhere. The same hollow eyes long devoid of hope and filled with despair and hatred. It wouldn't be long before Jesse lost his identity and became one of those zombies. He already was a puppet with others pulling his strings.

Depression was a companion and he often found himself languishing between self-pity and desperation. He was becoming not only a prisoner of the law, but of his mind. The shackles around him were tightening. Freedom was becoming just a memory.

What tortured him as much was there was nothing he could do about it. He couldn't adjust to his new environment and just accept it for what it was, consider it a temporary interruption of his life. Conformity wasn't part of his life. He had created his own lifestyle, his own morality, but now that too was taken from him. His only future was parole, whenever that might be.

Jesse had too much time on his hands, too much opportunity to brood. Many of his thoughts centered on Long's and Vitale's betrayal. He didn't deny his own blame for being in prison. He committed the crime and had to do the time. But it was Long and Vitale who stole his life from him with their duplicity. There was no solution other than revenge.

Berne also was the target of his rancor. He, too, had displayed disloyalty. "I always gave Art a piece of my action. It was what I had to do out of respect for him. He said he would help take care of my families while I was away. He never gave them a cent or even called them. He was the stingiest and greediest man I ever knew. That was one thing Ellington wasn't wrong about. I mean, here I'm loyal to him and the mob and then they turned their backs to me. I began to hate their guts, especially his."

A Hit From Prison

Jesse called Dorothy collect every Sunday afternoon at 1:30. On the third Sunday he was in prison he got no answer. She usually was home from church by then. He called again at 2 o'clock, then 2:30, and still no answer. At first he was suspicious. Was she seeing someone else? Then he worried. Had the Leisures or Flynn gotten to her? That made no sense. She didn't have anything they wanted.

Finally, at 3 o'clock she answered. She was hysterical. A man accosted her on the church parking lot, grabbed their adopted daughter from her arms and ran off. She didn't know where to look for him.

"Should I call the police, Jesse?"

Jesse raged. "No, I'll take care of it."

"But how can you when you're in prison?"

147

He screamed at her. "I said I'll take care of it, Dorothy!" She began crying and he tried to console her. "Look, I'm sorry. I know you're upset, but just let me take care of it. Just don't call the cops. You think they'll be much help looking for Jesse Stoneking's daughter?"

Time in prison didn't assuage Jesse's desire to kill. He called Stram, who was on his visitors' list, and told him to come to the prison the next day. He couldn't tell him why. Prison authorities might be monitoring his calls. When Stram came, he told him to contact Matt, a friend of theirs' and a giant of a man. The mere sight of him was menacing. He gave Stram the address of the girl's father.

"Get this straight, Mark. I want you and Matt to go get my daughter. Then you crack that (expletive). I don't care how you do it. Just hit him. Make him hurt a lot."

"You think that's right, Jesse?"

"Right? What do you mean right? He's got my little girl!"

"We'll get her back, but I'd think twice about hitting him, Jesse."

Jesse was furious. "Do what I tell you! I want her back with Dorothy and I want this guy dead. I don't want him breathing. Understand?"

Back in his cell, Jesse slumped deeper into despair. Everything was out of his control. He was to be transferred in several weeks to a federal prison in Wisconsin, even farther from his families and his friends. He would be more isolated and alone.

Stram came to see him on Friday. He was excited. "We got her, Jesse. She's back with Dorothy."

Jesse laughed with relief. "She was okay?"

"Not a scratch on her. Nothing wrong."

"That's great. I owe you guys a big one. What about the guy?"

"That's taken care of, too."

"You crack him?"

Stram paused. "I told you, Jesse, it's taken care of."

Stram was being evasive and Jesse was irritated. "Answer me! You crack him?"

"Not exactly."

"What do you mean not exactly? I told you I wanted him cracked."

"It wasn't right. But we whipped his ass good. He ain't gonna be walking for a long time."

"That's not what I wanted, Mark!" Jesse shouted.

"Maybe later, Jesse."

Jesse said nothing. His silence conveyed his anger over Stram's disobedience.

Stram was uneasy. "You should have seen Matt. I mean he went bananas when the guy mouthed off to him."

"I'm not hearing what I want to hear, Mark."

"Well, Matt just tore him up. It's a wonder he didn't kill him after all. He had him up against the wall pounding him. His face was so beat up you couldn't tell what he looked like. Matt was like a crazy man. He broke both his legs and one of his arms. Just like they were tooth picks."

Jesse thought for a moment and then laughed. "The guy probably wishes he was dead right now, anyhow. Well, maybe that's the best way after all. Let the jerk suffer. I'll send him a get well card to cheer him up."

The abduction tormented him. The inability to meet his obligations was deplorable. "A man has things he has to do in life, like take care of his family. If a man doesn't do that, he's nobody. I couldn't be my own man locked up like an animal in a cage. I couldn't even protect my families like a man should. The feds made a stooge out of me. I was a dead beat."

He would be unable to see his children for several more years. All he had now were memories and photographs in his cell. Carolee and Dorothy visited him, but he wouldn't permit them to bring the children. It wasn't the image of their father he wanted them to have.

And with that a sense of guilt, a feeling of remorse came over him. No one was to blame but himself. "I read somewhere that once you make a decision to do something you're stuck with it for the rest of your life and that other people can get hurt by what you do. I never thought anything about that until I ended up in the joint. It was true. I could never change what I had done in my life and my kids were hurt by it."

Jesse agonized over that and the hurt he had caused. The more he tried to penetrate the confusion and helpless in his mind, seeking a solution, the more desperate he became, the more chaotic his thoughts. There had to be a way out, but he couldn't find it. Worse, he soon would be transferred.

Time To Deal

The answer came to him one night. Maybe he could try to strike a deal with the FBI. He would tell them what little he knew about the bombings. All he would want in return was to do his time in a prison closer to home. He wouldn't be selling his soul for his freedom and become a stool pigeon.

"I'd only tell the "g" about the bombings. I didn't have any part in them and the Leisures weren't my friends, anyway. I'd convince the FBI that despite what Vitale had told them I wasn't involved in any of that. I was just trying to clear my name. I was sure he hadn't told them about offering me the fifty grand to whack Paulie Leisure."

Still, Jesse's conscience harassed him. Regardless of how little he told the FBI, he would be a detestable snitch. The law was alien to him, a ruthless, cunning adversary to be shunned at all costs. How could he cooperate with that enemy? He was balanced precariously on a thin line between his inbred personal loyalty to the mob and his own interests. He soon pushed himself over the edge.

God obviously told him the decision to make. Carolee visited him that weekend and he told her what he was going to do. She supported him. He told her to call Fox and Bohnemeier and tell them he wanted to meet with them. He trusted them more than he could any other officer of the law.

Fox talked to Carolee. She didn't want to tell him over the telephone why Jesse wanted to see them. Fox assessed this development. He had an idea why. He said they would go there in the next day or two.

Two days later they sat across a table from Jesse in a small room with a single barred window. They exchanged greetings. The agents weren't sure how to handle him. It was no less difficult for Jesse. He had to manipulate them.

Jesse now had second thoughts about what he was doing. "Here I was, sitting with the 'g' that had gotten me into this mess. I'm thinking, 'Jesse, you must be nuts. Tell 'em goodbye and forget about it'. But I couldn't do that. There was only one way to play this game. Let them know who's running this show. I had to control it because these people are treacherous and have a way of using you. They didn't know who they were dealing with."

Bohnemeier broke the silence. "What do you want to talk about, Jesse?"

Jesse cleared his throat and searched for words. He wanted them to think at first he was backing out. That would give him an edge, maybe cause them to beg a little and make a better deal. He had to be contrite, yet firm. After all, he had something to sell and he had to bargain for the best price. But he didn't know who he was up against.

"I guess you know this isn't easy for me. I'm not used to talking to you people."

"Try us, you might like us," Fox said, his voice challenging, yet gentle.

"I asked you to come here, but I'm not sure I should have."

Bohnemeier laughed. "You know what kind of weather we came through to get here? Ice on the highways you can't believe. We could have gotten killed and you're telling us you don't want to talk to us."

Jesse sighed and sat down. "Well, you guys treated me right, so I'll take a gamble with you. Maybe I can help you guys out on those bombings."

"No doubt you could," Bohnemeier said.

"I mean, I don't know that much about what was going on, but maybe I can clear some things up for you."

"Like what?" Fox asked.

"I'm not going to go into details right now." Fox shrugged his shoulders. "Well, I'll tell you one thing right now. That (expletive) Vitale is a snitch and I proved it." He snickered triumphantly.

"We don't know anything about that. Even if he was we wouldn't tell you."

Jesse went on the offensive. "Well, I know about it! He's a snitch and you guys know it! He sold you a bunch of nonsense about me. Nothing he told you was true."

Both agents remained non-committal. It agitated Jesse more. "I mean, Vitale tried to set me up and the 'g' knew about it. You know he offered me five thousand to get Ski Kowalski to bring him a bomb probably so you could bust both of us and then he wanted to give me a contract for fifty grand to crack Paulie Leisure."

Still, the agents said nothing, displaying no emotions. Silence was their weapon. It was Jesse's show. He had to open their mouths to learn what they knew about him. "He probably told you guys that I made the bomb and put it on Michaels' car. How can you guys trust that (expletive)?" he asked, challenging them.

The agents let the silence linger. Finally, Bohenmeier asked, "What do you want from us, Jesse?"

Jesse got up and paced the floor. "I guess you don't believe me. I don't know why I'm even talking to you. A lost cause." It was part of his act.

"We didn't say that. You're hanging around with the right people who could be involved."

"What do you expect me to do? Bum with priests?"

"It might do you some good," Bohnemeier said sarcastically.

"Aw, the hell with you guys."

They had played him far enough. It was time to challenge him. "So far, you haven't told us anything except that Vitale's a snitch and you're innocent," Fox said, pretending disgust. "If this is all you've got, we might as well go back home."

Jesse leaned back in his chair. "I can tell you about Spica and Michaels. Like how Tony Giordano put me and Spica in the unions and Spica was going to hit Ray Flynn." He stopped for effect.

"And?" Fox asked, still feigning indifference, as if they already knew that.

Jesse chuckled derisively. "You think I'm a hoosier and I'll tell you everything before we got a deal?"

"What do you want out of this, Jesse?" Bohnemeier asked.

"Not much. Just a transfer to a joint nearer home where I can be closer to my family. They're about to ship me up to Wisconsin."

Bohnemeier thought for a long time. Jesse was becoming nervous. "Okay, you got a deal," Bohnemeier said. Jesse shook their hands. "We'll be in touch with you. We can't make any promises. We'll give it our best shot."

"One more thing. I ain't going into any court and testify. That'll get me killed for sure."

Jesse realized he hadn't been in control. His gifted tongue and his imposing presence failed to influence them. Instead, he had been manipulated. He had played his trump card too soon. He should have toyed with them and tempted them. "Those guys were like stone. I couldn't read 'em out. I didn't know if they were sincere. It was like talking to a wall. I never met people like them before."

Government bureaucracy caused delays in getting Jesse's transfer to the medical facility at Springfield, Mo., about 225 miles from the East Side. Fox asked U. S. Attorney Thomas Dittmeier in St. Louis to intercede. He was anxious to prosecute in the gang warfare. By April, Dittmeier arranged the transfer. Jesse already was in Wisconsin and he was transferred temporarily back to Terre Haute before going to Missouri.

Fox and Bohnemeier met with him in Terre Haute. "We kept our bargain and got you transferred to Springfield," Bohnemeier said. "Now it's your turn."

Jesse told them what he had promised. It was the first hard evidence they had about Flynn's involvement in the Spica bombing, but it wasn't enough to initiate prosecution. Jesse relaxed now that he had crossed the threshold. The agents had led him over the first difficult hurdle. The others would be no easier.

"That was easy, wasn't it, Jesse?" Fox asked.

"I hope you're satisfied," Jesse said. "You made a snitch out of me. That's the first time I ever talked to the heat."

"We're honored," Bohnemeier teased.

All three laughed heartily. Fox leaned forward. It was time to nudge Jesse farther. "You know, you'd be more valuable out of here."

"What do you mean?" he asked, his instincts aroused. He suspected what they were hinting at.

"You could get more information if you weren't in prison. What I'm saying is that if you were out on the streets you'd be in a better position to get more on the bombings." Jesse said nothing. Fox proceeded cautiously. He didn't want to spook his quarry. "Would you consider working with us?"

Jesse shook his head and stood. This was more intricate than just talking about the bombings. "Ain't I snitched enough for you?"

"We need more solid information," Bohnemeier said. "We need someone who's on the inside and you're there."

"How am I supposed to get out of here? Bust out or just call a cab?" Jesse snickered.

"There are ways. We'll do everything we can. You have our word."

Jesse was flirting with disaster. He had to make a fateful decision. "I kept thinking, 'What are you doing here, Jesse? You got any idea what you're getting yourself into? Why don't you just put a gun to your head and pull the trigger if you want to die so quick'? I wanted to tell them this was enough. But the idea of getting out of here and back on the street was too much to ignore. And I couldn't help thinking it could be a way of getting even with Vitale."

Jesse knew when it was ended he would have to walk away from the mob. There was no way he ever could return to it, even if his work for the federal government remained unknown. Maybe it was time for him to get out. He faced the agents. "I got to be crazy, but, okay, I'll go along with you guys. I can do you a lot of good."

"We know that," Fox said, relieved.

"I gotta ask you something, though. How safe will I be out on the streets if I work for you?"

Fox and Bohnemeier didn't want to mislead him, but they couldn't tell him about the threats Paulie Leisure made that the bureau's bugs monitored. Their working relationship with him only was beginning and a lot of mutual trust still had to be built.

"Just as safe as if you were on your own. You'll be okay," Fox said. "You can handle anything that comes along."

Bohnemeier met with Judge Beatty and told him of Jesse's agreement to cooperate with the FBI if he was granted probation. The judge agreed to cooperate. Rice had filed a motion to vacate the sentence and grant probation, a routine but rarely successful legal maneuver. It argued Jesse's family was suffering hardship with his imprisonment.

Jesse was adamant he didn't want Rice involved except to pursue the motion. His agreement to become a snitch had to be kept concealed, even from his attorney. Rice was close to certain elements of the mob and he feared word of his subterfuge would be leaked, getting him killed.

Rice presented his case to the judge. Carolee testified their family was being disrupted by her husband's absence and he was desperately needed at home to help raise their children. The U. S. Attorney, fully aware of the deal with Jesse, vigorously opposed probation to help establish the cover. He argued he was a dangerous organized crime figure and nothing had changed to warrant probation by the court. Judge Beatty routinely took the motion under advisement.

While waiting Judge Beatty's ruling, Jesse set out to fulfill his commitment to Fox and Bohnemeier. He had a new loyalty, a new dedication and purpose in life, and he was eager to prove himself. He had incurred a debt to the agents and he wanted to begin paying it down.

"I'm on the phone constantly, calling my buddies collect and asking them what was happening on the outside. There was a guy working for the Illinois Division of Criminal Investigation who was stealing drugs that were evidence. He was also identifying undercover narcotics cops to the dealers. I found out a lot about scores that had been committed since I was in the joint and about a professional hit man who was arranging hits on the West Coast from prison."

Vitale died of heart disease on June 5. Jesse felt deprived. He had concocted a scheme to lure Vitale into admitting some kind of criminal activity and then report it to the FBI. That's what a snitch was supposed to do.

Judge Beatty granted Jesse's probation as expected and Jesse walked out of prison on September 17. He was liberated from prison confinement, but he was about to enter different captivity no less restrictive.

The Scorpion

Fox and Bohnemeier gave Jesse the code name "Scorpion." They hoped he would accomplish what the arachnid did best – sting its adversaries into submission. He assured them he would work under-cover for only a few months. They weren't sure they could control him even that long. In their brief exposure to him they learned he was a man of his word, but he also was his own man.

Jesse was making the transition from a hoodlum to a "square-john," just as Loretta Berne predicted and God had planned. And her husband was about to be exposed to a snitch, as she also foretold. It also was the beginning of his evolution from "Stone Killer" and criminal back to his childhood faith in Jesus Christ.

Part of that transition had to be his rejection of his past crim-inal life, although he would have to pretend he still resided there by living a double life. He would have to walk the walk, talk the talk, and continue displaying the "Stone Killer" image. He essentially had to be a ghost, an illusion – What you see is what I and the FBI want you to see.

Even so, he now viewed his former existence as repulsive and evil. He once charished that lifestyle, but now he pledged to himself to have no part of it. He had to live life on the straight and narrow. At first it was difficult for him to understand why he had made such a profound reversal of his life so quickly. He eventually accepted it for what it was – God's will.

What he also had to discard from his lifestyle was his tendency toward violence. He realized how heinous and shameful he had been, especially planning his massacre. Now, he had to make a com-mitment to God not to kill, except maybe if his own life was in jeop-ardy. Forgiveness had to replace violence and murder. It was what he had been taught when he a youth,

Jesse knew it wouldn't be an easy trek and danger would accom-pany him as he lived a dual life – the good guy and the hoodlum Jesse Stoneking. He would be back in his old territory where no mercy, no forgiveness, no second chance is granted to turncoats. If the truth about him was discovered, it would be open season on him, retribution sure and swift. He once would have done no less to a snitch.

Who would be a hero in the underworld over his corpse? What price would be put on his head? Would a hit man be brought in from Chicago? The outfit there would have a vested interest in his demise. Or would it be someone he knew? Perhaps Ray Flynn or J. D. Michels or Bill Politte. Forgiveness surely wasn't compelling in them. The government likely wouldn't admit he was an informant and he had gone straight. They would classify his death as just another gangland hit.

Jesse met with Fox the day after he returned home. He parked his car in a grove of trees alongside U. S. Highway 50 near Lebanon, not far from his O'Fallon home. Fox got into his car. A few minutes later Jesse glanced in the rear view mirror. A dark blue Buick was bearing down on them. It was Berne. It was too late to duck down. Berne looked over and waved. Jesse waved back.

"Aw, nuts!" Jesse shouted.

"What's wrong?"

"That was Berne. You guys'll get me killed before I even get on the streets. What's the odds of that happening the first time out?"

Fox tried to reassure him. "Don't worry about it, Jesse. There'll be other close calls. It's inevitable."

Jesse laughed derisively. "Yeah? Well, screw it! This ain't for me. I want out. I ain't gonna get hit for no one. It's stupid meeting here like this."

"We got a deal, remember?"

"A deal for me to get killed, huh? Judge Beatty said I could walk away from it any time I wanted to. Now's the time while I'm still able to."

Fox sighed. "You telling me this big time hood gets scared so easily?"

Jesse shook his head. "To hell with you, Fox." He was in no mood to talk and Fox left. They would meet three days later, this time in a city park in Belleville. The agents had to explain the ground rules.

Jesse met with Judge Beatty. The judge, realizing not only the danger, but the complexity of the arrangement, wanted the terms of the probation clearly understood.

"He asked me if the FBI agents were pressuring me to work for them or if they had threatened me. I said no. He was very concerned about what could happen to me. He told me I could walk away from the FBI any time I wanted to and it wouldn't affect my probation. He said, 'You know that you're life's going to be in danger, don't you? Do you realize that you can be killed?' I told him I understood that. So, he says to me, 'Personally, I think you probably will be'. That didn't help much."

The conditions of the probation were stringent. Judge Beatty told him he could violate no law unless authorized by the agents. He couldn't possess a firearm, regardless of the danger he faced. To be caught with a weapon would result in revocation of his probation and his return to prison. Jesse had no intention of honoring that restriction. The only exception was he could associate with convicted felons and persons engaging in criminal activity. That was the purpose of his release from prison.

A Dead Duck

The afternoon of the meeting, Fox and Bohnemeier drove through the park until they saw Jesse's car, but not their new asset. Panic flared in them. Had he been discovered so soon? Had Berne recognized Fox when he drove by? Then they saw him at the end of the lake, watching the ducks feeding in the water.

"Hey, Jesse, what's going on?" Bohnemeier asked.

Jesse turned around and grinned. "Just picking out my duck."

"I don't follow you."

"They're dead ducks." He pointed to one. "That's Jimmy Fratianno. And that's Vitale. And that big one by itself, that's me. All snitches become dead ducks. You know I'm gonna get hit just like all the others are."

Bohnemeier tried to humor him. "Tell me something. Are you hoods really tough?" He and Fox had heard of his prodigious strength.

Jesse grinned. He grabbed Fox, who was more slender and taller than Bohnemeier, under the arm pits, lifted him off the ground and heaved him a few feet. He did the same with Bohnemeier, who was about his height, but not as heavy. Fox landed in a sitting position and Bohnemeier stayed on his feet. Both agents laughed.

"Well, I guess they are tough," Bohnemeier said humbly.

Fox asked him if he would wear a concealed recorder at times and he agreed. He handed him $5,000, payment for information he already had given them. Jesse said it was a bribe. The FBI would pay him $1,600 a month for his undercover work plus expenses.

"Gee, can the government afford it?"

"We had to fight like hell to get that."

"I can make that much in five minutes on the streets."

It would put a financial burden on him. He had cash set aside, but it wouldn't last long. The months in prison with two families to support and no income depleted his assets. Living the Spartan life would be a difficult adjustment, although he had to display affluence as part of the drama.

Jesse pointed to the two-year-old Oldsmobile Cutlass he was driving. "I can't operate with that. It wouldn't be me. I need a big car, a Lincoln or a Cadillac. That's what people are used to seeing me in."

Fox and Bohnemeier had anticipated that. A new Lincoln Town Car could be leased for about $500 a month and the FBI would reimburse him.

There were inviolate regulations for working FBI informants, many embracing Judge Beatty's. Jesse would have to participate in criminal activities to maintain his cover and credibility. They would instruct him how far he could go. Crimes against property were permissible with FBI approval. Crimes against the person – robberies and assaults – were not. If a police officer arrested him – and there were many who would like that distinction – they could not come to his aid. To do so would blow his cover.

Jesse's priority was to build strong cases. He must be careful to do nothing to jeopardize a conviction. He still was a hoodlum and Berne's underboss, a hustler and a money-maker. Fox and Bohnemeier would have him on a short leash, but it was a pit bull they had to control.

Jesse wasn't unsympathetic. He accepted that the regulations not only were for prosecutorial purposes, but for his protection as well. But there was no way he would carry out his assignments unarmed.

"It was my life, not theirs'. Guys would get suspicious if I wasn't carrying a gun. I'd become an open target."

Another meeting was two days later in the park. Fox and Bohnemeier had to build a relationship with Jesse beyond the cold one of agent-informant. They wanted to show him they had a sense of humor. They bought two Donald Duck masks. As Jesse drove up, they put them on. He opened his door and they turned to face him. He laughed and shook his head. "You guys are weird." Their relationship went to a new level.

There would be many meetings in the park. There often were people around the lake and the ducks wouldn't be disturbed. Almost always when the agents and Jesse approached, the ducks would scatter and swim to the other side. Jesse said it was ominous, but the agents laughed.

Fox and Bohnemeier showed Jesse the recorder he would wear, a Nagra. He had the right to refuse to be wired up if he felt unsafe. It would be taped either to his abdomen or his leg and activated by pressing a switch attached to his upper leg. It was six inches long, four inches wide and three-quarters of an inch thick. Its size troubled Jesse. It also would be installed in his car's trunk with a small microphone and a switch to turn it on under the dashboard.

He could record no conversations without approval of the agents. They would wire him up or install it in the car and each time he would have to sign a form consenting to tape conversations. The recorder had to be returned as quickly as possible. The regulations were intended to preserve evidence and to counteract possible defense accusations he tampered with the tapes or acted on his own.

It was time for the agents to debrief him. For four days, they rented rooms in different motels around the East Side and in the countryside. They wanted every morsel of information he had about the mob and its operatives, especially crimes they had committed. They challenged him to educate them and he did.

A Partner In Snitching

Jesse debated whether to tell Stram he was an informant. It would be impossible to do his undercover work and keep him in the dark.

There was no way Jesse could explain his refusal to commit certain crimes, nor did he want to snitch on Stram. He would be obligated to inform the agents of felonies Stram might commit. The FBI wouldn't offer him protection. He wasn't part of the deal.

By bringing him along, he could control him and influence him go straight. It might be a lifesaver for Stram. Jesse picked him up for lunch. "I got something to tell you, Mark. You're not gonna believe it, but how do you think I was able to get out of the joint?"

Stram snickered. "The judge liked you and felt sorry for you?"

"I agreed to work for the FBI."

Stram was silent for a moment and then laughed loudly. "You still got your sense of humor, don't you?"

"I ain't kidding, Mark."

"Yeah? And I'm the pope and bears don't poop in the woods."

"I'm telling you, I got a deal with the 'g'."

Stram realized Jesse was serious. "Oh, man, why'd you do that? I can't believe this. Jessee Stoneking a filthy rat?"

"I just thought about a lot of things that happened while I was in the joint. Vitale. Long. Everything. I'm just going to work for awhile on the streets for them and see what I can come up with on the bombings across the river. Nobody can operate with all this crap going on. Maybe we can help stop it. Besides. I'm going straight."

"They'll drag you in deeper and deeper until you can't get out. And you'll end up getting cracked over it."

"No way, Mark," Jesse argued. "I can control it."

"Listen to what I say, Jesse! Going clean will get you killed."

"I'm not gonna be dirty anymore. I want you to come in with me, Mark. I'm not telling you to do it. Just asking you. I don't want to see you get hurt. I can't protect you if you're not with me on this."

Jesse knew it was no easy decision for him. What he didn't tell him was he, too, would be on everybody's hit list if their dual role was discovered. He assumed he knew that.

Stram thought for a long time. Finally, he turned to Jesse. "Okay, I'm in with you." He laughed. "Someone's gotta take care of this crazy man."

Jesse now understood his undercover work wouldn't be limited to the bombings. He had planned to reverse roles with Fox and

Bohnemeier the dogs on his leash. Only, now they had a choke chain on him. Even so, the glamour and intrigue of undercover work was intoxicating.

Fox and Bohnemeier were apprehensive. They had jumped into bed with one of the most notorious and dangerous hoodlums in the metropolitan area. There would be many sleepless nights as there would be for Jesse. They would not be few carefree days for him. He still wouldn't enjoy a walk in the park.

God would allow adversities to come into his life. He would want Jesse to use them not as stumbling blocks to self-recrimination and hatred, but as stepping stones to greater faith in, and greater love of, Him. At the same time, God would protect him from the many perils he would face.

Still, Jesse would have decisions to make – whether his resolve stood firm and he would shun Satan's temptations or succumb to them. They would not be easy choices as he continued his return to the Lord.

CHAPTER SEVENTEEN

"Just Kill The Snitch"

Without warning, the casual, friendly conversation turned potentially deadly. Jesse's life was in the hands of a Mafioso who vowed to kill snitches.

It was the first time Jesse was wired up. Would it be the last, his career as an undercover operative ending before it really began? Judge Beatty's prediction of his imminent death might be coming true.

Trupiano had wanted to see Jesse shortly after his release from prison. He suggested they meet at the Banana House on Produce Row. A wire with a miniature microphone was attached to each side of Jesse's chest. The recorder was taped to the upper left side of his chest near the arm pit. The weather was warm, but he wore a wind-breaker over his shirt to help conceal the equipment.

Jesse wasn't at ease. "That was the worst feeling I ever had. It was like I had a sign on me that said, 'Hey, Jesse Stoneking's wired up'. I kept worrying that the thing might fall off onto the ground or start making a squeaking noise and my life would end."

Trupiano hadn't arrived yet. Jesse chatted with Pat Lopicollo, a soldier in the Mafia. The conversation turned to Jimmy "The Weasel" Fratianno, the highly placed hood who was a government informant. His biography, "The Last Mafioso," had been out for some time, but it still evoked great anger in the underworld. Lopicollo had just finished reading it.

The lumbering Lopicollo was demonstrative in words and actions. "That (expletive) Fratianno, he oughta get hit in his head," he said angrily. "Can you imagine a guy like that? One of us!"

"He's no good, Pat. He's a (expletive) rat."

Lopicollo became more agitated. "Somebody'll crack him, Jesse. You go against omerta and you gotta die." He clutched Jesse's shirt. His beefy hands held the microphones, but he didn't detect them. "Jesse, you gotta watch out for all these snitches these days. If I ever catch a snitch, I'll kill him with my own hands. I won't say a thing. I'll Just do it. Right there on the spot. A man's gotta have honor. You know that. Just kill the snitch."

Jesse tried to back away, but Lopicollo held on. He commanded the panic to stop, but it wouldn't. Lopicollo's fingers felt of the microphones. A puzzled look came to his face. "What's that, Jesse?"

Lopicollo was about to kill him. His undercover work was at an end before it got started. There was little he could do to defend himself except shoot Lopicollo and that would sign his own death warrant. Just then, Trupiano drove up and honked his car's horn.

Lopicollo took his hands from Jesse's shirt and waved as Trupiano got out of the car. Trupiano laughed. "What're you doing, Pat? Hugging Jesse? You two got something going?"

"Naw, we're just talking about that weasel, Fratianno," Lopicollo answered.

"You don't have to worry about snitches around here. There aren't any."

Jesse's first undercover excursion in the mob was for naught. The agents wouldn't hear how he almost was killed. He had forgotten to activate the recorder.

A few days later, Jesse and Berne attended a wedding reception. Trupiano and Anthony "Nino" Parino, the vice- president of Teamsters Local 682 in St. Louis and his "consigliere," or trusted advisor, were there. They called Jesse aside and handed him an envelope with 10 hundred dollar bills. Trupiano said it was a gift from them.

"We know you're a little hard up just getting out of the joint," Trupiano said. "We thought this would help you out a little."

Jesse shook their hands and thanked them. It was an act of fraternal friendship and Jesse momentarily regretted snitching on them.

Trupiano had just returned from a command appearance in Chicago before mob boss Joey Aiuppa, who ordained him as don of the St. Louis Mafia. He now occupied the most prestigious seat of power in the underworld. What he lacked in criminal acumen and leadership talents he made up with bravado. A few days later, the author wrote a story about Trupiano's ascension to leadership published on the front page of the St. Louis Post-Dispatch.

Jesse described the reaction. "Joey Aiuppa knew that Trupiano liked to brag so he figured he leaked the story to the paper. I was there when Art called Joey and told him about the story. Well, Joey is really upset. He calls Mike and tells him to get his sorry ass up to Chicago.

"Aiuppa must've had one hell of a prayer meeting with him. Mike came back like a whipped dog. Art said they told him he couldn't talk to the papers, especially that guy Lawrence, about what goes on in the outfit. He said it's the same as snitching to the 'g'. Mike just denied it. It's a wonder they didn't whack him."

A Sucker Bettor

Jesse repaid Trupiano's generosity a week later, but not out of a sense of gratitude. FBI agents in St. Louis learned he was running a large handbook and his bookies frequently changed telephone numbers for security. The agents needed to know the permanent telephones being used and the extent of Trupiano's involvement so they could prepare affidavits requesting wiretap authorization.

Jesse visited Trupiano at his house in south St. Louis County. "Mike, I got this guy across the river who's a sucker for betting on football games. He's crazy and dumber than hell. It's a chance for somebody to pick up some money. Where can I send him?"

"I'll take his bets," Trupiano said eagerly. "I got this book going and I'll take whatever action he's got."

"How do I put him in touch with you? Give him your number?"

"You can call his bets in to me. We'll split what he loses. And I'll be sure he loses." He gave Jesse a telephone number, one he used only for his bookmaking.

The sucker bettor was Fox. Each week he selected a team on which to bet $100. Jesse called Trupiano on Friday afternoons, first to get the point spreads, later to place the bet.

"The first time, Mike gave a spread that was bigger than it actually was and it was so against the bettor there was no way he could win. But Tom won anyhow. The next week, Mike made the spread even bigger and Tom won again. Mike says, 'Is this guy stupid'? I said, 'He's pretty stupid, Mike'. Then, he'd say, 'Well, try this spread on him. There's no way he can win with that'. And Tom won again. I couldn't believe it. It got to be embarrassing."

Fox won eight bets, Trupiano only one. With Jesse's information and Fox's bets, FBI agents had enough probable cause and applied for wiretaps. Trupiano had no felony convictions and they were anxious to give him one.

Jesse, The Bug Detector

Trupiano suggested Jesse move across the river and work with him. "You'll have a better future with me. You gotta get away from Art, Jesse. He's an old man and he ain't got much going for him no more. I need a good strong arm, a sneak guy, who's there when I need him. I can trust you."

"I don't know about doing that, Mike."

"You can still work for Art, but you'll really be my man."

"Maybe so, Mike. Give me more time. Let me think about it."

The agents told Jesse to agree with Trupiano. He was concerned Berne might consider him disloyal and even have him hit. He told Berne he was moving to St. Louis because there was too much heat on the East Side. Berne wasn't upset and said it was a bad move, but told him to do what he thought was best.

Trupiano was running scared. He was sure the law was after him. His worst fears came true on January 23 when FBI agents executed search warrants for his person and his house. They were served on him at Lambert International Airport as he returned from a trip to

Pompano Beach, Florida, where he met with Jack Tocco, a Detroit Mafia boss, and Sorkis Webbe Sr., the St. Louis manipulator. The author published a photograph of that meeting.

Agents confiscated $15,627 in cash from his coat pocket they believed was part of the proceeds from the sale of the Aladdin Casino. They also found $11,000 in cash in his house. Nine members of his handbook ring also were served with search warrants.

Trupiano correctly suspected the telephones in his home were bugged by the FBI. Agents were monitoring his calls and conversations in his family room. He trusted no one anymore, convinced someone in his inner circle was betraying him. How else could the feds have connected him with his bookmaking operation?

He was determined to find out who the snitch was. He searched every person, including his associates, who came into his house. Jesse no longer wore a wire when visiting Trupiano. It was a prudent decision. Trupiano also patted him down. He wasn't apologetic for doing it and Jesse said he didn't blame him.

One afternoon early in March, Trupiano complained to Jesse. "It's terrible what they're doing. Invading a man's privacy like this. It ain't right, you know."

"Yeah, Mike, it's a shame."

"I know they probably got my phones tapped. They got 'em all over."

"Think so, Mike?"

"Sure. I was wondering. You know anybody who's got one of those things you can sweep your telephones with to find out if they have a bug on them?"

Jesse thought for a moment. It was an opportunity to ingratiate himself further with Trupiano. "Yeah, I think I know a guy who's got one."

"Can you borrow it and check my phones out?"

"I don't see why not."

The next day Jesse brought a detector the FBI gave him. Agents had electronically deactivated the bugs on the telephones and the monitor in the family room so they wouldn't be detected. He and Trupiano went from room to room, but the detector was silent. When they got to the kitchen, it sounded.

"What'd I tell you, Jesse? They got this phone bugged."

Jesse was confused. "Sure as hell looks like it, Mike."

That wasn't part of the scenario. Unknown to Jesse, but observed by FBI agents who had the house under surveillance, a St. Louis County Police Department helicopter hovered above. A cable with a microphone to monitor conversations inside dangled 20 feet above the roof. It set off the bug detector. It was believed police had observed Jesse's car there.

Trupiano ranted. "What am I gonna do now? I got business to take care of."

"Maybe you should replace the phones, Mike."

"How am I going to do that without the feds finding out?"

Jesse had an idea. "I know this guy over on the East Side who works for the telephone company. He owes me. He can get you new ones."

"What happens when they don't hear anything on the bugs?"

"They'll know you found them."

"So, they'll just put new ones in and I'm back where I started."

"You don't understand, Mike. They got to get in your house to put them in."

"So what? They did it before."

Jesse was enjoying this mind contest. "They had to break into your house, right? All you have to do is have someone here all the time."

"Yeah, that makes sense. But why don't we just take the bugs out of the phones?"

Jesse was getting in deeper than he intended. He was running out of answers.

"You know what a bug looks like? I don't know anything about them."

"I guess I need new phones, huh?"

Fox and Bohnemeier had taps installed in three new telephones. Trupiano now was confident of the security of his house. He talked freely about sensitive matters no prudent mob boss would have discussed over a telephone. He was indebted to Jesse, whose prestige in Trupiano's outfit soared. Others begged him to get the detector and sweep their homes, but he declined, saying his friend would resent being asked for it too often.

The "Mud Dauber" Score

George Eidson, a proficient burglar and safe cracker connected with Berne's outfit, called Jesse late in March. He and Anthony Leisure had a score possibly worth as much as $1 million lined up. They needed his expertise and offered to bring him in for an equal share.

The target was an antique and jewelry shop called "The Mud Dauber" in rural central Illinois. Eidson was told much of the owner's fortune was in rare coins he kept in a safe in the shop. Jesse didn't tell Eidson he knew the owner and there would not be nearly that much loot there. Most of it would be in bank safe deposit boxes.

They cased the store and Eidson believed there would be little difficulty by-passing the burglar alarm system. He suggested they make the store the coming Saturday night when the owner who lived next door would be out of state. Anthony Leisure would be with them.

Eidson was a prize catch, but Anthony Leisure outranked him on the FBI's target list. Fox and Bohnemeier were enthusiastic, but the final decision for Jesse to participate was with their immediate supervisors and those in Washington. They weren't optimistic.

Jesse asked the agents what excuse he could use to back out of what appeared to be an easy, relatively risk-free heist. Since the owner wouldn't be present, no crime against a person would be involved. He assured them there would be no more than $15,000 to $25,000 in cash and rare coins in the safe.

Fox and Bohnemeier considered the risks to Jesse. They weren't concerned he was being set up. If Eidson and Leisure suspected he was an informant they wouldn't have invited him on a score. Jesse's credibility was a major issue. His underworld integrity would be at risk if he declined to participate in such an easy score. Questions would be asked and doubts raised.

There were other complications. If Jesse wasn't permitted to participate in the burglary, they would be obligated to catch Eidson and Leisure in the act. Failure to do so could cause them to be accused of negligence, even complicity. But if Eidson and Leisure were arrested Jesse would be exposed because it was assumed only the three of them knew of the score. He would be the only possible informant. The agents had little choice. They would seek authorization for his participation.

It was decided to let the score come down unimpeded. Leisure was too important a target to pass up. Agents would keep the store under surveillance, but would make no arrests until Jesse's covert operation was ended.

The operation still presented a risk. Whatever the financial loss in the burglary, the government would have to indemnify the owner if the stolen property wasn't recovered because the FBI knew about the crime in advance and didn't intercede. In effect, the theft would be committed with the government's tacit approval, making it liable. With arrests not made for months or longer, jewelry and coins would be fenced and cash would be untraceable.

If the loot was less than $25,000 as Jesse predicted, there would be few problems. But what if Eidson was right and it amounted to $1 million? Or if Jesse was accurate, but the owner claimed a much larger loss? How could he be disputed? Washington would have their heads and throw Jesse to the wolves.

Jesse accepted all those possibilities, but he wasn't that concerned. "I wondered what the big problem was. They had a chance to nail George and Anthony and they're worried about the regulations. Sometimes rules were meant to be broken if the prize was big enough. I guess they played by different rules than I did."

Authorization from Washington came Thursday afternoon. Bohnemeier surveyed the area of the store Friday morning for surveillance locations. Local police radio communications would be monitored so agents could divert any authorities who wandered into the area while the burglary was in progress.

The agents had a contingency plan if the property was worth more than anticipated. Jesse needed to insist his car be used, arguing it had an Illinois plate and wouldn't be as noticeable as a vehicle with an out-of-state tag. A transmitter would be installed so conversations before and after the burglary could be monitored.

If the loot was as Eidson predicted, agents would let them cross into Missouri, arrest them and confiscate the valuables. Jesse would make a run for it and agents would chase him, even fire a few shots in the air, but allow him to escape. He would go into hiding until the heat was off. They still might be able to salvage his covert operation.

All the planning was for naught. Washington rescinded its approval late Friday afternoon. The Leisures and members of their outfit were to be indicted in a few weeks on charges growing out of the warfare. The cases against them were solid. An interstate transportation of stolen merchandise charge against Anthony wasn't needed.

Washington also argued making a case against Eidson wasn't worth the risk to Jesse. Fox and Bohnemeier couldn't tell him of the impending indictments. It wasn't included in his need-to-know information. They only told him the big-shots in Washington changed their minds. Government bureaucracy was at work.

Jesse reacted predictably. He was furious. "What's wrong with them people? Don't they know a good deal when they see one? They must be a bunch of jerks. It ain't their butts on the line. It's mine."

"They don't look at it that way," Fox said plaintively. "They just said it wasn't worth the risk. The guy said, 'Kill it. You turned it on, you turn it off'. They don't have to explain."

Fox and Bohnemeier had to develop a new game plan and quickly. They must abort the burglary and preserve the integrity of the undercover work. Eidson and Leisure were to meet Stoneking at 7 p. m. Saturday at a restaurant on the East Side for dinner before the score.

Fox called Eidson's home in St. Charles County in Missouri at mid-morning Saturday to learn if he was at home. Eidson answered and Fox asked for "Lorraine." Eidson said there was no one there by that name and asked what number was being called. Fox made up a number.

The agents watched Eidson's home the rest of the morning and into the afternoon. He left at 3 o'clock and drove east on Interstate 70 through downtown St. Louis and then south on Interstate 55 toward Jefferson County. They wanted to spook him and they didn't conceal their surveillance.

If Eidson was aware of the surveillance, he didn't indicate it. He drove to Twin Cities Auto Auction in Barnhart. He left with Leisure 30 minutes later and went south to Festus where he owned a pawn-shop. Two other FBI cars joined in the bumper tag.

Eidson detected the surveillance. He accelerated to 100 miles an hour for eight miles, but he couldn't shake his pursuers. He parked in front of his pawnshop. He and Leisure casually walked inside without looking around. The agents parked conspicuously nearby.

Eidson called Jesse at home at 5 o'clock. "This thing is a no-go. I got heat all over me. They're following me and Anthony wherever we go."

Jesse feigned disappointment. "Aw, hell, man, I'm ready." He hadn't known how Fox and Bohnemeier would interrupt the score, but that must have been how.

Jesse Stoneking in an Arizona park not long after
turn of the century.

An FBI photograph of Jesse Stoneking not long before
he was arrested and turned an informant.

CHAPTER EIGHTEEN

"You're Dead, Jesse"

J esse was to die at the hands of Anthony Leisure. He had been unmasked, his cover stripped from him, the snitch exposed. And it was because of the FBI's cancellation of the Mud Dauber score and the surveillance scheme.

The death duel began when Jesse, Eidson and Leisure had lunch in a south St. Louis County restaurant two days after the aborted theft. Jesse wore the recorder. The score wasn't discussed until they finished eating when Eidson said he dialed the number Fox gave him and learned it was non-existent. He was curious, but not alarmed, until he left the house and was tailed.

"They were probably the 'g'," Jesse said. "Why would they have been following you?"

"Who knows. Maybe there's a snitch somewhere and they found out about the score? You think?"

"It wouldn't surprise me. I'd like to know who it is and I'd crack him, myself." Jesse hoped he was convincing.

Leisure said little during lunch. Now he stared accusingly at Jesse. He knew something was wrong and he had to get rid of the recorder.

"Let's go for a ride and talk," Leisure said. His voice was icy.

"We can talk here," Jesse said calmly.

"It's more private," Leisure insisted.

"Sure. Too many people in here, anyhow."

Jesse was sure he was being lured into a trap. "I have to go to the john," he said. It was his only chance to get rid of the recorder.

"Yeah, me too," Leisure said.

They walked side by side to the restroom, neither speaking. Jesse couldn't let Leisure search him. A row of urinals was on the right and three stalls were to the left. The wash basins were to the right near the door. Jesse hurried to the middle stall. Leisure walked to the urinals.

Jesse closed the door and quickly dropped his trousers so Leisure could see them. He tried to make the sounds appropriate to a bowel movement, but he couldn't. He reached under his shirt and yanked loose the recorder and the microphone. Leisure walked back to the wash basins but he didn't turn on the water or pull any paper from the dispenser. He hadn't urinated. He was just standing there, waiting for Jesse.

"Hurry up, Jesse," Leisure called impatiently.

Jesse laughed. "You can't rush these things." He ordered the panic in him to subside.

There was no way to hide the recorder in the stall. The only place was in the trash can next to the wash basins, but that was where Leisure was. A .38 snub nose was in the right pocket of his jacket. He would have to use it.

The restroom door opened and someone walked in. Then other footsteps and the door opened again as Leisure left. The man who had just entered was at the urinals. It was the opportunity Jesse needed. He quickly buckled his trousers and went to the used paper receptacle. The man's back was still toward him as he zipped up his fly. Jesse plunged the recorder and microphone under some used towels and washed his hands.

Leisure and Eidson were waiting outside the restroom. They got in Eidson's car. Jesse was fearful. "I knew I shouldn't be getting in that car. I wouldn't have much room to maneuver and I'd be trapped. I had to think of some way to get out of there. But there was only one way. Run like hell. If I did that, the game would be over. They'd know I was a snitch and I'd be a dead man."

Leisure opened the door on the rear passenger side. "Get in the back," he ordered, motioning to Jesse.

Jesse stood firmly, defiantly. "No way, Anthony."

Leisure was six inches taller than Jesse and outweighed him by at least 30 pounds. He shoved him into the rear seat and got in before Jesse could resist. Jesse knew he was facing death. He had one chance to live. He scooted to the far side, drew his .38 and leveled it at Leisure as he reached under the seat and grabbed an automatic.

"No offense, Anthony," Jesse said, smiling. He grabbed the automatic from Leisure's hand and put it in his jacket pocket. Leisure stiffened, but said nothing.

Eidson sat impassively behind the wheel. He looked over his shoulder. Leisure nodded and he started the engine.

Leisure laughed weakly. "What can I say, Jesse?"

"A man can't be too careful. What do you want to talk about?"

Leisure regained his composure and was menacingly calm. "You're a snitch," he snarled.

"Why you think that?" Jesse asked derisively

"Because of what happened yesterday."

"Why would that make me a snitch?" Jesse asked.

"The cops were on to George heavy and they were too obvious. I think they knew about the score and they wanted to stop us. The only way they could have found out was from one of us. Only the three of us and Paulie knew about it. I ain't no snitch. Paulie sure ain't, either."

"Maybe George is. You a snitch, George?" Jesse asked.

"You gotta be kidding!" Eidson said, insulted.

Leisure tensed. "That leaves you, Jesse, and there's only one way to find out. I'm gonna search you. I figure you'll be wired up for a meeting with us if you're working for the feds."

"Like hell you are," Jesse said calmly.

"Then you're a snitch as far as I'm concerned."

"And what if I am?" Jesse challenged.

"You're dead, Jesse" Leisure said matter-of-factly.

Jesse's eyes didn't leave Leisure. Nor did his .38. "Pull in that side street up there, George," he instructed.

Eidson drove into an apartment complex and Jesse told him to pull behind one of the buildings. He motioned Leisure out of the car with his pistol. He followed and stood before him. "Do what you gotta do, Anthony."

Leisure quickly patted him down. He seemed disappointed when he found nothing.

"Satisfied?" Jesse asked.

"Just because you're not wired up doesn't mean you're not a snitch."

"Screw you, Anthony."

"There's one more thing, Jesse. We know you met with Vitale a couple of times. We know he was working with the Michaels crew against us."

"Yeah, when was that?"

"After Michaels got hit and after Paulie got bombed." Leisure glared at him, daring him to answer.

Jesse had to make a snap decision. Was Leisure just fishing or did he really know? There was no way of telling how much he knew. A lie would get him cracked. He had to level with him.

"Yeah, I met with him, Anthony. You know what he wanted me to do? He wanted me to set up Ski Kowalski. Have him make him a bomb. He offered me five grand. I told him no way. Then after Paulie got bombed, he offered me fifty thousand to crack him in the hospital. I just laughed at him. He said the money was from Michaels' family. He really hates you people."

Leisure said nothing, doubt still etched on his face.

"I'm gonna tell you something else, Anthony. Vitale was a snitch for the FBI."

Leisure looked at him in disbelief. "You're conning me, Jesse."

"Yeah? Well, the day before he offered me the five grand for Ski, two FBI agents come to my house and offered me the same money for the same thing."

"Why didn't you come to us?"

"I just didn't want to get involved in what was going on over here. I still don't. That's your business."

Leisure thought for a long time. Then he spoke cautiously. "Maybe I had you figured wrong, Jesse. I guess I gotta apologize to you."

"Naw, Anthony. I'd have felt the same way. I might have cracked you, too, if I thought you were a snitch."

They shook hands. Jesse's other hand still held the .38. A handshake could be an invitation to death. Jesse drove around for awhile after they left and went to the restaurant to retrieve the recorder. He considered ending his work as an undercover operative. This proved it was far too dangerous. He lived because he broke an FBI regulation about owning and carrying a gun. He wanted to tell Fox and Bohnemeier how dangerous that rule was.

"But then I thought, I can't say much to them. They would know I had a gun. They'd get real upset about that. These guys went strictly by the rules. I could lie about it, but they had a way of reading me like a book. They'd know I was lying and that would make it worse. I'd just keep my big mouth shut. I'd tell them I didn't turn on the recorder because nothing important was talked about."

He only told the agents Leisure had accused him of being an informant, but he convinced him he wasn't. Perhaps they would relax their regulations governing him, but they didn't.

After that close call, Jesse realized God was the only sure source of solace and protection for him, as he wished it was for his former criminal associates. "If they would ever stop and look at themselves, I wonder if they wouldn't go to the Lord and change their ways and get scared to see what they really are. Like I did."

He admitted revenge against them initially had tremendous influence on him. "But I didn't do that when I first got out. I'm not going to sit here and act like a priest. When I first got out of prison I had revenge in my heart. Get back at those people for putting me in the situation I was in. As time went by, say six months or a year, after reading the Bible and just looking back at my life, I saw all the things I did against the Lord. And society, itself."

It was then Jesse realized the part God plays in man's life. "So, you know, the Lord, He programs all our lives. I think He's projected my life. You know, I was a hood for so long, but he's going to get me out of that mess and give me another chance. Yeah, He's going to protect me until the day He wants me to come home. That's the way I look at it. He'll keep my straight. Jesse Stoneking can't. He's been too bad too long."

Jesse realized it was time for him to return to God and Jesus. He knew it would not be an easy, carefree journey. It would require much concentration and devotion. He would pursue that when his undercover work was over, when survival didn't occupy much of his mind.

CHAPTER NINETEEN

Beneficial Scams

There was no way knowing if Anthony Leisure believed Jesse or he still was suspicious. Jesse devised a complex scheme of false illusions and duplicity to protect himself and preserve his underworld credibility, but it also almost got him exposed and killed again.

Jesse's subterfuge and manipulation, once for the sole purpose of self-enrichment, were necessary elements of undercover operations. Now it had another mission – possibly getting him elevated to outfit boss with access to the powerful Chicago Syndicate, a major FBI triumph.

Attention would be focused on Jesse and Berne by a federal grand jury investigating the Spica killing. Jesse believed invoking the Fifth Amendment and refusing to answer questions would enhance his reputation as a stand-up guy who protected his outfit and his comrades. Those who had secrets to share would know they would be safe with him.

Just as significantly, Berne no doubt would refuse to testify, even if granted immunity. He conceivably could be held in contempt of court and sentenced to jail. Jesse then would become boss of the East Side Outfit, giving the FBI access to the seat of power in Chicago.

U. S. Attorney Thomas Dittmeier, known as the "Pit Bull" for his tenacious prosecution, was eager to help. The current grand jury was to expire in a few weeks and a new one impaneled after the first of the year. He warned entrapment could be a defense issue if Berne was given immunity and held in contempt.

Berne soon learned of the impending grand jury inquisition from a close friend, a doctor in south St. Louis connected with someone in Dittmeier's office. He was unsure of the reason for his subpoena, but he suspected it was because of his position with the Pipefitters Union.

"They're liable to say it's some kind of racketeering, but I don't know how they can do anything about that," he told Jesse. "That's legitimate. I earn that money. What the hell, I've been there all these years."

Jesse feigned concern. "Maybe it's about something else."

"Yeah, but what? I only worry when you get a bad feeling."

"The only bad feeling I got is that maybe there's somebody around who might be talking to the 'g'."

Berne was confused. "I don't go around anybody. I talk to you and Mike, but I don't talk much to other guys."

Jesse laughed. "Maybe I'm a snitch, Art."

"Yeah, maybe Loretta was right about you," he responded jokingly. He said he was concerned about being held in contempt of court and a high bond being set.

"Don't worry about it, Art. If you go to jail I'll get you out. You won't be there one day. You think I'll let you just sit there? Hey, have I ever been wrong?"

"No, I guess not." Berne wasn't convinced.

Jesse didn't tell him there was no bond for contempt of court. He would stay in jail for the duration of the grand jury, which would be 18 months, until he testified or a judge released him. The seeds of Berne's discontent and possible departure to jail had been sown and Jesse nurtured it.

By the time the new federal grand jury was impaneled in January, Berne assumed the government had lost interest in him, but his attorney assured him it had not. He told him if he took the Fifth Amendment the government could have him immunized from self-incrimination and cited for contempt of court if he persisted in silence.

Berne now was convinced the government wanted him behind bars with contempt of court apparently the most convenient way.

"They'll call me in there and I take the fifth," he confided to Jesse. "Then they bring me out and the judge will say, 'Well, Berne, you're not the target here so I'm granting you immunity'. Once you go back into the grand jury you can say you killed people and there ain't nothing they can do. But you still got to answer about this guy, about that guy, whatever they ask you. Well, (expletive), them. I won't answer. All I'll give 'em is my name and address."

"That's what I'll say, Art. Don't tell 'em nothing. They can immune us all they want."

"If I go to jail, all I want is a clean place with no hoosiers."

"I'll take care of that."

"Well, Jesse, there's nothing you can do about it. Anyhow, you'll have to be boss over here. You'll just move right in. You get some solid guys around you. It'll just be business as usual, only without me. Aiuppa's already approved you."

Both were served subpoenas on February 21 and were to testify two days later. Berne was in the grand jury room 45 minutes, invoking his Fifth Amendment privilege 22 times. When he came out he was visibly shaken and angered. His face was pallid and his lower lip trembled. Jesse asked him what had happened, but he didn't answer. He slumped in a chair and shook his head. Jesse gloated over his distress.

"Was it about Flynn and Spica?" Jesse finally whispered.

Berne nodded. He said he would meet him and Flynn at 2 o'clock the next afternoon in the doctor's office.

Jesse was in the hearing room only 30 minutes. He, too, refused to answer any questions, as previously arranged with the prosecutor.

The next day the recorder was taped to Jesse's lower inside right leg under his flared trouser leg. There was a remote chance Flynn might say something incriminating about the Spica hit.

Flynn was waiting for Berne and Jesse. They used a small room with one window. Flynn sat in a chair against the window and Berne was in front of the door. Jesse's chair was against the wall, opposite Flynn. He was effectively trapped. A .38 was in the waistband in the small of his back under his black leather jacket.

Berne was agitated. He now knew Vitale had been a snitch. "The roof caved in on me. This guy from Dittmeier's office says, 'Did you go to Chicago with John Vitale and discuss two bombings, Spica and Jimmy Michaels, while you were riding'? I took the fifth. I thought, that dirty (expletive) Vitale. There was only him and me in the car and he was doing all the talking. He kept bringing Jesse's name up and Ray's name."

"Unbelievable, isn't it, Ray?" Jesse said disgustedly.

Flynn just shook his head. Berne continued. "Then he asked me, 'Were you and Ray Flynn against Spica getting that job in Local 42'? So, I took the fifth again. Now, I'm wondering if Vitale was wired up when we were in that car going up there because we talked about that. I remember him trying to get me to say a lot of things."

"Yeah, he's the one who put that Spica rap on me," Flynn said angrily. "He's the only one who could have."

"You sure were right about Vitale, Jesse," Berne said.

"Yeah, but nobody listened to me."

Flynn was staring at Jesse's right leg. The trouser leg had pulled up, exposing the bold outline of the recorder under the stocking.

"What's that on your leg?" Flynn asked, leaning forward.

"What do you mean?" Jesse asked.

"That," Flynn said, pointing. He moved closer to Jesse.

Panic threatened Jesse. He desperately needed a logical explanation or he was dead. He laughed weakly. "Oh, that. I hurt my ankle a few years ago and it's been bothering the hell out of me lately. The doctor told me to wear a weight on it to strengthen it, but it still hurts like hell." He shook his leg. "What'd you think it was? A tape recorder?"

Flynn shifted in his chair, doubt etched on his face. His coat opened. The pistol in its holster on his belt was in plain view. He moved his hand closer to it. Jesse reached down and rubbed his ankle, replacing the trouser leg as he did. He wouldn't be able to get to his gun first.

"You want to see it?" Jesse asked jokingly.

Berne leaned closer, staring at the device. Flynn frowned and then chuckled. "There ain't no worse pain than in your bones. I know about that."

The crisis was over. Jesse was near death one more time, but he had survived again.

The grand jury scheme accomplished part of its purpose, although Berne was home free and Jesse remained second-in-command. Prosecutors decided not to grant him immunity for fear of being accused of frivolous prosecution and entrapment that might jeopardize a future case. But Jesse's reputation in the underworld as a standup-up guy increased.

"Guys came up to me and said they were proud of me, the way I stood up to the 'g'. They said there was no way I could be a snitch. A couple of them even said I would make a hell of a better boss than Art and they were behind me. They wanted to work for me."

The grand jury on April 14 indicted the three Leisures and most of their outfit members in the killings of Michaels, Faheen and other acts in the Leisure War. Their cash bonds were so high there was no possibility they would be released.

Jesse now understood why the score with Eidson and Leisure was canceled. "When I heard that it was like a big weight off me. I wouldn't have to be looking over my shoulder any more for the Leisures. Ray Flynn wouldn't be much of a threat any more without the Leisures. It was like I was a free man again."

Jail Instead Of Death

Since Jesse now couldn't kill Flynn for his treachery, he and the FBI decided to give him a Christmas present. It was intended to be viewed as an offer of forgiveness. Rather it was part of scheme to get even in a different way – put him behind bars.

Fox and Bohnemeier suggested Jesse try to re-establish a rapport with Flynn. Since the assassination attempt on Jesse, their relationship had been cautious at best. The government was having trouble making a case against him for the Spica bombing. Perhaps Jesse could open his mouth. Besides, they had no other cases against him to prosecute.

Jesse dropped by to see Flynn. He said he wanted to buy his wife a new washing machine for Christmas. Jesse volunteered to try to find one. Fox had researched a state law recently upheld by the

Missouri Supreme Court making it a felony to acquire goods even if one only suspected it was stolen. It would be a minor charge against Flynn, but a necessary one. The agents gave Jesse $500 to buy a new washing machine. It was imperative Flynn believe it was stolen.

Jesse again met with Flynn several days later. He gave him an expensive bottle of wine as a Christmas present. Flynn was grateful. He told Flynn he and Stram had stolen a new washer from a house under construction. Flynn insisted on paying him, but Jesse refused the money.

It was a solid case, but the value of the property barely constituted a felony. The agents asked FBI officials in Washington for several unclaimed stolen diamonds Jesse could sell to Flynn. They sent four diamonds, each a carat or more, worth $18,000. Prosecutors assured the agents entrapment was not a concern.

Jesse told Flynn he had four diamonds from a home invasion he and Stram had committed in Tennessee. He would let him have them for $8,500. He invited Flynn to his home the next day to inspect them. FBI technicians had installed an electronic monitoring device in the kitchen and rigged a video camera in a briefcase on the dishwasher.

There were three chairs at the kitchen table. Jesse and Stram sat on either side, leaving Flynn sitting at one end facing the video camera. The diamonds were in a cloth bag. Flynn looked at each with a jeweler's eyepiece and then weighed each one with a scale he had brought. He was satisfied with what he saw.

"How much you say you want for them?" Flynn asked.

"Eighty-five hundred."

Flynn said he couldn't pass up the deal. He counted off the money from a wad of bills he took from his pocket. He was as good as in jail, Jesse thought.

CHAPTER TWENTY

"The Little Bomb Maker"

L ucas Brazil was a virtuoso in the art of death by bombs. To him, they gave efficiency and anonymity to murder.

Car bombs had significance in the St. Louis underworld. The terror they inspire is the ultimate tool of intimidation and retribution. But they are not a clean method of execution like a bullet in the head. Victims are mutilated, their bodies unrecognizable masses of flesh and bones. Expensive cars are reduced to charred rubble in an instantaneous burst of unleashed energy.

The carnage bombs leave is a grim reminder of revenge and sins not forgiven as with Spica, Faheen and Paulie Leisure. The message they convey is unambiguous: Cross us, be disloyal, and your body disintegrates.

Unlike a pistol requiring the hit man to be close to his target, explosive devices are more impersonal. The killer can be remote, perhaps not even seeing his victim die. He can be far away when the ignition is turned or the brake pedal is touched, detonating the charge. With a bomb activated by remote control, he can remain concealed and be gone before the dust settles.

The nature of a bomb shields the executioner from implication if properly constructed. Little evidence is left except residue from the explosive material and a few minute parts of the device. A bullet can be recovered from the body, identified and connected to a single gun which can be put in the hands of the killer.

Brazil, born Robert Allen, a name he rarely used, perfected murder by bomb. What attracted him was the required expertise. Little talent is needed to chamber a bullet in a gun and pull the trigger or plunge a knife into the heart. The precision necessary to construct a bomb without blowing oneself to eternity and ensuring it works is the real state of the art of murder.

Brazil went undetected for years. He first came to the FBI's attention during the surveillance of Ski Kowalski's mobile home in 1980 after the Michaels' bombing when agents observed him deliver a package they assumed was a bomb. They had more than Vitale's word Kowalski was involved in bombings. Telephone records disclosed Flynn called him six times in the week preceding the Spica hit. There were no calls after it.

Brazil drove an older model Mercury Cougar with Missouri license plates issued to him at an address in St. Louis. He was slightly built, short, weighing 150 pounds, with his short grayish brown hair parted in the middle. The resident at the address, the sister of Robert Allen, didn't know her brother's alias. Brazil's name and the car's license number and model of the car were filed and forgotten.

Kowalski introduced Jesse to Brazil a few years earlier. Jesse sold him a stolen diamond ring. Brazil had worked as a pipefitter with Stram and they were friends. His intelligence was reflected in his IQ of 160. His tastes were simple and he lived unpretentiously in a cluttered mobile home near Belleville.

Brazil met Stram by chance and he casually discussed a bomb he was making. Stram wasn't aware he made explosive devices. Jesse told the agents. Fox was interested but Bohnemeier contended he would be a waste of time. Jesse ignored him. He had a gut feeling Brazil was worth pursuing.

Kowalski admitted to Jesse that Brazil was a "master bomb technician" who had been making them for years. Jesse called Brazil and said he had a hot diamond – in fact a "c-z," a fake made of cubic zirconia – he might be interested in. He went to see him. Brazil was working on a timer for a bomb for which he would be paid $5,000. Jesse's instinct had been right again. He was surprised Brazil talked so freely, but his reputation and stature in the mob unsealed many lips.

Brazil demonstrated how it worked. He set the timer for 15 minutes and attached it to a detonator cap. He put two telephone directories and a pair of blue jeans over it to muffle the explosion. The cap detonated exactly 15 minutes later. Brazil grinned smugly. He had displayed his professionalism.

Jesse decided not to sell him the fake diamond and possibly jeopardize the investigation. Fox suggested he get Brazil to repeat the demonstration and tape it. He also should try to obtain the telephone books as evidence. The next day Jesse told Brazil he didn't understand how a timing device worked so accurately. Brazil repeated the demonstration. Jesse said he had a proposition from Art Berne and needed the telephone books to prove Brazil's expertise. He gladly gave them to him.

Jesse turned conspiratorial. "Lucas, me and Art might have a little piece of action for you every once in awhile. What I'd like to do is have you as our silent guy. You ain't gonna be seen or heard, you're just gonna be there when we need you."

Brazil was elated. "I've been low profile all my life. That's how I've been able to get by and why nobody knows about me."

"This way, we can come to you and say, 'Lucas take care of this for us', and bang you got your pocket full of money. With your talent we'll make some bread together. Just remember, these are things you got to keep to yourself. You don't tell Ski or anybody else about our deal."

Brazil savored the intrigue. "Oh, no. You can count on that."

"And I want you to know that you're not obligated. If something stinks, you back off. That's the way we want it."

"Well, you're not dealing with an amateur, Jesse," Brazil said proudly. "You know, a thief's got some morals. A thief is a gentleman with intelligence. He's smart enough to have a deep instinct. Now, a crook, he just runs into a drug store and robs it without planning. That's where we're different."

Brazil further promoted himself. He said he made a device for Kowalski and delivered it to him at the trailer court. Jesse knew it was the package agents saw him giving to Kowalski.

Brazil reminisced. "You see, I try not to make anything for use around here. I do once in awhile, but I never want to know what happens to it. I don't care where it goes or who it's for. You heard of Machine Gun Kelly, haven't you? Well, he told me never to shit in your own nest. I knew what he meant by that. I done time with him. He was one great guy."

"Was he?"

"He died in my arms. We were out walking on the cinder track and he threw his arms around me and his head went back and he died. He had a heart attack."

Jesse continued exploiting Brazil's vanity. "I hear you're a hell of a technician, Lucas. And that's good enough for me and Art. But I still don't understand how those remote controls work."

Brazil pointed to a car a block away. "Take that one over there. Say that's the guy you want to hit. You got your little box here. You throw the lever and the jay bird's got a nest in his ass before he even comes down."

"What distance can you blow him up at?"

"Up to eighteen miles. See, the beautiful part about it is a lot of guys have their cars wired up so that there's always at least twelve volts going through it. If you hook wires to that car, well, you'll blow yourself up. That's why you use a magnet to attach it to a car and with a remote control you're safe."

"Now, say we got a guy who wants to buy one from you. What does that cost?"

"It's worth five, six grand to me. I got people mostly in Ohio that get them for that price."

"What did they call you, Lucas?"

Brazil chuckled. "The little bomb maker."

Jesse needed to induce Brazil to talk about the bomb he made for Kowalski. "This one you said you made for Ski. Can I get something like that?"

"Like I make? Yeah, you could."

"How long would it take?"

"I'd want two weeks at least. I don't rush it. See, my life and my reputation is at stake, too."

"This one will go out of town. I guarantee you that. I'm pretty sure this guy is going to want one. I'll let you know as soon as I hear."

"I'm glad it isn't going around here. I knew I screwed up when I made that thing for around here. I didn't ask where it was to go because like I told you I don't want to know."

"Did you get all your money for that bomb?" Brazil said he had. "I mean, did you get half up front and half later?"

"I got it c.o.d."

"Was it five thou?"

"A little better," Brazil said, annoyed at Jesse's persistence.

"Ten grand?"

Brazil paused. "No, seven."

"Seven thousand? See, everything I heard was right on the nose." Now for the clincher. "Was it for old man Michaels?'

Brazil's face contorted. "I like you, too, Jesse."

It was a dangerous mind game Jesse was playing with him, but he couldn't stop now. "How many remote control bombs has Ski had you do?"

"Just that one."

Jesse needed to build a background profile of Brazil and learn more about Robert Allen. He told him he always tried to maintain a low level of identity, but Vitale had ruined that and had brought attention to him.

Brazil agreed. "That's the way I am, too. Like when I go somewhere I leave my real identification at home. I don't want to be caught with it."

"That's one thing I don't understand. It's none of my business, but why do you go under the name of Lucas Brazil and you write your checks out in your other name, Robert Allen, or whatever it is? That don't make sense."

"I keep my money in my own name for one reason only. If something should happen to me my sister can get it with no hitch."

Jesse asked if there was a real Lucas Brazil. A young boy with that name died many years earlier. Brazil got his birth certificate and was issued a Social Security number in that name. He had driver's licenses in both names. He also had a passport in the name of Lucas Brazil while he was on the run from a robbery in which a man was killed. It was why he still didn't use his real name. He wouldn't admit specific involvement, but he did obliquely admit another homicide.

"You know, I've never got caught on any job I ever did. I always got ratted on. I had this guy down in New Orleans. They had him hid out. He had an assumed name and different identification. Three years I looked for him."

"The guy snitch on you?" Jesse asked

"It was a half-assed burglary rap. I got hold of a guy I know down there and he put the word out on him. He found him. That's all I wanted him to do. The case against me was dismissed for lack of evidence."

"The guy went bye-bye. One of those little old remote control jobs, huh?"

"I didn't have to worry about him anymore," Brazil said emphatically.

Jesse was surprised how Brazil opened up. "He was mine now. I owned him. The rest would be easy. He was a marked man. He trusted me and that was his big mistake."

Fox and Bohnemeier decided to ignore Brazil for awhile. They didn't want Jesse to appear too aggressive and spook him. He told Brazil he would be out of town for a week and when he returned they would have dinner. By then, Berne might have something for him.

The agents checked out Brazil's story about "Machine Gun" Kelly, the infamous bank robber and kidnaper. He died of a heart attack in the federal penitentiary at Leavenworth, Kansas, in 1954, as Brazil said. Brazil also was an inmate there, serving time for bank robbery.

A Child Witness

Despite FBI restrictions about criminal activities, Jesse took a contract from Kowalski the day after he met with Brazil. A drug dealer and pimp owed him a lot of money and refused to pay. He wanted the man beaten badly. He offered Jesse $3,000, but he turned down the money.

Jesse didn't consider he was breaking his contract with himself not to kill. He just would hurt the guy. He deserved it. Besides, it was an obligation to Kowalski.

"Ski was a good friend of mine and did me a lot of favors over the years. He'd be insulted if I said no and probably be suspicious too. And if Tom and Terry found out, I wouldn't be working for them anymore. I'd be out on the streets by myself. If not back in the pen. This guy, he was nothing but a low-life bum. You could kill him and the world would be better off."

The man lived in a trailer in a small court. Kowalski didn't offer a name and Jesse didn't want to know. It made no difference.

Jesse parked his Lincoln at 11 o'clock the next night in front of the man's mobile home. Lights were on in one room. He turned off the engine and opened the hood. Stram pretended to inspect the engine. Jesse knocked on the door of the trailer, while Stram stood to the side in the shadows with a baseball bat.

"What you want?" a voice with a deep southern drawl asked through the door.

"The battery on my car's dead," Jesse said. "You got a jumper cable."

"Go away," the man ordered.

"Look, I have to get my car started. Can I use your phone?"

The door was unlocked. It opened a crack. It was enough. Jesse was through it in an instant, knocking the wiry, almost bald, man to the floor. He cringed in fear, scooting back against the far wall. He opened his mouth to protest, but there were no words. His eyes were hollow from drugs.

Stram closed the door. Jesse was emotionless as he reached down, grabbed the trembling, sobbing man by the shirt and pulled him up. His fists were jackhammers, slamming into the pimp's face, flattening it into an unrecognizable mass of blood, flesh and bone. The man slumped to the floor, able only to whimper. He tried to talk, but his jaws flopped as if on strings.

"You owe Ski Kowalski some money, (expletive)," Jesse said calmly. "This is how you're gonna repay it."

Stram handed him the bat. The pimp raised his hands in front of his face to ward off what he knew was coming. The first blow landed on the man's right forearm and the bone shattered. The second blow broke his other arm. Jesse raised the bat again. It hovered over his head aimed at the pimp's right leg.

A scream pierced the room. A black-haired girl, not more than three years old and dressed in raggedy pajamas, stood in the doorway. Her hands covered her contorted face. They didn't hold back the stream of tears.

"Daddy! Daddy!" she screamed. She ran past Jesse and stood between him and her bloody, beaten father.

"Oh, hell," Jesse said to Stram. He handed the bloody bat to him.

He went to the girl, but she backed away. "Come on, honey. It's okay. I'm not going to hurt you." She shielded her face with her hands. He took her in his arms and held her to him. Her sobbing eased. He took her to the bedroom and gently placed her on her bed, covering her with a torn, dirty blanket. She held her hands to her ears.

Jesse returned to the living room. The pimp was unconscious and bleeding profusely. Stram searched drawers in the kitchen. He opened a coffee canister and found $3,000 in hundreds and fifties. Jesse stuffed the bills in his pocket. It was Kowalski's money.

Jesse found a phone booth not far from the trailer court. He dialed 911 and reported a burglary at the trailer. It was the least he could do. He had committed a terrible wrong. What he had done was not much different than murder. The man might be alive, but he was near death and in terrible pain and agony.

Jesse knew controlling his inbred instincts to kill was a monumental task he had just failed. Would he one day in the future be tempted again? He surely would, but could his sense of decency - his commitment to himself and to God - prevail?

"I hated myself. I hated everything I was. Not only because of what I did to him, but that little girl. I asked myself, 'You a man or an animal, Stoneking'? I knew I had to ask God to forgive me and to help me get over this thing about killing."

Another Snitch Exposed

Jimmy Giammanco took over the vending machine company in Fairmont City after Giordano died. Jesse dropped by to chat with him not long after the Kowalski contract. He didn't like Gimmanco that much. He was a loudmouth with the personality of a rattlesnake. His intelligence and his abilities earned him no greater rank than a mere soldier in his Giordano's army. Giammanco seemed unusually moody.

"Something bothering you, Jimmy?" Jesse asked.

"Yeah, it's this guy that keeps hanging around here. This Louie Morales. I heard yesterday that he's a snitch."

Jesse knew Morales was a street-level drug dealer. "Why's he hanging around here, then?"

"He's just a nuisance. I give him a couple of odd jobs to keep him occupied. He ain't gonna find out nothing, anyhow. We don't talk about nothing in front of him. I guess I ought to have him cracked."

"You don't wanna do that, Jimmy. If he is a snitch, it'd just bring a lot of heat on you. You want me to find out for sure if he's a snitch?"

"Sure. Go ahead."

When Morales showed up, Jesse chatted with him. "Hey, Louie, you want to make some money? I got this grass I'll sell you cheap. I got to get rid of it."

Morales was eager. He didn't even bother negotiating a price. He would buy all he had. Jesse told him to meet him there at 3 o'clock that afternoon.

Giammanco was concerned. "Jesse, you better watch out, messing with that stuff. I don't want it around here."

"Don't worry about it, Jimmy. It won't be anything."

Jesse went home and raked the back yard until he had two black plastic trash bags full of dried grass. At 3 o'clock he pulled up in front of the vending company. Morales was waiting outside for him. Giammanco was inside the office watching through the window.

As soon as Jesse turned off the ignition of his Lincoln he was surrounded by five Illinois Division of Criminal Investigation agents, their revolvers drawn. "We have a search warrant for your car, Stoneking," one agent said.

"What for?"

The detective didn't answer him and handed him the search warrant. He and another agent searched the interior, but found nothing. "Open up the trunk," he ordered.

Jesse complied. The officer beamed at the plastic trash bags. He reached inside one and then the other, each time pulling out a fistful of dried grass clippings and leaves. He was disgusted.

Jesse turned to Morales. "I told you I was going to bring you some grass. What'd you think I meant? You a snitch, Louie?"

Morales, embarrassed, walked away. Giammanco said he was eternally grateful for exposing him. The incident was the topic of conversation for weeks in the underworld. Jesse had enhanced his standing with the Sicilians.

CHAPTER TWENTY-ONE

A Litany Of Murder

Lucas Brazil showed no emotion except pride as he recited his litany of murder to Jesse. At least 30 people died because of his bombs.

They were words the FBI agents needed to hear to establish Brazil's expertise in homicide. He admitted he had been making bombs for a long time. He had gained his basic knowledge as a military demolition expert and he improvised from that.

"How many people you think got cracked because of them?" Jesse inquired casually.

Brazil didn't hesitate to calculate. "Probably thirty. A lot of them in Ohio." His voice was as emotionless as an accountant reciting numbers from a spreadsheet. Death to him obviously was trivial, murder methodical.

Jesse assumed it was an accurate body count. He prodded him further. With great relish, Brazil recited some of his lethal masterpieces. Not all were car bombs and some were innovative. One device inside the victim's mailbox exploded when the door was opened. Another in the reservoir of the commode detonated when the victim flushed the toilet. One blew up when the light switch was turned on in the house.

"I've got my specialty model, too, that's in a briefcase. Once I set it there's no way it can be disarmed."

"Does it go underneath the seat, or what?"

"No, you just take it to the guy's office or wherever."

"Is it remote control, too?"

Brazil was impatient with Jesse's lack of knowledge of bombs. "No, he thinks it's a present. You put a happy birthday card on it and then when he opens the briefcase up, why that's the last birthday he ever has."

"You got a pretty good name as a highly ranked technician, don't you?"

"I don't know about being high ranking and all that, but there ain't nobody better than me."

Jesse probed deeper into Brazil's trade secrets. "Let me ask you a question. The government comes in and they go through this car real good after it blows up, like Michaels, and they find no fingerprints or nothing. Is that because everything is blown up?"

"What I do is take this super glue and put it on each finger. That way there won't be any prints on anything I touch. The glue coats your fingers. I can't work with gloves on. I got to use my fingers."

"I've sure learned a lot from you, Lucas."

Brazil said he once made a "double bubble," containing two bombs, one for under the front of the car, the other for under the rear. He had yet to build a "triple bubble" made of three bombs, the third under the center of the car. He was looking forward to a contract for that.

"If you want complete obliteration then you want the triple. You might want me to make you one sometime. That costs a bundle, though. But, you know, it's worth it to save people from going to jail if it's a snitch you're going to hit."

Jesse laughed. "One thing I learned about you, Lucas. You like company and you like bombs, don't you, Lucas?"

"I like it because it's ..." Brazil seemed at a loss for words.

"Devastating. That's the word you're looking for?"

"Yeah, and it's a good living," Brazil said cockily. "That's the survival of man, you know. I don't like to harm people. I love people and I love life. You don't bother me and I won't bother you."

"That's the way I think. Don't shake my tree and my peaches won't fall on you." Jesse chuckled. "If them peaches fall on you they'll blow up, won't they?"

"Each peach will be loaded. Right."

It was time to lure Brazil into the trap. "The main reason I wanted to see you is that this guy I talked about who might want a remote control called me. He's ready. It's for a car." Brazil grinned broadly. "Now, how much did you say you wanted for one just like you made for Ski?"

Brazil thought for a moment. "Seven grand."

"Seven. How about six? That's what I told the guy."

Brazil sighed. "Okay, you got a deal. Six grand."

"You said you needed two weeks?"

"Yeah, depending on how quick I can get the parts."

Brazil asked Jesse how he could afford two families. "It's brutal," Jesse replied."I got four, five thousand every month to pay in bills. I don't have nothing in my pockets anymore."

"I figured that. Well, I don't need no broads."

Jesse had wondered about Brazil's sexual persuasion. He never talked about women. Stram complained his women were keeping him broke, too.

"Why don't you get a young boy, Mark? They don't cost much."

"See, Mark, what've I been telling you?" Jesse said, pretending seriousness.

"And they're loyal to you, too." Brazil wasn't joking.

"I've been trying to hit Mark for years and he won't let me," Jesse teased.

Jesse complained jokingly to Fox and Bohnemeier. "I don't mind hanging around with these killers for you, but not these guys. That's asking too much."

"We'll give you a bonus for hazardous duty," Fox said. "Just watch yourself. If you drop a twenty dollar bill, don't bend over near him to pick it up. You'll become his sweetheart." He patted Jesse on the buttocks. "You do have a nice little butt, sweetie."

"Get out of here, Fox," Jesse said disgustedly.

Jesse's enthusiasm for his undercover work reached a new level. Brazil was a worthy challenge. "I hadn't accomplished much except gather a lot of information on people. I hadn't made any big cases yet. The gambling case against Mike Trupiano wasn't really mine. But now I was about to get Lucas Brazil all by myself."

"You Just Got Me Killed"

Trupiano told Jesse two days later he had found a house for lease. It was in south St. Louis County not far from his. It had four bedrooms and the rent was $750 a month. They inspected the ranch house and Jesse signed the lease. The FBI would reimburse him.

Jesse's relationship with Carolee was deteriorating. She was moody at times, argumentative and defiant at others. He didn't understand how distressing he was for her. He considered women subservient to men. Their purpose in life was limited to child-rearing, cleaning house, cooking dinner and providing sexual gratification. He was the classic male chauvinist.

Nor did he perceive Carolee's indignity of having to share her husband's love, attention, time and assets with another woman of equal status in his life. He didn't comprehend the jealousy that often turned into rage, the crippling pain of self-reproach for having to compete with his illicit lover. Now that he was an informant, the cold, hard reality of sudden, violent death, not only his, but perhaps hers as well, was just as crippling.

Jesse explained: "What could I do? I had two families and I had to support and love each of them. I loved both Carolee and Dorothy. I had an obligation to take care of both of them. I just couldn't walk away from one of my families. What man could do that? My kids in each family needed a father. That's what I was. Their father."

He spent the night of June 5, the day before he and Carolee were to move to St. Louis, with Dorothy. He went home the next morning to help finish packing. The house was empty except for his belongings and a few pieces of furniture. Carolee's car and the children were gone. A neighbor said she and a man loaded a U-Haul van. The man left in the van and Carolee followed in her car.

"I looked all over for her. I talked to everybody we knew, but no one knew anything. I was frustrated at first, not knowing why she had left. The more I thought about it, the madder I got at this guy who stole my family. That's all I thought about. When I found him I'd hurt him real bad."

Jesse learned where the truck was rented. A man named Arnold Johnson leased it for a one-way trip to Las Vegas. The name meant nothing to Jesse. The employee said the van broke down near Joplin, Missouri. Johnson chose not to unload the belongings into another van and was waiting while it was being repaired.

Jesse arrived in Joplin late in the afternoon. They had left three hours earlier. The manager of the rental agency refused to give him the van's license number or the Las Vegas motel where they would be staying, but $100 loosened his tongue.

Jesse considered trying to overtake them, but they probably were at least 150 miles away by then. The thought of going to Las Vegas tempted him, but that would require too much continuous driving. He already had been out of contact with Fox and Bohnemeier too long.

The agents were deeply concerned. Jesse had standing orders to contact them at least once a day. Calls to him were unanswered. His houses in O'Fallon and in south St. Louis County were vacant.

They feared Jesse either had been discovered and killed or he had walked away from the operation. FBI field offices in Missouri and Illinois were alerted to watch for him and detain him if he was located. The agents doubted he would be found. If he was on the run he would be far away by now and using an alias. If he was dead his body eventually would be located. Corpses of snitches were intended to be found to send a message. They would wait another 24 hours before putting out a nationwide alert.

Jesse called Bohnemeier from Joplin. He had debated whether to be truthful. His manhood had been insulted, his pride badly bruised and he was embarrassed. Revenge seemed so sweet, but he decided to tell him. It would deter him from harming Johnson. He expected Bohnemeier to be angry, but he wasn't. He sympathized with him.

Jesse called the motel in Las Vegas. Carolee and the children were in two rooms registered to Johnson. He demanded no explanation from her. That would come later. He told her if she didn't immediately return home with the children he would come to Las Vegas. She wouldn't want that. She didn't argue with him. She promised she would be back as soon as possible. He told her he wanted to talk to Johnson.

"You know who I am, don't you?" Jesse asked. His voice was calm, but conveyed a threat.

"Not really," Johnson said.

"I want to know why you stole my wife and children."

There was a long pause. "She asked me to drive her here. That's all, Mr. Stoneking. Just drive her. She begged me and gave me a thousand dollars."

"Nobody messes in my personal life, Johnson!" Jesse's anger almost was out of control. "You got any idea what I'm going to do to you?"

Johnson couldn't conceal his fear. "Just try to understand, Mr. Stoneking. I think you're wife's got mental problems. I only tried to help her."

"I'll look you up when you get back, Johnson."

Jesse cooled down by the time Carolee and the children returned three days later. Johnson didn't accompany her. The furniture was in storage. She explained she just wanted to get away for awhile, that his undercover work was too stressful for her.

There was nothing between her and Johnson. He was just someone she knew. Her profuse apologies seemed sincere and Jesse accepted them.

As time passed, she seemed more troubled and deeply in thought. Jesse tried to talk to her, but she shunned him. Finally, she said she had something important to tell him and began weeping. "I told that man who took me to Las Vegas that you were an informant," she blurted out.

Jesse was stunned. "You did what?"

"I told him how you got out of prison and everything, Jesse. I don't know why I did it."

Jesse raged. "You just got me killed, that's what you did!" He slapped her several times and threw her to the floor. She didn't try to defend herself. It would be futile. He stormed from the house and didn't return for two days.

He had to tell Fox and Bohnemeier. What she did posed a real danger. They checked out Johnson. He had no known organized crime connections and no arrest record. He was just an average, law-abiding citizen who made a bad decision. She was an attractive, alluring woman and they understood why he got involved.

The agents assessed the danger. If Johnson believed Carolee was delusive he probably would say nothing, perhaps too embarrassed to tell anyone he helped a woman flee her husband, a notorious, dangerous hoodlum. However, if they talked to him it would confirm what she told him and there was a likelihood he might brag about it in a moment of weakness or after a few drinks. They decided not to pursue the matter, but warned Jesse to be more alert. They didn't have to tell him that.

Jesse visited Brazil to check on the bomb. He still was working on it. "You gonna get the plastic explosives?" Brazil asked.

Fox and Bohnemeier warned Stoneking not to procure any bomb components. The defense could successfully claim entrapment. Jesse was indignant to Brazil. "You mean for six grand I gotta supply the stuff too? I don't know anybody who's got that. Why do you think I'm having you make it?"

"The bomb will just have to be bigger, then, if I have to use dynamite. With plastic, I can make it real compact. I ain't got either one right now."

"You got any contacts to get any?" Jesse asked.

"Yeah, in Kentucky. Maybe we'll have to take a ride down there. I'll use eight sticks. You just put it right under his ass."

"He'll be going to heaven, won't he?"

Brazil giggled. "He'll be shaking hands with St. Peter. He'll have a nest full of jaybirds in his ass before he even hits the ground."

"Is that all you know about them damned jay birds?" Jesse said, irritated. The cliché made no sense.

"Well, it's true."

"I don't know what you mean when you say that." Brazil didn't answer him. Jesse said he was concerned about handling the bomb. "It'll be completely disarmed, won't it?"

Brazil laughed. "Sure. I'll give you instructions. Matter of fact, when we get the dynamite you can stand way off when I hook it up."

The Wayne Newton Hit

Brazil said he was awakened at 2 o'clock that morning by a telephone call from a friend who had a contract for him. Entertainer Wayne Newton with a partner had bought the Aladdin Hotel and Casino in Las Vegas after the St. Louis and Detroit mobs sold it. There were allegations he had underworld connections, which never were proven and which he denied. He filed a defamation of character suit.

Now, Brazil said, the mob wanted him hit. "This guy wanted me to help shut that Newton up. He's running his mouth off about the mob and he won't shut up. This guy's got a contract on him for a million dollars."

"The Mafia does?" Jesse asked, not sure he should believe Brazil.

"Because he wouldn't let them come in the joint. He's just being a nuisance."

"The hit's coming out of St. Louis?" Brazil didn't answer. "You know, the people in St. Louis and Detroit used to have it. I hear maybe they're wanting back in." Brazil remained silent. "A million dollar contract, huh? Hell, for that much I'd crack him."

"They want him so bad they're going to give half up front," Brazil finally said. "It'd be easy. He's got three bodyguards and all you'd have to do is grab one of them guy's wife and kids and then have the bodyguard set Newton up for you. I turned it down. I won't want to mess with them people."

"You don't know who to trust, is that what you're saying? They'd probably give you half the money and then hit you."

"That's exactly the problem. These guys are playing for millions. They don't take no chances. They're not gonna leave witnesses around."

"The person who told you that, is he a good source or do you think he's just playing with you?"

Brazil just nodded. Jesse assumed whoever offered him the hit was someone of importance and he didn't want to talk about it. During the trial of Newton's suit there was testimony that, indeed, a murder contract on him had been considered by the underworld.

CHAPTER TWENTY-TWO

A Hit Disguised

L ucas Brazil issued Jesse's death warrant and prophesied it, but it was disguised and unseen until almost too late. His execution was to be with the remote-controlled bomb he bought from Brazil.

Brazil told Jesse the bomb was completed, except for the dynamite. A friend, Pat McAtee, who lived in Smith Mills, Kentucky, just south of Evansville, Indiana, would provide the explosives.

"You sure you can trust this guy?" Jesse asked.

"I been dealing with him for years," Brazil replied. "I got too much on him. He knows I'd kill him if he ever opened his mouth."

Brazil was to pick up the dynamite the next afternoon. Jesse said he wasn't sure he could make the trip because he might have business to take care of. Traveling with Brazil and the dynamite was the last thing he wanted to do.

Fox consulted an agent in Washington who was an explosives expert. He explained the dynamite used in bombs often was old and its nitroglycerin unstable. It would be dangerous for anyone, especially a novice, to handle. The decision whether to accompany Brazil was entirely Jesse's.

"That cinched it. I didn't have to think twice about that decision. There was no way I was going to get blown away for the FBI. Brazil could go get it on his own. Let him get blown up. Nobody would miss him, anyhow."

But the special agent in charge of the Springfield, Illinois, FBI field office ordered Jesse to accompany Brazil. Putting the dynamite in Brazil's hands would enhance the case. Jesse was angry and confused. Where Brazil got the dynamite would make no difference. A bomb was a bomb and Brazil was making it. He reluctantly agreed to drive Brazil to Kentucky.

Precautions must be taken. The dynamite's stability was unknown and it would assumed to be dangerous. There was no way to control that. It was imperative to record conversations with Brazil during the drive, but the tape could not be changed when it ran out halfway through the trip. A transmitter could detonate the dynamite.

Fox and Bohnemeier decided the transmitter would be used on the way down and the recorder on the return trip. For Jesse's security, Fox would maintain vehicular surveillance and Bohnemeier would be in an airplane overhead. It was the best they could do. It didn't satisfy Jesse.

"I don't know why you're so worried," Bohnemeier said. "You'll be safer than me in that plane."

"Yeah. You want to trade places?"

"No way."

Fox parked in a secluded area not far from Brazil's trailer. Jesse would drive that way and as soon as he was on Route 15 he was to signal Fox, who would notify Bohnemeier to take off from a nearby airport.

Jesse activated the transmitter before he got to Brazil's trailer. After they left, he said, "Well, Lucas, I'm glad there ain't much traffic on the highway. We'll make good time."

It was the prearranged signal he was on his way. Fox didn't hear it. For an hour there was nothing from the transmitter. Punctuality was a way of life for Jesse and he never was this late. Fox called Dorothy, who said he left the house at 8 o'clock. The pilot of Bohnemeier's plane flew east over Interstate 64, but Jesse's Lincoln couldn't be located.

The worst case scenario gripped the agents over what might have happened to him. He could be dead, but Brazil would have no reason to kill him. Jesse had developed a working relationship with him. There was nothing more they could do. They awaited his return and braced themselves for his wrath. If he was alive.

The agents didn't miss any incriminating conversations. Just a lot of idle chatter. Jesse tried to induce Brazil to discuss the bombs he made for his clients in Ohio, the witness against him who was killed in New Orleans and the Michaels bombing, but he wouldn't talk about them.

When they arrived in Kentucky, Jesse waited in the car while Brazil went into McAtee's house. They came out and Brazil motioned to Jesse. McAtee, dressed in bib overalls, led them to an old pick-up truck parked in the back yard. He retrieved a burlap sack with 10 sticks of dynamite and a grocery bag with 13 blasting caps. Brazil offered him $50, but he refused the money.

Jesse looked at the dynamite. It was sweating nitroglycerin and was soft to the touch, indicating it was highly unstable. Brazil told him to put the dynamite in the trunk and the blasting caps on the floor in the back. They had to be kept apart to prevent the caps from accidentally detonating the dynamite, he said. Jesse activated the tape recorder as they left McAtee's house.

After they crossed into Illinois, Jesse called Dorothy from a telephone booth at a service station. She told him Fox was concerned. There was no surveillance of Jesse.

As anticipated, he was furious at the agents. "Here I am with a crazy man and a bunch of dynamite ready to blow at any time, and there's no FBI around. You talk about being all alone in the world. We'd have a little talk about that later. I had bigger problems now like not going up with a bang."

Jese turned to Brazil. "There ain't no chance that dynamite in the trunk will get too hot and blow up, is there, Lucas?" Brazil assured him there was no danger of that, but Jesse wasn't convinced. "It's like nitroglycerin, isn't it?"

"It's close to it."

"Maybe we ought to put it inside the car where it's cooler and put the caps in the trunk."

"No, it'll dry out back there."

"I'm not talking about it drying out, Lucas! I'm talking about it overheating."

"It won't overheat. That's not the problem. When it gets in the state it's in it can't stand too much of a jar. Not more than 45 to 50 pounds of pressure."

"What do you mean by that?" Jesse asked, alarmed.

"Don't worry about it, Jesse, but right now we're riding on a bomb," Brazil said, amused. "Just don't go running into a brick wall or a tractor-trailer. If it goes off, you and me will never know it."

Jesse knew Brazil was playing with him. "Lucas, why did you say that? I think I'm going to let you drive and I'll take a bus home."

"Well, if it goes off, we'll get home a hell of a lot sooner. You want to stop and get some insurance?"

"Don't be messing with me, Lucas."

A Prophesy Of Murder

As they neared the East Side, Brazil said he was concerned about Jesse handling the bomb. Although Jesse had told him he only was the intermediary and the purchaser would use it, Brazil believed he was going to install it himself. Jesse wasn't sure what he was driving at.

"There ain't no friction or nothing between you guys, is there?"

"No way. These guys, Tom and Terry, they're my partners. Why?"

"Well, what better way would there be to get rid of a guy? While you're hooking it up, all your guys have to do is throw the switch."

Jesse understood Brazil's concern. Trust no one. "I'll have that remote control in my possession at all times. They'll have to hit me in the head to get it out of my hands."

"Yeah, whoever has it is in control. I heard a story once. I guess it's true. A guy had the load and as he was putting it under the car his partner threw the switch and he got rid of the witness and the car. Bang! It's a done deal."

"Why would he do that?"

"I guess the partner had a bitch of some kind against him. Maybe he thought he was a snitch."

Jesse was curious why Brazil told him that. It probably was his paranoia or just a story. He left Brazil off at the trailer. He promised the bomb would be ready Tuesday morning. It now was time to give the agents a piece of his mind for their carelessness. He called Bohnemeier from a pay phone. "Where the hell were you guys?" he shouted.

Bohnemeier said Fox hadn't received any transmissions. He suggested there had been a malfunction in the transmitter.

"Malfunction, my ass!" Jesse shouted.

"You know we were there. Tom called Dorothy."

"You leave me go down there by myself with that lunatic and come back with the bad dynamite. Bull!" He slammed down the receiver before Bohnemeier could respond. There was nothing else to say.

Brazil on Monday confirmed the bomb would be ready as promised. He assured Jesse it would be unarmed, but because of the instability of the dynamite, Fox and Bohnemeier planned delivery of the bomb to them. Jesse was to drive five miles from Brazil's trailer to a deserted excavation site, where it would be given to Army demolition experts for examination. The dynamite would be disposed.

Jesse would have to use the heavily traveled Route 15. There could be no radio communication with him once he had the bomb because of the danger of detonation. It also could be set off by a signal from a citizen's band or a police radio. There was no way to control that. To have local authorities close the highway would raise suspicions and Jesse could be identified.

Jesse was on edge. "I'm nervous as a whore in church on Sunday. I told Tom and Terry they could get the bomb themselves. They said something about the chain of custody. I was worried about a chain of death, not chain of custody. I said something doesn't feel right. They told me not to be worried. It would all be over in a few minutes. Yeah, it might. Permanently."

Ride To Hell

He met with the agents at the excavation site at 9:15 a. m. Tuesday to begin what he called the "ride to hell." There were procedures to ensure the integrity of the evidence. They didn't want to give defense lawyers opportunity to contend Brazil had been entrapped with a bomb Jesse made.

While Bohnemeier installed the recorder in the trunk, Fox counted the $6,000 Jesse was to pay for the bomb. The serial numbers were recorded, not that the agents hoped to recover the money. Jesse signed a receipt.

"I don't like this at all," Jesse said when they were finished.

"I can't say that I blame you, Jesse," Bohnemeier said. "It'll be over in a few minutes and then we all can relax."

"Something tells me this ain't right."

"There's nothing we can do about it now. You got to go through with it."

"Yeah, I know."

As Jesse drove to the trailer, he was relieved the case was minutes away from being finalized. He was home free now. No more concerns about being blown away. He had made a good case against Brazil. It was cut and dried. Brazil no doubt considered him a trusted friend, but that relationship would end.

Despite his confidence, Jesse took one precaution. He told Stram to get to the trailer before he arrived. He was to stay with Brazil until he delivered the bomb to the agents. He was not to let Brazil out of his sight. "It was my insurance. I didn't tell Tom and Terry about it. They always talked about need to know. Well, they didn't need to know about this. There was no way they'd have approved bringing Mark into it."

Stram and Brazil were outside the trailer when Jesse drove up. A black lunch box containing the bomb and a brown paper bag with the remote control were on the steps. Jesse turned on the recorder and motioned Brazil to the car.

Brazil extended a hand, but Jesse didn't shake it. He didn't want to ever touch him again. Brazil opened the lunch box, pointed to the bomb, then quickly closed the lid. Jesse couldn't make out what was inside. Brazil placed the lunch box on the rear floor behind the driver's seat and the bag on the front passenger seat.

Jesse counted aloud the $6,000 in hundreds. "There's your six grand, Lucas, for one bomb."

"Thank you, Jesse."

Brazil handed him a sheet of white paper on which he had printed step-by-step instructions for arming and detonating the bomb:

"1. Plug wires from package to cap wires.

"2. Turn on transmitter.

"3. Push switch from off to on (on package), then go to car and proceed with four and five.

"4. Attach antenna and extend full length.

"5. Push handle on left side of transmitter up quick. Boom. Boom."

That was an important piece of evidence. "You wrote this out, huh, Lucas? You think of everything."

"Yeah, I did."

Brazil once again assured Jesse the bomb wasn't activated and was safe. "You ain't got nothing to worry about. You're home free."

"You got this thing wiped clean of prints, don't you?" Brazil insisted he had. "Okay, you got your six grand, you've counted it and everybody's happy."

"Everybody except the guy who's going to get it with that. And I'm not charging you any taxes."

"Okay, Lucas, I'll see you later. I got to go see Tom and Terry." He laughed. "You'll probably end up seeing them in court sometime on something. They're always in and out of there for one thing or another."

Jesse was backing out of the driveway when Brazil stepped up to the door of the trailer to open it. Stram blocked his way.

"I gotta go inside and take a leak," Brazil pleaded.

"Later," Stram said, gripping Brazil's arm firmly.

Brazil sat on the steps. He was preoccupied. "I got a remote control I got to get done. I'm way behind on it."

Stram pushed Brazil inside the trailer. "Where's it at?"

Brazil reached for an oblong device on the kitchen table. Stram grabbed his arms and stopped him. He gingerly picked it up. The switch was pointed to the "on" position. Stram switched it to "off." He flipped open the panel on the back and removed the batteries. He handed the device to Brazil. "Now work on it,"

Brazil put it down. A look of disappointment flashed across his face. Stram knew he was going to detonate the bomb Jesse was carrying. Stram had saved Jesse's life by a few seconds.

As Jesse left the driveway of Brazil's mobile home, he looked over his shoulder at the lunch box with the bomb on the back seat. Brazil had assured him it wasn't activated and Jesse had no reason to think otherwise. It wasn't because he trusted Brazil. There just was no reason it would be armed. Brazil didn't hate him. Not yet. He was a professional and didn't make that kind of mistake.

The agents had insisted Jesse make sure the wires on the bomb were disconnected before he delivered it to them. They didn't want to take any chances. Jesse considered it a waste of precious time. He wanted to unload the bomb as soon as he could. It wasn't necessary to check it out.

Jesse went several blocks and pulled to the side of the street. Maybe he should do what the agents told him. He really hadn't seen the bomb. Brazil closed the lid too quickly and he couldn't see that the wires were disconnected.

Jesse got out of the car and opened the back door. He flipped open the lid to the lunch box. A tremor slammed through his body.

The wires Brazil said were unattached were connected. The bomb was armed and ready to kill! Brazil planned to hit him. Fear then anger surged through him. He had to control himself. His life now was in his own hands.

He wasn't supposed to touch the bomb once it was in his possession for fear of leaving his fingerprints and contaminating the evidence. He got a tissue from the glove compartment. Clutching it, he disconnected the wires. The bomb couldn't be detonated now except by accident.

Revenge consumed Jesse. "My first impulse was to go back to the trailer and kill Brazil with my bare hands. Beat the hell out of him. But I couldn't do that. I wasn't going to kill anymore. Not even someone who about killed me. I had to get rid of that bomb. I'd take care of him later in court."

Jesse composed himself as he drove the short distance to the highway. The two escort cars were on an overpass nearby. He turned on the headlights to signal he had the bomb.

When Jesse got to the excavation site, Bohnemeier took the bomb and Fox carried the remote control device far into a field. They wouldn't call the Army bomb disposal unit Jesse left. Who brought it had to be unknown. The bomb was photographed and dusted for prints before the demolition experts examined it and detonated it.

By the time Jesse got home his fury at Brazil had subsided and he was enthused. He had been working for the FBI for almost a year and this was the first major case he made, mostly by himself.

"But what almost happened wasn't a mistake. They didn't call Brazil the master technician for nothing. He was a professional and he knew what he was doing."

When Mark told him what happened at the trailer he had no doubt Brazil planned to kill him. What was confusing was Brazil's motive. Then he realized the irony of what Brazil had told him. The tale about the partner who killed his associate as he installed the bomb was a prediction of Jesse's death so well disguised he didn't recognize it. Brazil was the deadly partner.

But why? Did Brazil harbor a grudge against him? Would killing Art Berne's lieutenant, a man of great stature in the mob, satisfy Brazil's consuming passion for prominence? Was he acting in behalf of someone else? Jesse never would know.

CHAPTER TWENTY-THREE

The Mob's Tariff

If governments impose taxes on people and companies, so can organized crime. Decline to pay the government and you likely will be sued or prosecuted. Refuse to kick back a piece of the action to the mob and calamity awaits you.

Just like the owners of topless night clubs on the East Side who were caught in a mob shakedown. It began late in the fall of 1983 when Mike Trupiano summoned Jesse to a meeting at the Banana House. Jesse was to be the extortionist.

Trupiano was upset with progress of his new protection racket. Dennis Sonnenschein, owner of the Golden Girls night club in East St. Louis, was being shaken down for a percentage of his profits. He already had paid Trupiano $2,000 for what he was told was the mob's help in getting the club's liquor license.

East St. Louis city government had enacted a law banning issuance of liquor licenses to topless night clubs. Sonnenschein, unable to open his club, paid Trupiano $2,000 for help in obtaining the license. The money was to be used to bribe officials and influential politicians.

During recorded conversations between Jesse, Trupiano and Jimmy Kostoff, an associate of Jesse who had considerable political connections, a number of prominent politicians and officials were considered possible sources of help in obtaining the license.

According to an article by Thomas C. Toban in the former St. Louis Globe-Democrat, those sources included a prominent Belleville attorney and Democratic state committeeman; the mayor of East St. Louis; the former chairman of the Madison County, Illinois, Democratic Central Committee; an influential township supervisor; a former St. Clair County, Illinois, state's attorney; and a well-connected state employee.

In a conversation recorded by Jesse on September 25, 1983, he and Kostoff discussed ways to get the license approved.

" … He (the state employee) told me if (the former Democratic Central Committee chairman) can't get it fixed … you give me a call," Kostoff explained. "He says, 'I'll get hold of (the mayor)'. And I told him we want topless, you know, we're gonna have topless joints."

"He said he'd do it though, huh?" Jesse asked.

"He said he'd call up (the mayor) personally and talk to him."

"Oh, beautiful," Jesse said. "Did you offer him any money?"

"I told him, I said there'll be a little, huh, political contribution. He said, 'Don't worry about it'."

"They'll give him a grand," Jesse said.

A day later, Kostoff told Jesse the mayor had refused.

The tapes didn't reveal to whom the $2,000 bribe was paid, but the Golden Girls night club eventually was issued a liquor license. After the initial payment, Sonnenschein balked at any further squeeze by the underworld. He claimed inability to pay, which angered Trupiano and Berne. There were other clubs to shake down.

Fernando "Nando" Bartolotta, one of Trupiano's enforcers, told Jesse of the boss' anger. "He wants me to choke this guy and strangle him, or something." He feared excessive force could have a negative effect. "What can I do? What can you do? Beat a guy and you'd never get it. Just be careful, be careful this guy don't go to the 'g'."

"Well, if he don't pay, come up with so much every week, all his joints are going to be wiped off the map," Jesse offered.

Berne was entitled to half the payoffs because he controlled the East Side. He was no less irritated by Sonnenschein's resistance. "You tell him my (expletive) is hot," he instructed Jesse. "If he thinks Mike Trupiano gets mad, tell him they (expletive) with my money, I get all worked up. He'll pay or he's going out of business."

Trupiano wanted to expand the extortion of Sonnenschein to include massage parlors he operated. But it became more complex when the Golden Girls night club was firebombed. Trupiano was convinced the owners of P. T's, a club also on the East Side, were responsible. He assumed it was in retaliation for the mob's extortion attempts on them.

Trupiano was infuriated and instructed Jesse tell the owners of P. T.'s the Golden Girls "belonged to the family" and any further damage to it would bring swift retaliation. Berne was just as adamant.

"What I'm gonna do is just throw one of them pineapples on that joint, not level the joint," he told Trupiano about using a bomb. "You generally throw it in the corner up in the air, you know, on the roof. Where it's gonna throw a lot of dust and it shakes up a guy. He's gonna run to you."

Trupiano agreed. "I'd say it's a good idea."

Whether the payoffs should be a designated amount or a percentage was discussed. Berne insisted it should be a flat rate. "One thousand a week. We give them a pass. We're just a nuisance payroll." It was agreed to attempt to collect $2,000 a week from Sonnenschein with Berne and Trupiano taking even shares.

But before any of the payoffs could be collected, Trupiano panicked. He learned Sonnenschein had found a recorder on a man he knew. Trupiano and Berne feared the FBI was onto them. They decided to abandon the extortion. Trupiano had become paranoid by then. He believed FBI monitors were everywhere around him.

A Snitch Exposed

A snitch was snitching on a snitch and that was unacceptable for Jesse. It could bring to an end to the FBI undercover operation. And to Jesse's life. There was one way to stop it. Confront him and expose him. It was what a snitch must do.

Bartolotta was a young Mafioso and an important FBI target. He was street wise beyond his 26 years. Chubby and gregarious, he had a pleasant personality and a good sense of humor, constantly wisecracking. He was a hustler and aggressive, always looking for a score, and he often was successful. But he was brash and sometimes reckless, a loose cannon. That made him susceptible to Jesse.

Vitale recruited Bartolotta with the traditional Mafia ritual of vowing eternal loyalty to La Cosa Nostra and took him under his wing. He became Trupiano's nemesis, a constant source of irritation and concern. He was big trouble waiting to happen, Trupiano complained. Bartolotta brought too much heat on him.

"I wish I didn't have to have him around me. I'm getting all the heat with him," Trupiano told Jesse. "If it was up to me, I'd never have made him. I don't even want to know what he's got going anymore. See, when you're the boss you got all these things to worry about."

Bartolotta was paranoid about FBI surveillance. FBI agents interviewed him recently. "The FBI came to my house and blackmailed me and told me that if I cooperated with them I wouldn't get indicted on the credit card scam. All I had to do was help them burn Trupiano. So, I go and tell Mike about it. Man, he jumped all over me. He was more worried than me."

Jesse tried to sympathize with him, but to no avail. "That's all we need is for the FBI to have a super snooper on us," Bartolotta said.

"What's this super snooper nonsense, Nando? I don't think those things can go through a car. Calm down. You and Mike, you're both paranoid anymore."

Bartolotta wasn't convinced. "Houses are bugged, phones are bugged, cars are bugged, people are bugged. The whole world's bugged. I'm afraid to talk to myself anymore 'cause maybe they got me bugged. I don't trust nobody."

"I never heard of a car being bugged, Nando. Only the phone or a house or a person."

Jesse wasn't wearing the recorder. It was installed in the car. Bartolotta playfully slapped Jesse on the side of the chest where the microphones would have been taped.

"Am I right, sweetheart?"

Jesse was surprised. "Get your hands off me, boy, or I'll break your neck. I could be wired up, you know. Check me out good."

Bartolotta did. He jokingly patted his back and chest. "Looks like you're clean."

Bartolotta had been a partner with Richard Beck, a notorious criminal, but ended the association because he believed he was a snitch. "I'll tell you something, Jesse. He's been running around town talking that you're a snitch, too."

"Really? I'll have to have a little talk with Mister Beck."

Jesse didn't know Beck that well. He had to learn if he was an informant. Beck had served at least six federal and state prison sentences and was considered one of the more dangerous criminals in the area. He had no murder convictions on his record, but officials suspected he was involved in a number of homicides.

Jesse put out word he wanted Beck to call him and he did two days later. He denied saying Jesse was an informant. They agreed to meet the next day. As Jesse waited for Beck, a car with just the driver passed and parked down the street. It was a dark brown Ford sedan, a typical police surveillance car. Jesse jotted down the license number.

Beck was amiable and patronizing as they drove in Jesse's car. He told Beck about the police car to see his reaction. There was none. Beck asked if he had the license number and Jesse gave it to him. He got out three sheets of paper stapled together and studied the letters and numbers written on them.

"Well, it ain't no cop car, that's for sure," Beck finally said.

"How do you know?"

Beck hesitated. "I got a list."

"A list of what?" Jesse grabbed the papers from Beck and pulled the car to the curb, studying the lists of license numbers. The plate number of the police car was there.

"Here it is," he said, pointing near the bottom of the first page.

"Oh, I must have missed it," Beck said nonchalantly. "You got one of these?"

Beck said it was it was a list of license numbers of all detective cars and undercover vehicles in the St. Louis Metropolitan and the St. Louis County Police Departments. It was valuable, he said. A friend got it from a police officer. He gave it to Jesse as a peace offering.

"You'll say, there's the dicks and you'll be able to check it and find the number on there," Beck explained. "I've found ten of them already."

"Maybe I'll find your number there, Rich."

"I don't get it," he said, a puzzled look on his face.

"Nando says you're a stool pigeon for police intelligence."

Beck laughed, but he wasn't convincing. His concern was obvious. "What the hell, they're trying to put me in jail. Okay, I'll say this. I'm in this car with you and I want you to know what I got on me. I got a piece in my pocket here. That's illegal, especially with me, an ex-con. If I was a rat I couldn't carry it."

It was the opportunity Jesse wanted. He reached over and opened the glove compartment, exposing his .45 automatic. "That's my angel. That baby goes everywhere I go in this car. There's a shotgun in the trunk, too." It was intended to impress Beck and it did.

"Look, I want to say this, man, so you know where I'm coming from," Beck said. "I was kind of paranoid about getting in your car and talking. You never know." Jesse knew Beck was playing the game of accuse your accuser. "It ain't no secret to them bums if they're listening, but I've whacked quite a few people. And I think you're in the same way, okay?"

"Right. Okay," Jesse said.

"I come to you and I appreciate talking to you. I want to be a hundred percent with you."

Beck said Bartolotta was a thief without a conscience. "He wanted to break into his sister's father-in-law's house while her mother-in-law was in the hospital. It just turned my stomach. He even talked about breaking into John Vitale's house where there was supposed to be a big stash of money, but he couldn't get it done. Nobody wanted a piece of that."

Jesse laughed to himself. Bartolotta wasn't the only one who couldn't rob Vitale. "I guess a lot of guys were trying to get to Vitale's money. He shouldn't have been so greedy and showed it to everybody."

Jesse had lunch the next day with Trupiano at a fashionable restaurant on The Hill, an Italian settlement in southwest St. Louis. A city police intelligence detective pulled him over several blocks after he left. He asked if he could look in the trunk. Jesse unlocked it. When the officer found nothing he asked if he could inspect the glove compartment. Again, he gave his permission. The angel wasn't there.

"What's wrong?" Jesse asked. "Beck give you bad information?"

The detective shrugged his shoulders and laughed. "Well, you know, we got our snitches."

"You got a hell of a one this time."

It came down the way Jesse had planned. "It only proved what I already knew. Beck was a snitch. If I had my gun with me, I'd have been busted and my probation would have been revoked and it would have been all over."

Jesse considered spreading the word Beck was an informant, but he couldn't. It likely would get him killed and he didn't want that. Maybe Beck would be able to trap a high-level hoodlum. Good luck, Beck!

"I really wasn't upset with him. He was doing what I was doing. He was trying to score some points against his next arrest. Only he wasn't all that smart."

Jesse was allowed to keep a copy of the list. It helped him a number of times detect police surveillance.

CHAPTER TWENTY-FOUR

To Save An Agent

The FBI agents told Jesse to talk Nando Bartolotta into committing a robbery, but not to let him go through with it. Merely planning a felony by a person crossing a state line was sufficient for federal prosecution.

Fox and Bohnemeier had no indication that when they tried to prevent Bartolotta from pulling off the score he would try to kill one of them and Jesse would save him at the last second.

Jesse didn't have to induce Bartolotta to do a score. He already had one lined up and he wanted Jesse to help him. He wanted to rob a Venture store in the St. Louis suburbs. It was the height of the Christmas shopping season and the take would be at least $300,000. Jesse agreed to participate, saying he would bring Stram along.

Bartolotta wanted to case the store and Jesse drove him there. He grinned when he came out. "I tell you, brother, I was back there by the office and I saw this lady counting money like you wouldn't believe. The whole desk was piled with money. I almost went nuts. I wanted to dive right through that window. I want this place bad."

"What does she do with the money after she's done counting it?" Jesse asked.

"She just leaves it there and waits for the manager to come in and put it inside the vault. It doesn't have a combination. They use a key." Bartolotta said they could get in the vault one of two ways. His friend was a manager and could make a duplicate key or they could accost him and force him to open it. He preferred they used a key.

"Won't your friend be suspected if we have a key?"

"We can just leave pry marks on the door so it looks like we had to force it open. Now, they got a cop in the store so we'll have to be carrying. If he comes back there we'll have to blast him. Either that or we get caught. What do you think, brother?"

"It's what we have to do," Jesse said dispassionately.

Bartolotta caressed Jesse's vanity. "Berne, he's getting old and he don't have that much longer to go and then you'll be boss. Just remember me when you're boss, will you?"

"I don't want no part of you," Jesse teased.

"I just want to kiss your ring every once in a while. Can I call you Don Jesse?"

"Sure. And I'll even let fat little dagos like you kiss my ass."

"Can I be your bodyguard?"

"If you think you're tough enough."

"I can be tough as hell."

They met the manager on December 19. What he told them wasn't encouraging. Because of the seasonal increase in sales, security at the store had been upgraded. There now was an electronic locking device on the office door and there were several more armed guards. The day before there almost was $400,000 in cash in the store and there should be nearly that much each day until Christmas.

"I don't know what to do about that electronic lock now. It was a cracker box before," the manager said.

"What do you think, Nando?" Jesse asked.

Bartolotta thought for a moment. "It's just a little more complicated than it started out to be, but nothing's impossible. It can be done." He turned to the manager. "You just be outside the office when we come in. We'll put the gun on you and force you to open the door and the vault."

Bartolotta wanted to case the store again. He kept looking behind as they drove in Jesse's Lincoln. He said he had been under surveillance again recently by FBI agents. One car followed him from his home and by the time he got to the East Side for a meeting there were several more cars tailing him. "It was like a convoy behind me. I couldn't believe it. Why would they make it so obvious?"

Jesse laughed. "They wanted to spook you, let you know you got problems and the heat's on you,"

"Everybody's afraid to make any moves anymore. Everbody's paranoid about the FBI and snitches. I mean, they're all over you. How come the 'g' ain't on your butt all the time?"

"They've been there plenty of times."

"I don't see any."

"You ain't looking in the right place, Nando."

"Well, you're getting me popular, too."

"Before I get through with you, you'll be so popular you'll be getting your toilet paper free."

"Will I? Where?"

"In the joint," Jesse joked.

"Why am I going to the joint?"

"Some snitch will get you."

"Like maybe you?" Bartolotta asked, enjoying the bantering.

"You never know, Nando. I might be an FBI agent."

"Boy, if you are, I'm screwed, ain't I?"

"You better believe it, fat boy."

Bartolotta went inside the store. When he returned he said there were three security guards inside. "I'll set some dresses on fire to cause a commotion at one end. Everybody'll be yelling and screaming and those coppers will run there and we'll be home free."

Jesse didn't like the idea. "Somebody might get hurt doing that."

"Maybe we'll just throw some firecrackers, then. The cops will think there's a shoot-out going on."

Bartolotta planned to do the heist two nights later, but the robbery couldn't be allowed come down. The agents' denial of Jesse's participation was a foregone conclusion. For one reason, he would have to be armed and they couldn't allow that. Bartolotta's participation only made it more hazardous. Jesse laughed to himself. There was no way he wouldn't be carrying even if the score was canceled.

The agents already had their case made. They told Jesse it was up to him to abort the robbery. They would give him the opportunity by placing them under close surveillance, as they did with Eidson.

"Just look what almost happened with that scam," Jesse recalled. "It almost got me whacked. They should realize doing that can be dangerous."

The Heat Is On

Jesse and Stram picked up Bartolotta at 7 o'clock the night of the robbery. Jesse was to wait in the car while Bartolotta and Stram pulled off the heist. They would force the manager to open the door. The element of surprise, as usual, was their major asset. They would be in the office only a few minutes.

"If there's a guard there, we'll just take him out. Got your piece?" Bartolotta asked Stram.

Stram said he did. Bartolotta took a .357 magnum from his belt and showed it to him. "That'll keep us out of trouble, huh?" He had two ski masks in his coat pockets. He brought two briefcases. Each would take one to carry the money.

Fox and Bohnemeier and agents in three other cars put them under tight surveillance. They passed Jesse and pulled in front as they drove on Interstate 70. The other agents' cars stayed in back.

"Check that green Ford out," Jesse said, pointing to the agents' car. "That's got to be the 'g' or city intelligence." Bartolotta agreed it looked like a police car. "We're walking right into this, aren't we?" Jesse said, pretending he was nervous.

Jesse drove around the parking lot until he saw Fox and Bohnemeier's car. Bartolotta didn't notice it as Jesse parked 40 feet away. Bohnemeier got out and walked in front of Jesse's Lincoln toward the store.

"That's the guy that was in the green Ford," Jesse said, faking alarm. "You can tell a mile off he's a cop. What the hell's going on? They got us surrounded."

"Let's not panic, fellows," Bartolotta said. "If they were on to us they'd be swarming all over us. He's probably just going shopping. Come on, let's go get our money. It's Christmas time for us. If that guy is a cop and he gives us trouble we'll just waste him. No big deal."

Jesse assumed Fox would accompany Bohnemeier, but he remained in the car. Bohnemeier could be walking into a trap. Jesse knew Bartolotta would shoot if he felt threatened. He had to accompany the two and somehow protect Bohnemeier. It might be a way of aborting the score.

"Let's check it out first," Jesse insisted.

Bartolotta was impatient. "The hell with it. Let's go now."

"No way," Jesse commanded. "Let's make sure nothing's changed."

"What the hell?" Bartolotta argued. "We'll just be exposing ourselves more. I'm gonna go in and get my money."

As Bartolotta started to open the door, Jesse pulled his pistol from his waistband and leveled it at him. "Do it my way or you're on your own."

Bartolotta sighed disgustedly. "I ain't going in there light," he said defiantly.

It was futile to argue. Jesse put the pistol back in his belt and so did Bartolotta. They went into the crowded store, pretending to be shopping. Stram lingered a few yards away. Jesse stayed near Bartolotta.

Bohnemeier made his presence obvious. He was all over the store. He bumped into Bartolotta and excused himself. Bartolotta tensed, anger etched on his face. Jesse, 10 feet away, moved his hand toward his automatic. Bartolotta backed off.

They went to the glassware section. Bohnemeier was 20 feet away, inspecting a wine glass. He suddenly dropped it.

Bartolottta spun around and drew his pistol before Jesse could stop him. He concealed it with his jacket as he moved a little closer to Bohnemeier. He took the gun out. It was a few inches above the counter as he aimed it at the agent. His finger tightened on the trigger just as Jesse grabbed his wrist and twisted it. He grabbed the gun from him. Bohnemeier walked away, unaware of how near death he had been.

Bartolotta had enough. He made for the entrance. Bohnemeier hurried in front of him. He stopped at a telephone near the doors, lifted the receiver and began talking into it without inserting any coins. Bartolotta went to the parking lot. Bohnemeier followed them.

"Give me my gun," Bartolotta whispered. "Let's take him out when he gets close."

Jesse shook his head. "No way. It's over."

"What's a matter? You a pussy or something?"

"Want me to show you?"

"Man, I don't get it," Bartolota said, confused. "I'd see this guy way over on one side and then he'd pop up where I'm at. And dropping that glass! I was a second away from blowing him off and you stopped me. Then he's on the phone when we come out and pretending he's talking."

"I think he was a store detective," Jesse offered. "I'm passing on this one. I wouldn't do it for a million bucks".

"That's right, Jesse," Stram said.

"He shouldn't be breathing," Bartolotta said accusingly. "You gave him a pass." He was silent for a moment. The money inside the store apparently still tempted him. "Well, I'm not going for it either, guys. Not now. It ain't right."

Jesse wasn't sure Bartolotta, as impetuous as he was, wouldn't try it on his own later. "Don't go on your own and get your ass in trouble, either, Nando. And don't trust your friend. You hear me? He maybe snitched on us and that's why the heat was on."

A Better Score

Bartolotta promised not to try again. He had a scheme that could earn them as much money, but was less risky. Bank presidents were easy marks for extortion because they have access to money, he said. He explained how the extortion worked.

"You case the guy and learn his movements. After he goes to work one morning and his wife leaves you go to his house and cut the telephone wires. You call the guy up at his office and say, 'I got your wife here. I'll kill her unless you get fifty grand right now. If you don't believe me try to call your wife up. I'm going to call you back in a couple of minutes. You got only one chance'.

"The guy'll go crazy. He'll call his wife right away, but there's no answer. Now, you call him back within a couple of minutes because you can't give him time to call the police. You tell him to put the money in a bag and drive somewhere and leave the money and get out of there. He's got all the money he needs right there in the bank.

You got your guy waiting and when he leaves off the money he picks it up and takes off."

Only 15 minutes should elapse from the first call until the banker left with the money. "He's got to think these guys will kill his wife in a hurry. See, you got to play a game with him."

"Don't you think these bankers are onto this scam?"

"Yeah, it's been done a lot," Bartolotta said confidently. "Beck did a lot of them."

Bartolotta wasn't lying. Fox and Bartolotta said Beck was convicted of such an extortion.

"Did you help him on any?" Jesse asked. Bartolotta didn't answer. "Don't you think he might call the cops and they'll be there when you pick up the money?"

Bartolotta sighed. "Don't you see? You don't give him time. He's got to love his wife and you make him think you're going to do a number on her. So, he's only got one choice. Get the money. If he doesn't come out of that bank in a few minutes then it's over. Forget it and walk away."

"What do you do if the guy says to hell with you?"

Bartolotta chuckled. "We had that happen one time. The guy said, 'My wife, you keep her'. And one banker had a heart attack."

Jesse said he didn't want to get involved in that kind of score. It was too dangerous. He was thankful the case against Bartolotta was wrapped up. "I didn't need to hang around him anymore. I got what the FBI wanted. The conspiracy to rob the Venture store and the credit card fraud he talked about would put him away."

The agents were more than a little grateful to Jesse for saving Bohnemeier. Their relationship moved a degree closer to personal.

For All To See

Loretta Berne had a Christmas party for friends and relatives the next night. She invited Jesse to show him off. He was attractive and charming in a rough sort of way and he would impress her female guests. Fox and Bohnemeier wanted him to wear the recorder. It might just be one of those fortuitous occasions when Berne, in a festive mood with a few drinks, might open up.

Jesse was reluctant. He had a bad feeling that afternoon when the agents brought the recorder. "I don't feel right wearing it," he told them.

"Why not?" Fox asked.

"I just got a feeling something bad will happen."

They argued with him, but in the end, as always, it was his decision and he declined. Jesse was at the party only a short time when Loretta took him aside and introduced him to several women. She talked about her gall bladder operation several years earlier.

"Jesse's had a gall bladder operation, too," she said. She stepped toward him and grabbed his shirt, yanking it out of his trousers. His midsection was bared. The recorder would have been exposed.

"See Jesse's scar," she said. "Mine's a little different." The women stepped closer and inspected his abdomen.

Jesse smiled. "I won't ask to see your scar, Loretta." She and the other women giggled.

Now he knew why he had declined to be wired up. God once again had protected him.

CHAPTER TWENTY-FIVE

A Passion To Kill

U ncertainty and turmoil began battering Jesse at the beginning of the new year. His mere existence was becoming burdensome and too unpredictable, his temper more incendiary.

A confrontation with someone over something was brewing. Would it be impiety clashing with Christian faith and values? Forgiveness versus revenge? Vanity brawling with compassion. Love or hate? Life or death? Who would be the saint and who the sinner? Would he be able to honor his commitment to grant life and not death? It depended much on Jesse's priority at the time of the conflict, the degree of tolerance.

His and Carolee's marriage, always tenuous, was more contentious lately. It was strained to the breaking point with frequent showdowns and shouting matches. It wasn't only because of the stress of his undercover work. There was another encumbrance on their marriage more intrusive and challenging to Jesse.

Carolee had become a born-again Christian and was doing the soul-searching accompanying that. She regularly attended church services with their children and was devoted to Jesus. He was her Savior, not Jesse. She wanted to follow in His footsteps and bring Jesse along.

But Jesse wasn't sure he wanted to accompany her at this time. It was something he must do himself. She would be too demanding, too restrictive, and it wasn't time yet. He had too much to do, too much on his mind.

He hadn't told her yet of his conversion from crime to God he wanted to make. He still was working on that rebirth. Nor had he told her about his commitment not to kill or do violence. It would be an admission of what he had done in the past unacceptable to her. Carolee apparently saw no change in him. He was his same old criminal self.

She brought up the subject of religion one night after dinner. He wasn't in the mood for it. "You know, Jesse, you can be forgiven for even your worst sins," she offered.

"Of course I know that. It's true." He laughed. "You got a few of those. Running off to Las Vegas with that man is about as bad as you can get."

"It doesn't matter how bad your sins are. Jesus forgives them all, even the things you've done. Even you having two families and living with two women at the same time."

Jesse didn't want to get involved in her soul-purging. "Just leave me alone if that's all you want to talk about."

Her patience waned. "I don't know all your sins and I don't want to. But I'm not ashamed to talk about my sins. I'm not ashamed to admit that I had an affair with Jake when we lived with him. The Lord has forgiven me. He'll forgive you, too, Jesse. Just go to Him. Listen to me!

Jesse now realized why Jake had let them live rent free in his house years ago. Rent was paid with his wife's body and love. The time bomb ticking in Jesse detonated. He shook his head violently. "How long did you do this?" he demanded threateningly.

She didn't hesitate. "Two or three years." She sobbed. "I'm sorry, Jesse. Really."

"You're nothing but a two-bit whore," he screamed.

She stared at him. "I'm not lying. You can't lie about your sins either because God knows them all."

He knew she wasn't lying. His fury raged out of control. "You know what I'm gonna do? Huh? I'm gonna cut your boyfriend's head and his (expletive) off and give them to you on a platter. You think I won't?"

"I know you will," she sobbed.

Jesse snapped. He slapped her as hard as he could. She reeled backward off the chair against the wall and slumped to the floor. He beat her face with his fist, almost knocking her unconscious.

Their younger son and daughter watched from the doorway to the living room. The boy was petrified with fear. She screamed and covered her face with her hands. Jesse ignored them.

He went to the bedroom and returned with his angel. His hands were steady as he cocked it and aimed it at her head only a few inches away. She didn't back off. His eyes reflected his instinct to kill. His finger tensed on the trigger.

The children ran into the living room. He was calm. He was ready to kill. He was justified. His commitment to no longer kill didn't matter. He discarded it.

Carolee looked up at him, but didn't cringe. "You haven't changed, have you, Jesse? You're still a hoodlum. Nothing but a killer. And you're going to kill me in front of our children. I hope God has mercy on you. He will on me."

There was no hatred in her voice. She was ready to die if that was what the Lord wanted. She had made her peace with Him, but not with her husband.

Jesse stepped backward. His finger eased on the trigger. Suddenly, he turned and left the house and got into his car. Confusion and his shattered pride joined the anger. His body trembled. He had been humiliated, his manhood defiled. He willed calm to return so he could think clearly, but his emotions were rampant.

Despair replaced his anger. Shame about what he had done to his wife and what his children witnessed overcame him. They had seen the beast in their father. Their real father. He was within seconds of killing their mother in front of him. It was a miracle he didn't.

"I just hadn't been able to think straight," he recalled. "I knew I probably lost her and the kids, too. My God! What had I done? Somehow, I'd have to make it up to them. It took lots of guts for her to tell me, of all people, what she had done. She did what was right."

Death On The Prowl

Jesse might have forgiven Carolee, but not Jake. He, not she, was the real culprit. Revenge was mandatory. "It was more his fault than hers. She was still guilty, but she was young then. What he did was no different than rape. I could think of only killing him."

Jesse would butcher him as he told her. He deserved no less. Only he wouldn't give the body parts to her. That would be a confession written in blood.

The next day he bought an eight-inch double-edged butcher knife and honed it until it was razor sharp. He put it under the front seat of his car. He lined a sturdy cardboard box with plastic trash bags and placed it and a spade in the car's trunk. He would put the body parts in it and bury it somewhere in the woods out in the country. Jake would disappear, never be seen again.

Jake lived in the same inexpensive, run-down house where he had sex with Carolee. It was the appropriate place for him to die. Jesse watched the house until dawn, but Jake didn't come home. A .45 semi-automatic was under the seat with the knife. It wasn't his angel. That one was for protection. This one was for extermination.

Jake didn't come home the next two nights. Had Carolee tipped him off? It made no difference. Jesse would find him. His patience and his determination to kill steeled. Wreaking vengeance on Jake was an obsession he could satisfy only one way.

A car pulled into the driveway of the house near midnight the fourth night. A man, tall, slender and hunch-backed, got out. Jesse hadn't seen Jake for a long time, but he immediately recognized him even in the darkness. He staggered, obviously drunk. That was an advantage. He would be less alert and more vulnerable.

Jesse waited 30 minutes after the lights went out in the house. Jake should be passed out. He put on a pair of plastic gloves. He didn't need an elaborate plan. Not for the swift and sure death he would deal Jake. No torture. Just a quick slash across the throat, cutting the carotid arteries. Life would flow instantly from him. He decided not to dismember the body. He now wanted the body to be found. Only the real reason he died wouldn't be known.

The knife was in his left hand, the revolver in the small of his back as he made his way to the front porch. He took a deep breath. There was no sound from inside. He turned the doorknob slightly. The door was unlocked. Another fatal mistake by Jake.

He pushed the door open several inches. The porch light suddenly blinded him. He stepped to the side. Jake, wearing shorts and an undershirt, stood in the doorway.

Jesse lunged at him. Jake shoved him backward, knocking him off balance. He fell off the porch onto his back.

"Jesse, what are you doing here?" Jake's voice was choked.

"You screwed my wife! You're gonna die for that."

"You're crazy, Stoneking."

"You're gonna die, Jake."

Jesse started to push himself up. Jake kicked at his hand with the knife. He missed and his foot struck Jesse in the abdomen. He jumped off the porch and ran to the rear of the house into the darkness. Jesse fired two shots, but missed. He heard Jake stumble through the brush and then there was silence.

Jesse started to chase him, but stopped. His passion for vengeance suddenly disappeared. It was replaced by the reality of what he was doing and the inherent danger. Lights in nearby houses flashed on. Police soon would be there. He had to grant Jake a stay of execution. At least for now.

He drove around for a few hours trying to clear his mind and to decipher what he had done. "It hit me how stupid I was. The minute Carolee heard Jake was dead she'd tell the cops about me. No way would she cover for me for that. It would be the end of everything. And I would have deserved it."

Jesse met with Fox the next morning in the park. As usual, the ducks scurried across the pond. His voice hoarser than usual, he told him what Carolee confessed and that he tried to kill Jake. He didn't tell him how he would have done it or about firing the shots for obvious reasons.

"You don't have to do anything like that," Fox said. "You know that."

"You don't understand. He ruined my life. He started me in all this when I was a kid. I wouldn't be here right now if it wasn't for him. Then he does my wife on top of it. How much can a man take? What would you do?"

Fox realized their relationship was at a new level. Jesse no longer was just an informant, he a professional, callous FBI agent. They now were friends. "Why are you telling me that you were going to kill him?"

"I guess I figured that if I told you I wouldn't be able to do it." He laughed feebly. "I'm not that dumb to come in on myself on a hit."

"What can I say, Jesse? You can't throw everything away, including your life, for something that happened years ago when you two were kids. Try to understand why she told you. Maybe it's been bothering her all these years and she wanted to talk about it. Sure, you're hurt, but you got to go on with your life. Forget about your pride." He reached out to shake his hand. "And don't forget about forgiveness."

"Yeah, I know about that. But it's not easy."

Fox, a religious man, thought for a moment. "You ever think about asking God for help?"

"I've done that, but you don't know how hard it is. I keep goofing up and ignoring God."

"God's not ignoring you, Jesse. Trust me. Trust Him."

Jesse knew he was at the crossroads. There was only one road he must take – the one back to God and to his commitment. But before he could accomplish that he had to subdue the evil still at work in him.

He stared at the ducks. Finally, he said, "You should have brought your duck mask along."

Jesse neither offered an apology to Carolee nor demanded one from her. There were no appropriate words. This rupture in their marriage probably never could be repaired. Their marital vows now seemed meaningless, a source of conflict, not love. Perhaps time would heal the wounds, but he doubted that.

Jesse's children said they were happy to see him back, but he saw through that. He knew they feared him, wondering if he would lose his temper like that again and go that one step further, killing their mother. He hugged them often, talked more to them, but their rejection of him was obvious. Would they ever forgive their father? Somehow, he had to make it all up to them. He had no idea how or when.

Russian Roulette

By spring, a sense of urgency settled on the undercover operation. Jesse had worked for the FBI for a year and a half. With each passing month the chance of exposure increased and Scorpion's life expectancy declined proportionately.

It was a game of Russian Roulette. The hammer had struck too many empty cylinders and there were too few left. A slip of the tongue. An overheard conversation. A chance observation of him and the agents together. Any one of those mishaps and others could bring quick and deadly retribution down on him.

Fox and Bohnemeier knew the clock could be their worst enemy. Jesse's safety and welfare rested with them, but they couldn't anticipate every contingency. The one they couldn't foresee could have disastrous consequences. This kind of work didn't permit the luxury of even a single miscalculation.

They had made good cases, but from their training and personal experience, they knew they couldn't allow themselves to become over-confident, apathy and carelessness success can breed. There were other areas they wanted to explore, other possible defendants they would like to bring down, but unless there was an emergency situation and they had to extract him immediately the decision to quit was his alone.

Jesse didn't delude himself, either. "I knew what the risks were. I knew that going in. You don't make these kinds of cases and do this kind of work without taking chances. The secret is trying to anticipate trouble. Sometimes, you can tell what a guy is thinking by what he doesn't say and his eyes. It's the times you can't tell that worry you."

CHAPTER TWENTY-SIX

An Unholy Alliance

It was almost two years since the last shot was fired in the Leisure War. An uneasy peace had settled on the underworld as it sought to return to some semblance of normalcy, but it wouldn't last long. Strife was on the horizon.

The Leisures were to be tried in a few months and it was a foregone conclusion they never would know freedom again. The government's case, bolstered by wiretaps and testimony from many of their outfit's key players turned snitches, was too strong. Even if they were set free, they never would be the power brokers they had envisioned. They would be branded pariahs.

By the spring of 1984, Bill Politte, a volatile, calculating member of Berne's outfit, was fanning the winds of war. He was mobilizing his forces in what Jesse assessed was a move to take over Berne's outfit and ultimately the underworld on both sides of the Mississippi River.

Politte saw the underworld foundering in a sea of uncertainty, buffeted by dissidents and incompetency within. He let it be known with him at the helm, it once again would be steered in the right direction. But he wouldn't make the same mistakes as the Leisures and go on a killing rampage. He was more sophisticated. Violence probably would be necessary, but not indiscriminate. Those who opposed him would be dealt with firmly, but quietly.

The FBI was getting similar reports confirming its fears of renewed underworld bloodshed. It desperately needed intelligence. Fox and Bohnemeier assigned the mission to Jesse. He was to try to ingratiate himself with Politte, even align himself with his coup d'etat if necessary. Jesse hopefully could build a case on him and eliminate the problem before it happened.

Had Jesse been able to pull off his massacre there would be no problem now. "Politte didn't know how close he came to being a dead man. Well, if I couldn't kill him I could at least maybe put him in jail."

He didn't have to make contact with Politte. He reached out for Jesse. Politte had a problem and needed Jesse's muscle and stature in the mob. His crew swindled Tommy Manion, an East Side dope dealer, out of $640,000 in two drug scams. Now Manion was threatening retaliation. His henchmen were watching Politte and two of his lieutenants. He wanted Jesse to lean on Manion.

Jesse wondered why Politte didn't take care of it himself. His appearances were as threatening as Jesse's. He stood six feet tall and was muscular with graying black hair combed straight back. His voice was gruff. And he had the necessary enforcers. Jesse suspected Politte wanted him as an ally, but he didn't eliminate the possibility he was trying to set him up. Either way, it was the opportunity Jesse needed.

Appearing conciliatory, Politte called Manion and convinced him it was time for a peace conference. Slender and boyish in his early thirties, Manion seemed anything but the threat he tried to project. His scowl and arrogance were patent, but Jesse knew he still was dangerous.

To ease Manion's concern about being set up, the confrontation was scheduled for noon the next day in a private room at a popular restaurant whose owner was friendly to the outfit. Manion could bring his own security guards.

Jesse sat next to Politte and Manion was across the table. One of Politte's men stood guard at the door and another sat at a nearby table. Three of Manion's bodyguards were at another table. The opposing forces watched each other warily, ready to react spontaneously.

Politte introduced Jesse only as "one of my people." A few pleasantries were exchanged as the three of them ate lunch. When they finished, Jesse leaned toward Manion, his hands folded in front of him. His eyes were orbs of steel and his stare was frigid, devoid of any emotion, except contempt for Manion. His lips were slightly snarled, his breath barely disturbing his massive chest. It was intended to intimidate.

"Let me tell you who I am," Jesse said. "I'm Jesse Stoneking. You know who I am?"

"I got an idea," Manion said defiantly.

"In case you don't, I'm Art Berne's right-hand man through the outfit in Chicago. I guess you know who he is." Manion nodded. "Now, Bill here is in our outfit, too. You understand that?" Manion again nodded. "What's the problem here?"

"He ripped me off. Not once, but twice. I lost over six hundred thousand that wasn't all mine. All I want is my money back."

"You know for a fact he did it?"

"Of course."

Jesse leaned back in his chair, glaring at Manion, mustering all the intimidation he could command. "Now you want to cause him trouble? Hit him, maybe?"

"That's not true," Manion said, his arrogance fading under Jesse's wilting stare.

"Let me tell you something, Tommy. First of all, you don't go threatening one of our people, staking him out and all that. You'll get a war you can't handle. It'll be the shortest war in history and you'll lose." He paused for effect. It worked. Manion weakened. "You got scammed in a dope deal. So what? That happens. It's over. Forget about it. Or else."

Manion remained silent. It was time to put the hard squeeze on him. "You got another problem," Jesse said. "What makes you think you can operate in our territory without giving us a cut?"

"Nobody said we had to," he answered weakly.

"Well, I'm telling you from now on you have to or that (expletive) war's going to start and end the same day. We want twenty-five percent of all your action. And we'll know everything you got going."

"I don't have anything going right now," Manion said, almost pleading. "I have to raise the money that I lost to pay back my partners."

Jesse stood. The meeting was over. The message had been conveyed unmistakably. "You'll think of something. Just don't forget us because we're always here. We'll be in touch."

Politte and his crew were impressed. Intimidation was what Jesse did best. He had lived up to his reputation. They would have more business together, Politte promised.

Jesse had doubts about the confrontation. Politte should have resolved it himself. Were he not trying to get closer to Politte, he wouldn't have gotten involved. Jesse knew dope dealers were unpredictable and there was no telling how Manion would react.

"I'd just rather crack him and forget about it," Politte said.

Jesse couldn't have cared less if a drug dealer was hit, but he had to try to prevent that. "I don't think it would be wise to crack him," he told Politte. "Too many people know you scammed him and he's been blowing his mouth off about you. I'm not trying to tell you your business. Instead, maybe we can get some more of his money."

"If we can use him we'll use him. All I want is somebody's money. The only difference between us and him is if we get scared we get mean. He gets scared and he gets stupid. We can just drain him of his money and then throw him to the dogs."

"If you kill him, Bill, how would you get his money?"

"I'm just saying, if he's a threat, kill him. If a dealer is a dog, and most of them are, and I get a crack at him I'll get him. If the guy is flaky, when we come to get his money he gets hit. That's just the way it is."

Jesse agreed. "These people, they got no morals. You can't trust them. It's dangerous these days. Everybody wants to hit you in the back of your head. You don't know who to trust anymore."

Spying On The Spy

The next afternoon while driving on an interstate Jesse saw in the rear view mirror a dark gray Chevrolet following him, but he couldn't identify the two men inside. The Chevrolet approached to within 100 feet and then dropped back. Jesse accelerated to 70 miles an hour and it kept pace. He took his .45 from the glove compartment and put it on the seat beside him under some papers.

The tires of the Lincoln screeched as he turned the wheel hard to the right and entered the exit ramp. The Chevrolet continued on past. The two men inside didn't look in his direction. Another false alarm, Jesse assumed.

Jesse left his house in south St. Louis County late the next morning. Two blocks later the same gray Chevrolet pulled out of a side street behind him. Two men were inside, but he still couldn't identify them. He made no effort to elude them. They probably were cops. They stayed with him as he drove north on the freeway toward downtown.

They were a nuisance. Jesse had a meeting with Trupiano and he didn't want them tagging along. He slowed near an exit ramp and turned on the right directional signal. The Chevrolet eased behind him, its right signal also blinking. He accelerated across the overpass. The Chevrolet went down the ramp and disappeared. He stopped on the shoulder of the overpass. The Chevrolet came up the entrance ramp on the other side and sped north.

Jesse caught up with it and noted the rear Illinois license plate. Before he could pass it and get a look at the occupants it lurched forward. He decided not to try to overtake it. Fox learned the license number was issued to a woman in Wood River near Alton. The address was a vacant tenement building. The title transfer showed the registrant purchased the car a few months earlier from a non-existent used car dealer in Granite City.

Jesse was concerned. "What does all that mean?"

"Probably nothing," Fox said. "You're getting too paranoid, Jesse. You're imagining things. Coincidences do happen."

"You think so? How do you explain that the plate can't be traced? A coincidence?"

"It was probably the cops," Fox offered.

"Since when do Illinois cops operate in Missouri?" he said, disgusted at Fox's indifference.

The car wasn't meant to be traced. Amateurs aren't that careful. Professionals, like hit men, are. "And Tom says it was just coincidental! I don't believe in coincidences. Not in this game. They were waiting for me. What bothered me is I didn't know who was behind it, but it probably was Manion's guys."

Saving A Drug Dealer

A week later, Politte told Jesse about a score in which he wanted Jesse to participate. The mark was a high-level drug dealer named Rick Pappas, who lived near Granite City and who probably had as much as $600,000 in cash in his house. Politte learned of the score from a lawyer, a former judge, who was doing the paperwork for Pappas' laundering of the money.

There was urgency to the score. Pappas had to be robbed before he could launder the money. But Politte saw a problem. The street in front of the house, which dead-ended a block away in the other direction, was the only escape route. A deep swamp was in the rear. "The guy's got natural protection and I don't think he realizes it,"

"I think the whole thing's bad, Bill," Jesse said. "Something could go wrong in there."

"We'll get him one way or another."

Jesse and Stram would follow Pappas for several days. Politte said Pappas had a girlfriend and perhaps they could snatch him while he visited her, call his family and tell them they would kill him unless they delivered the money.

Jesse agreed that might be the best way to do it. "You know, whenever you need me for anything, Bill, you just call me."

"That's the way I figured it, too, Jesse. We're partners now. If it comes to cracking somebody or anything like that, if you need me, fine. No problems."

Jesse laughed. "You can't forget about your silent partners, can you?"

Politte slapped him on the shoulder. The partnership was sealed. "You'll be my silent partner. The guy nobody knows about. My ace. You'll be with me all the way. You and me. I got plans that I don't want to talk about just yet."

"Not even Flynn or Art or Mike Trupiano or any of those guys will know," Jesse said.

"Least of all that jerk, Flynn. He ain't part of my plans. He's not going to bother nobody." He lapsed into silence and Jesse didn't disturb him. Finally, he said, "You know, if you get two or three or four of those good dope scams you got a bundle of money. Then you can get a nice little business and put your family in it. Once you get them situated you can start moving."

"I know what you mean, Bill."

"See, I'm not going to tie myself into a business. I don't have time for that."

Jesse knew what he meant. When his family needs were well cared for he would make his move to take over the outfit. He wanted nothing to distract him from that.

Politte changed the subject. "You ever met Joe Brooks? The bank robber?"

Jesse hadn't heard of him. "Is he good?"

"Well, he ain't ever been caught. He's got a partner who actually does the jobs. He just sets them up. They pick these small towns and they hit the banks. They been doing this for years. One day I'll introduce him to you."

Jesse and Stram followed Pappas, a gaunt, balding man in his early 40s, for the next several days, but they learned little. Fox and Bohnemeier as usual told Jesse to abort the robbery soon. It was too volatile to prolong. If Jesse didn't participate Politte would do it on his own and there was no telling who might get hurt.

Jesse wasn't supposed to meet Politte for two days, so he had time to think about how to stop it. But Politte called him that afternoon and insisted they meet in two hours to talk about the score. Jesse had no time to get the recorder.

He briefed Politte on his surveillance of Pappas. "It's no good, Bill, however you look at it. He's paranoid as hell and it'll be hard getting near him. We're gonna get in one hell of a shoot-out. If you ask me, we ought to walk away from it."

Politte shook his head. "I want that (expletive) bad. I need his money. Now."

"I think it's wrong, Bill."

Jesse's power of persuasion wasn't working. Politte became incensed. "Wrong, my ass! It's right."

"He'll have to be cracked," Jesse argued. "That's the only way. And those people in the house, too. Man, that'll bring some heat down."

"So what? As long as we get his money. Either you're in or out. I need that money more than you know." It was an ultimatum.

"Don't we all?"

"In not too long a time you'll understand why." He stared at Jesse, challenging him.

Jesse didn't answer him. It was obvious Politte wanted Pappas' money for his war chest and he would get it by whatever means. Jesse could stall no longer. He had no other option. "Okay, I'm in. Like you said, we're partners."

Politte said they would go for Pappas' money on Sunday night, four days away, even if there was an infant in the house. He would ask Pappas' lawyer to delay completion of the paperwork to ensure the money would be in there. He told Jesse to continue his surveillance, only keep it loose and not spook Pappas.

Jesse followed Pappas that night as he left his house at 11 o'clock and drove to one of two pay phone booths at the side of a service station and repair shop that were closed. He apparently was calling a connection or his girlfriend.

As Pappas hung up the telephone, Jesse grabbed him and pinned him against the wall of the building. He took a revolver from his belt and jammed it into Pappas' chest. Pappas showed no emotions.

"I'm not going to hurt you, Pappas. I don't want anything you got." Jesse's voice was commanding, but not threatening. Pappas remained silent. "What I'm going to do is save your life."

"Who are you?" Pappas asked.

"It doesn't make any difference. You got a lot of money in your house and some people are going to take it away from you. And they're gonna crack you when they do."

Pappas leaned forward and Jesse rammed the pistol harder into his chest.

"Whoever you are, you're nuts," Pappas whispered, half smiling.

Jesse slapped him hard with his left hand. "Look, (expletive), I don't give a (expletive) about you. You're just another piece of crap, a dope dealer, and dope dealers die all the time. You got six hundred grand in your house and these people are gonna take it from you.

They don't give a damned about anybody, even your baby and your wife. They'll kill them too, if they have to."

The mention of his wife and child had the effect Jesse wanted. Pappas became unnerved. "I don't understand this," he said.

"Understand that you'll be dead. Your baby, too. You don't have a choice. You leave town now with your family and don't come back for at least a year."

"Who's going to do this?"

"An outfit guy named Bill Politte. He's as mean as they come. And he's coming after you and your money."

"I heard of him. He ripped some people off."

Jesse took the magnum from Pappas' chest, unloaded it and handed it to him.

"Do what I tell you."

"Tell me, who are you and why are you doing this?"

Jesse chuckled. "I'm your angel and angels don't like to see people die."

Jesse knew he had played a deadly game. "If Pappas didn't listen to me, then it was his life. That was only part of the problem. If he didn't leave how could I walk away from the score? What worried me was that if he didn't do as I told him and went crazy and came after Politte, I'd be in deep trouble. Politte would know who had tipped him off. I'd join Pappas in the cemetery."

Jesse checked out Pappas' house several times the next day until he was sure no one was there. Neighbors told him the family moved out. He told Politte he couldn't find Pappas.

"He's gone?" Politte asked incredulously.

"Nobody's been there for two days."

"Hell! We needed his money, Jesse."

"There'll be other scores, Bill."

Fox and Bohnemeier asked Jesse about the heist. "I just told them it was done with and wouldn't happen. They wanted to know why. I told them he just up and left. There was nobody to rob. I know they didn't believe me, but I didn't care. They told me to stop it and I did."

CHAPTER TWENTY-SEVEN

A Deadly Mistake

Trupiano wanted to meet with Jesse. He had been out of town quite a bit and needed to be brought up to date on what was happening on the East Side. Fox and Bohnemeier installed the recorder in the trunk of Jesse's Lincoln. They brought along a technician to check the recording system in the interior.

Jesse picked up Trupiano and Giammanco that afternoon. Trupiano got in the back and Giammanco in the front. Jesse watched Trupiano in the rear view mirror as he picked up something from the seat next to him.

"What the hell is this?" Trupiano asked. He held a small black leather folder. Jesse was about to activate the recorder, but he stopped. He looked over his shoulder. Trupiano grunted. "It's a (expletive) identification card! Federal Bureau of Investigation. It's got the guy's picture on it."

He handed it to Jesse. It was the FBI technician's card. "I'll be! What the hell is that doing in my car?"

Jesse looked at the card and thought for a moment. "Okay, Stoneking, now what? What the hell's wrong with those guys? It's my life they're messing with. I wanted to turn the tape on to record my death for Tom and Terry, but it was too risky."

"You a snitch for the 'g'?" Giammanco asked.

"Sure, Jimmy. I'm really Agent Stoneking." He tried being sarcastic, but he knew it wouldn't sell.

"It ain't funny, Jesse," Trupiano snarled.

Another pang of fear ripped Jesse. What if Trupiano wanted to search the car? He might not find the microphone under the dashboard, but he wouldn't miss the recorder in the trunk. He had to mitigate this.

"It sure as hell ain't funny, Mike. I'll tell you one thing. I ain't talking no more in this car. The FBI's probably got it bugged."

"What's that got to do with the i. d.?"

"How in the hell am I supposed to know?" He didn't have to feign anger.

"Maybe we ought to check your car out," Trupiano said.

"Don't worry about it. The way they hide these things it's almost impossible to find them. I'm going to have my car inspected and see if it's bugged. The guy who gave me the sweeper for your house can do it."

"It don't make no difference." He and Giammanco got out of the car. He handed the identification folder to Jesse. "Here's your souvenir."

Jesse stopped at a telephone booth and called the FBI office in Belleville. His anger wasn't concealed. Fox came on the phone.

"You dumb (expletive)," he screamed. "You guys almost got me killed."

"What are you talking about?:

"The agent's identification card. It was on the back seat of my car and Trupiano found it."

It was difficult for Fox to find the right words. "I don't know about that."

Jesse cut him off. "I do! Meet me in the park. Now!"

The incident forced Jesse to make a decision. "I'm out of here. I'll say, 'Goodbye, nice knowing you guys. Find yourself another sucker. Make your own cases'. I mean, it's like I got a target on my back and every gun in the mob is aimed at it. It only takes one mistake like this to get me dead. They always told me it was my decision when to quit. Well, it is now."

Fox and Bohnemeier were waiting for him. They were visibly embarrassed. Before they could say anything Jesse threw the identification at Fox. "What the hell's wrong with you guys, anyhow?"

"I don't know what to say, Jesse," Bohnemeier said.

"I know what to say. Stupid mistakes like that get people like me killed. I quit. I've had enough of this."

"What did Trupiano say?"

"What do you think he said? He wasn't happy. He was suspicious. And so was Giammanco. I acted suspicious, too. I told them I'd have the car checked out to see if it was bugged."

"Maybe you should find a bug in your car," Bohnemeier mused.

Jesse snickered. "Sure. How in the hell am I going to do that?"

They told him to wait while they went to their office 15 minutes away. When they returned they had a miniature transmitter two inches long and an inch and a half wide. Bohnemeier gave it to Jesse. "You found this under your seat, okay?"

Jesse's anger subsided. Maybe it would work. "What do I have to lose except my life?"

Jesse called Trupiano and said he had something to show him. Giammanco was with him again when they met the next morning at the Banana House on Produce Row. Trupiano stared at Jesse, his suspicion still obvious.

"I found this under the back seat of the car," he said, handing the transmitter to Trupiano.

"What's that?"

"It's a transmitter, that's what it is. The guy I told you about, he checked it out. He said it's the kind the FBI uses in cars. Those (expletive) had me bugged."

Concern replaced Trupiano's suspicion. "It ain't broadcasting now, is it?"

"The guy took the battery out."

"How does that explain the card?"

"It must have dropped out of the guy's pocket when he was bugging the car. That's all I can figure out."

"Those dirty rotten (expletive)," Trupiano said. "How long you think it's been there?"

"They must have just done it yesterday because I cleaned the car the day before and the i. d. wasn't on the seat then." Jesse laughed. "I went to the FBI office in Belleville and gave the folder to the agent. You should have seen the look on his face. All I told him was to be more careful the next time. He had a fit."

Trupiano shook his head. "You got some guts."

Fox and Bohnemeier agonized over this latest threat. There was no way to determine what, if any, damage had been done. Jesse apparently had covered himself adequately, but had Trupiano bought his story? If he hadn't Jesse would become a leper and Trupiano and the entire underworld would shun him. He would be ostracized from the mob, become a pariah if he even lived that long. He would have to be extricated quickly.

A Search For Credibility

It was imperative Jesse's credibility be reinforced. The agents devised a drama. Jesse borrowed $20,000 worth of new diamond rings from a jewelry store owner he knew. He put them in a briefcase and went to see Giammanco at the vending company. Giammanco wore his usual perpetual scowl and Jesse couldn't tell if he still was suspicious.

Ten minutes after he arrived, Fox and Bohnemeier and two agents in another car drove up. Fox and Bohnemeir went inside the office and identified themselves to Jesse. The other agents stayed outside.

"Come outside with us, Stoneking," Bohnemeier demanded gruffly.

"What's the matter? You guys lose your i. d. cards again?"

"Just do it, Stoneking."

"I'm not going any place and I ain't got nothing to say to you."

Giammanco was worried. "Maybe you better do what they say, Jesse."

"To hell with 'em. I'm getting tired of them hassling me." He pointed a steady finger at Fox. "First these guys bug my car and now they try to bust me. They're just sore because they messed up with that i. d. A real bunch of pros."

"We just want to see if you got any hot merchandise in your car," Fox said. "We hear you do."

"You got rights, Jesse," Giammanco said.

Bohnemeier glared at him. "You got a license to practice law, Jimmy?"

Jesse laughed. "If you got a warrant I'll do what you want."

Fox gave him what he said was a search warrant. It appeared authentic, including a judge's signature, but it was faked. Bohnemeier had prepared it. Jesse looked at it and threw it to the floor in front of Giammanco. "Okay, I ain't got nothing to worry about. I'm just a diamond salesman, that's all. Legit."

"Hear that, Tom?" Bohnemeier said. "Mr. Stoneking's legitimate." He laughed.

"He never did a legitimate thing in his life."

Jesse and Giammanco followed them outside. Jesse unlocked the car trunk as ordered. Fox opened the briefcase and took out small cases, inspecting the jewelry in each. "We're taking these with us, Stoneking."

"You ain't gonna do nothing," Jesse said, grabbing the briefcase. Fox held onto it. The cases fell to the ground. Jesse pushed Fox away and they scuffled until Bohnemeier stepped between them.

"You want to get arrested for assaulting a federal officer, tough guy?" Bohnemeier said.

Jesse backed off and said nothing as Fox picked up the cases. Fox got a form from the agents' car, filled it out and asked Jesse to sign it.

"What's that for?" he asked.

"It acknowledges that we obtained this jewelry from your car."

Jesse signed the form. Fox gave him a copy. "We're just going to check them to see if they're stolen and transported interstate. If they're clean, you'll get them back. If they're dirty, you'll be hearing from us."

Jesse turned his back on them as they left. Giammanco was impressed. "I wouldn't have done what you did."

"You gotta stand up to them, Jimmy, or else they'll run all over you."

Fox and Bohnemeier returned the jewelry to Jesse later that day. Jesse was satisfied. "I told Tom and Terry we should get jobs as actors. We could be the Three Stooges."

The confrontation soon was known throughout the underworld. Jesse's credibility had been restored as intended. But the farce presented a new liability. Fox and Bohnemeier were exposed and identifiable. If Giammanco saw them with Jesse in anything but a confrontational situation, the undercover work would end abruptly – and perhaps fatally.

CHAPTER TWENTY-EIGHT

A Matter Of Honor

J esse didn't take his angel with him that Sunday night early in June when he went to the supermarket for a few items. He wouldn't need it. There were no threats, even from Manion, and he would be gone only a few minutes.

He routinely surveyed the parking lot but saw no cars he recognized. It was safe. He parked between two vehicles facing a four-foot-high concrete retaining wall. It offered some concealment. It was overcast and muggy from the impending thunderstorm. The nearest street light barely illuminated the area.

He was in the store 15 minutes. It was raining heavily when he came out and he sprinted for his Lincoln. His head was down and he paid no attention at first to the car driving slowly behind him. Someone looking for a parking space, he assumed.

As he reached his Lincoln, his intuition demanded attention. There were plenty of open parking spaces nearer the store. The driver of the car wasn't looking for one. He was following him!

Jesse opened the car door and placed the grocery bag on the back seat. He looked over his shoulder at the car. It was the dark gray Chevrolet that had tailed him before. He could see the outlines of two men inside. He reached for the .45 that wasn't in his waistband and cursed his carelessness. The Chevrolet stopped directly behind his Lincoln. The headlights went out.

His heart was a trip hammer, his breathing quick. He had only seconds to extract himself. He was trapped between the car on his left, his own on his right, the retaining wall in front of the Chevrolet. He knew there was a deep ravine on the other side of the wall. A creek with large rocks was at the bottom. There were broken tree branches sharp as knives on which he could be impaled if he jumped. There was no place to run, little room to maneuver. The inside of the Lincoln was a death trap

A man stepped out of the Chevrolet. He was one of Manion's bodyguards. He leveled an automatic pistol at Jesse. He couldn't rush him. Only a few feet separated them, but it was too much distance.

"Tommy Manion sends his greetings, Stoneking. Here's his answer to your shakedown," the bodyguard snarled.

He pointed the automatic steadily at Jesse's chest. Jesse reacted instinctively and fell to the pavement an instant before the loud crack of the gun. The slug embedded in the asphalt six inches from Jesse's head and the ejected empty casing bounced on the pavement.

It was time for Jesse to die. There in the pouring rain lying on a parking lot. He steeled his body. The next shot wouldn't miss.

Just then a car pulled into the parking lot, its headlights on bright, flooding the area with brilliant light. Jesse was in the shadows. The shooter scrambled into the Chevrolet as the engine accelerated.

Jesse was safe now, but he was mentally and physically drained. He had to leave. The last thing he wanted was to be questioned by police and a story in the newspapers about an attempted hit on him.

As he drove from the parking lot, the impact of what had happened seized him. "I couldn't go home yet. My mind was so messed up I couldn't think straight. My hands were actually shaking. I was angry at myself for being so stupid and not thinking. I walked into that with my eyes closed. I should have had my angel. I would have shot him and my work for the FBI would be over."

Dorothy screamed when she saw him. He looked in the mirror and realized why. He was dripping wet and his face was ashen. A cut on the right side of his forehead was oozing blood.

"My God, Jessie! What happened?"

"Someone tried to crack me, that's what."

"What are you going to do?"

"I don't know," he replied.

"You better call Tom and Terry right away."

He didn't answer her. "I couldn't tell them. Not when I had to deal with Manion. He's got to pay. They wouldn't understand. A man has to keep his honor. I wasn't going to go right over there and take care of him. They'd be expecting that. I'd wait and they'd be off their guard."

Jesse momentarily thought about his commitment not to kill. He again had to abandon it, at least for now. It didn't matter. They almost killed him. His revenge was what counted, not allegiance to God. "Didn't Manion know what happens when you crack an outfit guy, particularly Art Berne's right-hand man? There'd be a hit out on him so fast. I guess he thought he'd be a man if he whacked me. He'd be a man, all right. A dead man."

Jesse picked up Politte two days later. His Lincoln was being serviced and he rented a Mustang. The recorder was in the glove compartment concealed by rental documents and other materials. It was set for voice activation. Polite wanted to drive the Mustang. It hit a pothole in the road and the door of the glove compartment fell open. The recorder slid forward and fell to the floor.

"What the hell's that?" Politte asked.

Jesse picked it up, flicked the voice activation switch on and off. "Looks like a tape recorder."

"What's it doing in there?" Politte asked suspiciously.

Jesse continued to inspect the recorder. "Someone who rented the car before me must have forgotten it."

"Was it on?"

"Hell, I don't know anything about these things."

Politte reached for the recorder. "Let me see it."

Jesse snickered. "Probably the 'g' put it there. Let's see if it recorded what we said." He pressed the reverse button and ran the tape back to the beginning. Then he engaged the record button to erase the tape. There only would be a few minutes of conversation. He had to stall. He held it to his ear. "I don't hear nothing but static."

Politte grabbed it from Jesse and put to his ear. "You dummy, you got it on record." He ran the tape back and pressed the play button. There was only muted static and the few words they had said. He pressed the fast forward and let the tape run. When he activated the play switch there was nothing.

Jesse laughed faintly. "At least it wasn't the 'g'."

Politte handed the tape back. "Maybe we better put it back,"

"I don't want to get busted for stealing a lousy recorder," Jesse said.

"They're looking for something like that to violate me, too, and put me back in the joint," Politte said.

Jesse didn't tell Politte what happened in the parking lot. Politte asked him if he was going to lean on Manion again for the shakedown. He said he wasn't because it was too risky and he doubted much would be gained from it right now. Politte insisted Manion be pressured more. He needed his money. Jesse said he would next week. By then Manion would be dead.

Politte cautioned Jesse not to walk into a trap. "Make sure he's by himself. Just tell him the reason he ain't been messed with by the outfit for so long is because we've been giving him a pass, but the pass has expired."

"Yeah, it has expired," Jesse said.

Time For Revenge

Manion operated a health spa and gymnasium. Jesse went there the next morning, intent on carrying out his revenge. His only emotion was the rush of closing in on his prey. He was his former cold, calculating, deadly self, craving the satisfaction of watching him die. There was no hint of forgiveness.

No customers were in the gym. Manion's Corvette and the Chevrolet were parked in front. Jesse didn't want to confront Manion while his henchmen were there. He would be outnumbered and outgunned. They no doubt were expecting his retaliation.

Jesse parked down the street to observe the gymnasium. A few minutes later the two bodyguards got in the Chevrolet and drove off. The taller and younger of the two was the one who had shot at him. Jesse waited five minutes.

Jesse had to decide how Manion would die. Quickly or with terrible, lingering pain? A shot to the head or the heart with the magnum loaded with hollow points he had gotten for this purpose? A blast to the gut with the sawed-off double-barrel shotgun? He enjoyed the sadistic pleasure deciding which one.

Jesse made his decision. He got the loaded shotgun from the trunk and slid it down his right pant leg. He put the magnum in the small of his back under his jacket.

Manion was at the top of the stairway leading up to the gym when Jesse entered. He smiled and held out his right hand in greeting, the other reaching under his loose-fitting shirt.

Jesse pulled out the shotgun as he lunged up the steps. He was on Manion in an instant. He slammed the butt of the gun against the side of Manion's head, knocking him off balance. Manion screeched and fell on his back.

Jesse stood over him, his left foot firmly on his chest. He reached under Manion's shirt and yanked out the pistol, tossing it to one side. He put the barrel of the shotgun to Manion's nose, pressing it flat against his face.

"Big (expletive) hit man, huh, Manion?" Jesse snarled. "You ain't nothing."

"I don't know what you're talking about," Manion whispered.

"You made the biggest mistake of your life. Trying to crack me makes you a dead man."

Manion curled in a fetal position. In that instant, at the moment of Manion's death, the thrill of the kill, the hunger for revenge, vanished. It was replaced by a pang of pity for the man groveling and sniveling before him, not even begging for his life, meekly submitting to his own death without resisting. How could he kill a wimp like that?

Jesse moved the barrel from Manion's face to the left side of his head. He squeezed the trigger. The blast was deafening. Splinters tore into Manion's cheek and neck. He gasped and then whimpered. There was a bubbling sound and then the sickening stench as Manion lost control of his bowels.

Jesse put the barrel against Manion's forehead. "I'm leaving you for Politte. He wants you, anyhow. He won't be as nice as I am."

As Jesse drove away, he was confused. Had his commitment about granting life instead of death prevailed? "I don't know why I backed out at the last minute. It wasn't like me. I just couldn't crack him. It'd be like killing a kid. I made him suffer in the worst way. That's the lowest thing a man can do is poop in his pants in front of another man. But I couldn't tell anybody, especially Tom and Terry."

Two days later, Politte asked Jesse if he had visited Manion yet. Jesse said he had. "He got some balls all of a sudden. He said (expletive) Jesse Stoneking, (expletive) Bill Politte, (expletive) the outfit."

"You're kidding me."

"That's what he said. He wasn't kidding."

Politte laughed. "Well, it's his life. By the way, did you hear that there was some trouble over at his place the other day?"

"Trouble?"

"Somebody tried to blow him away, but missed. Neighbors heard the shot and called the police. Manion wouldn't say anything about it, but he was shaken up. They said he was crying and he crapped in his pants."

"That's a shame. Somebody must have really been upset at him."

Politte smiled knowingly. "It wasn't you, was it, Jesse?"

Jesse laughed. "Would I miss?"

"Just asking."

"Maybe it was some dopers. You know how they always kill each other."

"Yeah, maybe it was. But I doubt if they'd miss, either."

Jesse at last conceded to himself he had failed to reverse his lifestyle and turn to God. He really hadn't even tried, instead submitting to Satan as usual. Once again, he would re-evaluate himself and get back on the road to Jesus and salvation. There was much he had to do to accomplish that, mainly casting out the devils dwelling in him. When the time was right, he would confide in Carolee. She surely could be helpful. He hoped it wasn't too late.

Settling A Dispute

Lucas Brazil came to see Jesse. Politte had asked him to make a timer and it was ready. Jesse wasn't aware they were acquainted.

Was that why Brazil tried to kill him? Could Politte have given him a contract because he wanted Jesse out of the way? That seemed a real possibility.

Jesse offered to take Brazil to meet him. He needed to know why Politte wanted the timer.

Politte appeared to be troubled and he took Jesse aside. He was having problems with the Operating Engineers Local 520 on the East Side, which was competing with Local 513 from St. Louis. There was a jurisdictional dispute over a lock and dam construction project on the Mississippi River at Alton.

Both locals shared the project, but now Local 520 was claiming exclusive jurisdiction. It appealed to the International Union and if it ruled against Local 513, Politte's influence and power base would be eroded. Jobs he gave his cronies through Local 513 bought him loyalty. The construction was to continue for at least another five years and after completion maintenance of the facility was to be the Operating Engineers' responsibility.

"How you going to handle it, Bill?" Jesse probed.

"I'll take care of it my own way. Somebody just might throw something in that place, like maybe a hand grenade."

Politte instructed Brazil to bring the timer to a Howard Johnson Motel near Collinsville that night. Jesse offered to drive Brazil there. Politte was waiting for him. He got into Jesse's car. Brazil handed him a paper sack containing the timer. Politte gave him a wad of bills.

"How you know that thing works, Bill?" Jesse asked.

Politte snickered. "I've used them before."

"Looks like an egg timer with wires attached to it, doesn't it?"

Politte laughed and winked. "Well, you just listen to the news and see what an egg timer does."

At 11:04 that night an explosion extensively damaged Local 520's offices in Granite City. Bohnemeier told him to try to learn more about the bombing, but not be too aggressive.

Jesse waited a week before contacting Politte. "What's happening with those guys at the Operating Engineers? They tried to make peace?"

"No," Politte said curtly. "I kept telling them to get off this job but they didn't listen to me. So that night it happened. They got the message. Naturally, I get the sting over it, which I don't give a (expletive). I went to see my parole officer yesterday and he said, 'Bill, I hate to see you screw up'. I asked him what he meant, screw up. He said, 'Well, you better quit blowing up them offices'. I just laughed."

"So the timer worked okay with the dynamite?"

Politte said he didn't use dynamite. He decided at the last minute to use a hand grenade. "You get more concussion that way. What you do is have nails or ball bearings with it."

"How do you do that?"

"Well, you get a box of ball bearings or nails and tape it to the handle of the grenade and put it in a metal box. That's what does the damage. It's like shrapnel. It shoots them nails and bearings like bullets out of a gun. But you got to be careful. You got to bust out the window first because if you don't it might bounce off and come back at you. I've used fifty of them in my time. It gets a message to people."

"How much time do you have after you pull the pin?"

"Ten seconds. As soon as I pull the pin I get rid of it. I don't hesitate."

"I ain't got the balls for that kind of stuff. Give me a .45 anytime. Did it do a lot of damage?"

"Blew a five-foot hole in the ceiling. Blew one wall out."

"Can you get any more grenades? I'd like to have a couple. Never know when you can use one."

Politte gave one to Jesse a few days later. The FBI now had two solid cases against him – bombing the union hall and possession of an illegal explosive device. That would be enough to send him to prison for a long time.

CHAPTER TWENTY-NINE

To Kill A Whore

It wasn't an area of East St. Louis where Jesse felt safe any time, especially at night, and even while carrying his angel. Prostitutes, drug peddlers, thugs of all persuasions, roamed the streets, ready to steal, intimidate and kill.

But Jesse had a compelling reason to be there. He had to save the life of Sheila, a teen-aged streetwalker marked for death by Clinton Bramlet, a vicious killer and ruthless bank robber.

He normally wouldn't have cared if she lived or died. Why risk your life for a two-bit hooker who contributed nothing to society, except sex, and whose life expectancy was so nominal. But now he had a commitment to save life instead of destroying it and he needed to honor that.

That night Jesse went to the area near downtown. He talked to a dozen women, most of whom propositioned him. Three admitted a young girl named Sheila worked the streets. If they knew where she lived they didn't want to tell. Nor did they give him the name of her pimp. They knew better than to do that.

Jesse returned the next night and again drove and walked about the area, but he saw no girl with Sheila's name or description. He had one more chance to find her. Ham Bone Jefferson, an old numbers bookie who once worked for the outfit, might know about her. He now was a fence and Jesse had done business with him on occasion. A bear of a man in his 60s, he owned a tavern nearby and was behind the bar when Jesse entered.

"I need a favor, Ham Bone."

"It's yours, brother."

"I need to find a girl."

Jefferson gave a deep belly laugh that shook his entire body. "You don't need me for that in this part of town."

"It ain't for that, Ham Bone. I got to find her. She's a hooker named Sheila. About sixteen, or so. Got a knife scar on the right side of her neck. There's a hit out on her and I got to save her."

Jefferson thought. "Maybe I heard of a girl like that. Let me see if I can find out who her man is." He made several telephone calls. "Somebody'll be here in a minute."

They chatted until a young, gangly black man entered the side door. His gaudy clothes, the white wide-brimmed hat and his shuffle advertised his occupation as a pimp.

"My friend here wants to find a girl by the name of Sheila," Ham Bone said. "Young, small with a scar on her neck. She your girl?" It was more a statement than a question.

The pimp hesitated. Jefferson slapped him on the back. "He's okay. He ain't the law. He's people."

The pimp relaxed. "Yeah, I know her, Ham Bone. Why?

"My friend here wants to talk to her. He don't mean her no harm. And he don't want to lay her, either. He just wants to save her."

Jesse pulled a roll of bills from his pocket and gave a hundred dollar bill to the pimp. "Where is she?"

The pimp cautiously took the bill. "Wish I knew, man. I ain't seen her four, five days now."

"Where's she live?"

"She ain't there, either. Her mamma ain't seen her. She ain't run off. All her clothes are there. She wouldn't go nowhere without taking them. Know what I mean? Something's happened to her."

Jesse thanked the pimp. He knew what happened to Sheila. She was dead. Bramlet had killed her, as he had promised. "I knew I was too late. Hard telling where her body was. Even if her body was found it wouldn't be much of a story, if any, in the newspapers. It was like Bramlet said. She was just a hooker. No one would care."

Bramlet told Jesse the day before why he wanted to kill Sheila. While they were having sex she stole a thousand dollars from his billfold.

Jesse couldn't suppress his laughter. "What was her name?"

"She said her name was Sheila. It's probably not her real name. Sixteen years maybe. I doubt if she weighed eighty pounds. Kind of long face, kinky hair. Oh, yeah, she had a scar on her neck like from a knife. She was walking the streets and I just picked her up. You can get it any night right over there on Fifth and Sixth streets. Fifteen dollars is all I ever paid. I get it all the time."

"Relieves pressure from bank jobs, I guess," Jesse observed.

"Yeah, it does. Anyhow, I always take my billfold out of my back pocket and put it in my front right pocket, but for some reason that night I didn't. I guess she got it when she was doing it."

"A thousand dollars, huh? That was an expensive piece."

"She sold her ass for a thousand," Bramlet said acidly.

"No, she sold her soul. Boy, that'll be like looking for a needle in a haystack trying to find her down there."

"She'll be on the streets. I'm gonna kill her. I bought me a new ice pick, a big heavy one. Just for her."

"Put it in her throat, huh?"

"No, just stick it through her left tit right in her heart. She took me and she'll die for that." The only emotion Bramlet showed was hatred.

Rescuing Sheila immediately motivated Jesse. "This guy was a vicious killer, that's all. I knew he wasn't one not to carry through on a threat like that. Even though she was a hooker she didn't deserve to die like that. Sure she robbed him. He deserved it. I made up my mind. I wouldn't let her die if I could help it."

Jesse switched off the recorder. He didn't want the agents to hear what he was going to say. "You want me to crack her for you?"

"I can take care of my own business," Bramlet snapped.

"Yeah, but you told people about it and they'll be looking at you if she gets killed."

Bramlet laughed. "She's just a whore. Nobody'll give a damn. You don't understand, Jesse. I want to see her die myself."

Talking about killing the hooker primed Bramlet's ego and opened his mouth farther. He brought up another hit. "You remember when that pipefitter was killed up around Carlinville? Somebody shot him. Well, I was questioned pretty heavy on that."

Jesse knew the hit he was talking about. "This guy named Billy Belt was ambushed and killed at his house. An officer in the union accused Art's outfit of being behind it. Art was mad as hell. He told me to go lean on the guy. I told him we had nothing to do with it and didn't know anything about it. I said to him, 'Now, if you don't stop talking about us like that, we'll pay you another visit and you'll have more problems than you can handle'. He got the message."

Jesse needed to try to get Bramlet to talk about the hit for the recorder. "You use a silencer on that one, Clint?" he asked casually.

"I don't know," he answered evasively.

"How'd the heat get your name, anyhow?"

Bramlet said he had been helping dig a sewer trench at a friend's house when several union members tried to stop him because he and his friend didn't belong to the local.

"They beat me up real bad and this Belt was the guy that done the damage to me. He slammed my face into the outrigger on the tractor twice and kicked me in the face a lot. I never had a bruise below the chin. I nearly died. I was critical for three days and on the fourth day I had an operation to put my jaw back in my head. My left eye was out. Then someone killed him. I knew I would be suspected right off. The cops thought I was the obvious one."

"One thing about you, Clint, you're a capable man," Jesse said. "That tells me a lot."

Bramlet said no more. Jesse knew he had killed Belt. "I didn't blame him for not talking. What the hell. Who's going to come in on himself on a hit? Talking about scores you pull off is one thing, but not a murder. Nobody's that dumb. They never know when they might be talking to a snitch."

CHAPTER THIRTY

A Master Bank Bandit

It was near closing time on December 2, 1983, when Clinton Bramlet walked into the bank in the small, sleepy rural Illinois town of Irvington. He was there to make a withdrawal, but not the normal kind.

Wearing green fatigues, a dark parka and a ski mask, Bramlet's presence was threatening. He was armed with a sub-machine gun and a radio to monitor police calls. What wasn't obvious was a concealed handcuff with a hand grenade welded to it. If he was trapped he would attach it to the arms of an employee and himself and threaten to detonate the explosive.

When he walked out, he carried $34,293 in bank funds. An emergency call went out to the only law enforcement officer in town, an Illinois state trooper. He was eager to respond, but he couldn't. The rear tires of his squad car were slashed.

Four months later, Bramlet, again wearing a ski mask with a radio antenna protruding from it and carrying an automatic rifle, invaded the Bartelso Savings Bank in Bartelso, a small Illinois town southeast of the metropolitan area. His take this time was $20,000.

As with the previous robbery, a frantic call for help went out from the bank to another state trooper. He also couldn't respond. The tires on his squad car also were slashed and the mobile receiver antenna was broken.

Bramlet remained unidentified. He was no amateur bank robber. Practice apparently made him perfect. In 20 years he had pulled off at least 50 to 60 bank heists in Illinois, netting him at least one million dollars or more.

Bramlet's partner in the Bartelso robbery had purchased the getaway car from a couple in a St. Louis suburb and then abandoned it. Because of that, Bramlet found a new friend and partner – Jesse and the FBI.

He was waiting to retire as a snitch and had agreed to enter the government's Witness Protection Program. It was the opportunity he needed to walk away from his past, evil life. He realized just being in the mob, even as an informant, caressed his criminal vanity, especially his tendency toward violence. It probably contributed to his rejection of his commitment.

The couple told agents they sold the getaway car to a man for cash, but they didn't know his name. They signed the title and he said he would take care of the transfer, which he obviously didn't. They assumed he was from Illinois because he asked directions to their house from the East Side. He was heavyset, about five feet, six inches tall, weighing nearly 300 pounds and in his 50s. The description didn't match that of the robber, who was younger and smaller.

Bohnemeier asked Jesse if he ever met a bank robber with the older man's description and he said he had not. He suggested Jesse try to learn his identity while he still was on the streets.

It was by chance Jesse found Bramlet. The next day, Politte was going to check out a dope dealer he was thinking about robbing. Jesse went with him, more out of curiosity and boredom than expecting to learn something new. Politte wanted to use his untraceable "cool car" stored at a house owned by Joe Brooks. Politte had told Jesse earlier Brooks was a bank robber, but he had forgotten.

Polite introduced him to Brooks, an affable, loquacious man with gray hair. He almost was identical to that of the description of the man who bought the getaway car. Brooks was looking for an untraceable .357 magnum pistol. That opened the door for Jesse.

Jesse assumed he would have to put his retirement on hold. "I wasn't sure I should get involved at this late stage. I was only going along for the ride now. But I'm wondering if Brooks is in on those bank jobs. I didn't want to pass that up. So, I told him I'd try to get a clean magnum, but it might take some time. Tom and Terry wouldn't know. There was no way they would let me get a piece for a man they suspected of being a bank robber."

"I think I got one of your bank robbers for you," he told Bohnemeier, who was cautiously enthusiastic. Whoever bought the car surely was an accessory, but that didn't go very far in identifying the actual robber.

A Cop On The Take

A week later, as they rode in Jesse's car, Brooks said a friend of his was plotting to steal a million dollars worth of jewelry and gems from a man planning to fence them. "His dad's the one who does all the banks," Brooks said.

Brooks had all but given him the name of the bank robber. It was an indication of the trust Jesse had generated in him.

As they drove over a railroad crossing Brooks saw a parked pick-up truck with two men. They were near a warehouse and he was suspicious. They probably were burglars, he said, and he had a mind to call the police.

"You call the cops?" Jesse asked jokingly.

"I can call a Madison County cop. He's a pretty good guy. He's been on a couple of bank jobs with us. He likes to make a little extra money."

Jesse decided to leave it alone for the time being. Brooks said he and his partner had several bank robberies lined up for the coming months.

"You guys need a partner" Jesse asked.

"My guy wants somebody he can depend on and trust. I said, 'Man, I think I know just the guy'. He wants to meet you."

"Hey, I'm a stick-up man. That's my thing."

Jesse was amazed. Brooks essentially was making a confession. "Is this guy real good, though? I mean, if I go in with a guy ..."

Brooks interrupted him. "He's the best. You can trust him. He's not a squealer. If he'd get caught he wouldn't rat on you."

"You have to be that way. How do you think this guy would be in a shoot-out?"

"He'll shoot and he won't hesitate."

"But he's a good capable bank man, though, huh?" Jesse prodded.

"He's better than Jesse James."

"I need to meet him, Joe."

"You will. I told him I ain't got no guts anymore. I can't afford to leave any witnesses around because with my size they can pick me out easy. I said I don't want to have to go in and start butchering people so they can't identify me for no thirty, forty thousand dollars. The last job we done, the one up at Bartelso, we only got twenty thousand out of it."

"You got to split it up with that copper, or what?"

Brooks said they split evenly with the officer on the last two bank jobs. They normally give him only a few thousand dollars when he is the look-out.

Jesse debated how best to ask Brooks the name of the deputy sheriff. He didn't have to. Brooks volunteered it. He was Theodore Rousseau, a sergeant with the Madison County Sheriff's Department. Brooks said he also converted legal weapons into illegal automatics.

"Why are you guys messing with a copper? Once a cop always a cop."

"You get a crooked cop and you can trust him more being a crook than you can being a cop."

"Yeah, that's right because he can't say nothing. Why does he do it?"

"He likes women and they cost money."

A Gun Show

Jesse asked Brooks the name of his partner. Without hesitating, he said it was Clinton Bramlet, spelling the last name. Brooks called him, saying Jesse was interested in buying several automatic rifles. They picked up Bramlet at a restaurant he owned.

Soft spoken and timid appearing with black hair combed straight back, Bramlet was five feet, six inches tall and weighed 140 pounds.

He was 45, but he could have been in his twenties. He matched the description of the man who robbed the bank in Bartelso.

Bramlet had an M-16 and a Uzi, both fully automatic, he wanted to demonstrate for Jesse. They drove into the countryside far from any residences and stopped on a bridge over a small creek. Bramlet slammed a clip into the Uzi, cocked it and handed it to Jesse. He aimed at the water below and pressed the trigger. There was nothing. It was jammed.

Bramlet was embarrassed and apologized. He loaded the M-16. It was just like the one Jesse bought for the massacre. The rapidity of the firing, the flames licking from the barrel, the acrid fumes of the burned gunpowder were intoxicating as before. Bramlet reloaded and fired it himself. Jesse left the door of his car open, hoping the recorder would pick up the barking of the gun.

"You go in the banks with those guns?" Jesse asked.

"The one I used on the last job was the M-16. I got a lot of fire-power when I go in. You don't ever want to go in weak. Once you've put your cards on the table you got to play them. You don't back down for nothing."

Bramlet also took two hand grenades with him into the banks. "If a cop pulls up in front of the bank I just throw a grenade under his car. I got one of them welded to a handcuff. If I get hemmed in there I grab a girl and put the handcuff on her and pull the pin, but I'm holding the handle down. I say, 'Go on and shoot'. They'll know that after they shoot me that grenade goes off and there ain't nothing left of that girl. Me either, but it won't matter then. It intimi-dates more than a gun."

Jesse was impressed. "Boy, that's good insurance. You got your head together, that's for sure. You got a new partner, Clint." They shook hands.

Bramlet further outlined his strategy. It was a description of his last two scores. He communicates with his partner outside the bank with a walkie-talkie. It is as much intimidation as protection. His victims know he is not alone. As a diversion, he tells his victims he has a wife and three young children who are in need.

Although he wears a ski mask, making identification difficult, authorities would be searching for a much younger man with a family. He robs banks in small towns with only one or two police officers. If he finds their cars, he punctures the tires so they cannot respond.

He is on a strict time schedule, allowing him only a few minutes in the bank. Money in the tellers' cash drawers is left untouched. It often is bait, he said, with the serial numbers recorded or containing indelible dye. Instead, he orders the money removed from the vault.

Bramlet had a score in mind. It was a bank in Columbia, a small community on the southeastern edge of the East Side. He suggested they check it the next afternoon. After Jesse picked him up, he disclosed more about himself.

"How long you been hitting banks, Clint?"

"Since the sixties. I guess about 1961 I got my first one. I was just a kid. After the second one, I thought I'm getting pretty good at this. I'm making pretty good money out of it. I think this is the way I'll continue making my living. I never spent one night in jail for anything."

Jesse asked how many banks he had robbed.

"I never counted, except the money. Two, three a year for twenty some years. Figure it out. Maybe fifty, sixty." He chuckled. "Maybe I should have kept a scrapbook, huh? Only I couldn't show it to anybody."

Jesse mentally calculated Bramlet probably had stolen at least $1 million, maybe even $2 million.

Bramlet turned introspective. He said he had a reputation for being mean, but he was a compassionate and benevolent man. "I like people. As a matter of fact, and this is the honest to God truth, I gave a hundred dollars awhile back to this little girl that was living in a truck bed with her uncle. And you remember this little boy that was eaten up by the dogs? His mother put hamburger on him to attract the dogs. I sent him some money in a get-well card. I do have my good side."

Jesse drove around Columbia for 20 minutes, surveying the town, its streets, the police department and the bank. Bramlet directed him to a subdivision on a bluff overlooking the bank from where he could watch and keep in radio communication while he was inside. They located two shopping centers where they could kill time while the roadblocks were up.

Jesse agreed to case the inside of the bank. His cover would be to change a $100 bill. There were five tellers and atop the door was a video camera. Bramlet believed they might have to create a diversion. They could set off a charge of dynamite on the other side of town or they could call the police and report an armed man in a restaurant. Every available officer would respond.

Bramlet earlier showed Jesse a cabinet in a rear room of his restaurant where he said he kept a large reserve of money. While they were in Columbia, Stram broke into the room and stole $5,000 in cash. Bramlet suspected Brooks and said he never wanted to see him again. Jesse felt badly about that. Brooks was just an old man. Maybe he had done him a favor, after all, getting him away from Bramlet. But perhaps they had signed his death warrant.

Saved By A Cop

Bramlet called Jesse two days later and said it was important they meet that afternoon. Jesse started to make an excuse, but Bramlet said it was urgent. Jesse tried to call Fox and Bohnemeier, but they were out.

He and Bramlet met on a parking lot. He beckoned Jesse to his older, black Camaro. He was wearing a yellow sport shirt hanging out of his jeans. Jesse could see the outline of a pistol in his belt.

"What's up?" Jesse said as he got in the Camaro.

"I just thought we'd do a little work today."

"What do you mean, work?" Jesse asked, suspiciously.

"Let's take that bank in Columbia."

Jesse laughed weakly. "I didn't think you'd want to do it so soon. We haven't really planned it out. I don't like it like this."

Bramlet had made up his mind. "Don't worry about it. It'll be a cinch. I got the stuff we'll need in the trunk. The grenades and a .45 for you. And this is a safe car. It can't be traced back to me. Besides, I'm getting a little low on cash."

It was a 30-minute drive to Columbia. Jesse was trapped. There were too many complications. That he was an undercover operative wouldn't matter. He would participate in a robbery and be armed, both in violation of FBI and his parole regulations. The FBI never would have authorized his participation. If he was arrested it was unlikely the agents would rescue him. He would be back in prison.

Jesse pondered the situation. "You're in a real storm now, Jesse. I wasn't even wired up. Worse than that, I didn't have my angel. I don't know why I didn't bring it. The one he brought for me was in the trunk and there was no way I could get to it. I couldn't take his gun away from him because it was on his left side and I couldn't get to it. I was totally on my own."

As Bramlet outlined his game plan, Jesse had to work out his own scheme to extricate himself in less than a half an hour. Perhaps instead of taking his position on the bluff overlooking the bank, he could abandon Bramlet and call the police. When Bramlet called for him, he wouldn't be there. He would be arrested and Jesse would be a hero, although his cover would be blown. That didn't matter. His undercover career almost was ended.

But then a troubling thought. How would Bramlet react if he was trapped inside the bank? Would there be a blood bath if he shot it out? He had vowed to do that. And then the handcuffs with the grenade. Would he blow up himself and an innocent employee? It was too horrendous not to consider.

Bramlet looked at him. "You look worried, Jesse."

"Yeah, I am. I don't like this. It's like suicide."

"You worry too much. We'll be out of there in less than five minutes. What I want you to do is to watch the people so none of them sets off the alarm while I go to the vault. We'll get them all in the middle of the floor. I'll shoot out the camera as soon as we hit the door."

"I thought I was going to be your back-up man outside?"

"I changed my mind about that. I need you inside with me. Just remember, if we get in trouble grab the nearest woman and put the handcuff with the grenade on her. It's the only way. And we have to be ready to shoot it out if we have to."

Bramlet was putting Jesse to the test. "My plan to leave him there was shot down. There was only one way to get out of this mess now. When he gave me the forty-five I'd just come down on him and tell him who I really was. I'd handcuff him with his own cuffs. I'd be making a citizen's arrest. Politte would know about it in an hour. What the hell, it was all over, anyhow. The marshals would just have to get me out of town right now."

Jesse relaxed now that he knew how to extricate himself. It was risky, but it was the only way. They were only a few miles from Columbia and he ignored Bramlet's chattering. As they passed the city limits, Jesse steeled himself for his final act.

The traffic light up ahead turned red and Bramlet came to a stop in the inside lane. Jesse didn't see the police car until it was beside them. Bramlet stared straight ahead. Jesse glanced at the driver. He knew the officer. The policeman looked at him and waved. Jesse waved back.

The officer rolled down the window. "What are you doing in my town?" he asked, teasing.

"Just passing through."

"Make sure you don't rob any banks," the officer said, laughing.

The light turned green and the police car started through the intersection. Bramlet lagged behind.

"That settles it, Clint," Jesse said. "We can't pull it off now."

"No way," Bramlet said disgustedly. "Another time."

Jesse was pleased. "Who says there ain't no cops around when you need one?" he thought. "I was never so glad to see a cop in my life."

The Game Is Over

Jesse now was eager to retire as a snitch. The curtain was down on the last act of his drama. It almost was two years since he first went on the streets for Fox and Bohnemeier. He had set his course and stayed it. Scorpion had stung well. He accomplished more than he believed he would and he had taken a lot of chances. The agents' time and the government's money were well invested.

He soon would bring down many of the high and the mighty, the untouchables of the underworld. Criminals, some dangerous like Brazil and Bramlet, who escaped detection for years, would be exposed. The agents' careers would be greatly enhanced, thanks to Jesse. They deserved it.

And what had Jesse gotten out of it? Mission accomplished. The revenge that drove him to become an informant would be achieved, not in the manner he planned, but through the justice system. Except for getting even with Vitale. A higher authority took care of that. Jesse now was satisfied with not carrying out the massacre he had come so close to doing. Those men were alive today.

The game, the most deadly he ever played, was over and he had won. The glory days, however measured, were ended. He had walked the deadly line for much of his life, but this was the narrowest ever. Yet, it was a fulfilling experience like none other. The intellectual satisfaction of playing and winning dangerous mind games with adversaries. The emotional high of flirting with danger. The rush from staring death in the face and walking away from it.

It now was a matter of waiting for his transition to happen. Fox and Bohnemeier assured him his chances of surviving would improve once he entered the Witness Protection Program. He accepted that logic, but not necessarily the need. He could protect himself well, regardless of where he was and under what cover.

It was making the change that concerned him. He now began looking to God for the true assistance only He can provide. It was not God's commitment to him, for that he knew was absolute and guaranteed. It was his pledge to Him that wasn't yet written in stone. Until he accomplished that, he knew his existence would be tenuous.

CHAPTER THIRTY-ONE

Baptism By Fire

As the agents escorted Jesse late at night on August 14, 1984, it was with mixed emotions he watched familiar sights flash by and the lights of the metropolitan area fading behind him until there was only farmland and darkness. And uncertainty.

It was the beginning of his rebirth, his expedition to God. The old Jesse Stoneking, the "Stone Killer," was being buried, along with his vanity and tendency to settle disputes and seek revenge with bullets. The new Jesse was being born into the straight life with maturity in God.

He admitted it wasn't easy to turn his back on the enticing fame and fortune, albeit evil, he once savored and pursued. There were too many memories – good and bad. His former lifestyle still tempted him, beckoning him back, but now he was able to refuse it. There was no way he could return. Death would await him there.

He was relieved he soon no longer would be a puppet with the government pulling the strings. He again would be in control of his existence. He and no one else would make his decisions. But with that came the uncertainty of his new life, wherever and whatever it would be. Where would he live? How would he exist? His only talents and experience were criminal, not a good employment background.

He would return to the East Side before long to testify before grand juries and district courts. There would be two different Jesse Stonekings on display, one to be reviled, one to be honored.

And when it was all over he would disappear and enter another undercover life. Jesse Stoneking would cease to exist. In his place would be Jesse McBride with a birth certificate, driver's license, Social Security number and credit cards in that name. No one but the agents and a few others he trusted would know who he really was. He would become invisible in the Witness Protection Program. But it would take the government some time to build the new Jesse.

All traces of him would be destroyed except his fingerprints permanently on file. They would stay with him forever and couldn't be altered. That was another reason he had to live a clean life. An arrest would bring back the real Jesse Stoneking. A red flag was placed on his FBI fingerprint file. Any inquiries would be reported to the field office nearest the requesting agency. Agents would assess the circumstances. Access to the file would be denied unless it involved a serious offense such as murder in which Jesse was a suspect.

"It was like I was at a funeral for someone I loved and they were lowering the casket into the grave. You know, gone forever. Never seeing him again. That was me. Jesse Stoneking."

Jesse's two families were moved to temporary quarters at Kentucky Lake, a resort area about 200 miles southeast of St. Louis the day before he arrived. Neither family knew the other was there and the marshals put them in cabins miles apart. He and the agents spent three days reviewing the thousands of pages of transcripts of pertinent conversations he had recorded and other evidence.

And then the second phase of the relocation began. The families were to be situated in different parts of the country to avoid conflicts. Jesse could have no communication with them, not even know where they were. Long distance telephone calls could be traced. Nor could he call Fox and Bohnemeier, the only friends he had. Any contacts between them would be handled by the marshals. Jesse said it was unreasonable, but they told him it was for his own safety.

Back To God

Jesse understood the necessity for the separation from his families, but it was with trepidation he said goodbye to them, particularly Carolee. He wondered when he would see his children again. It wouldn't be soon enough.

"Something just wasn't right. When I held Carolee and kissed her it was like she wasn't there, that she was somewhere else. She seemed so cold. Her mind seemed to be on other things and not me. I couldn't blame her. Our life together hadn't been too great, especially in the last year, but I would make it up to her."

Jesse knew it was time to apologize to Carolee and confide in her his decision to convert to Christianity, especially his commitment to himself and God never again to invoke violence and death. That surely would reunite them and improve their relationship. After all, she advocated forgiveness, not only by the Lord but by humans. She would provide the necessary assistance he desperately needed.

Two marshals escorted Jesse to Philadelphia on the first leg of the trip to Boston. A new person might have been created, but the old defiant one was alive and kicking. While in the terminal, he bolted from the marshals for the nearest telephone, ignoring their protests. He dialed the number of the motel where Carolee was to be staying temporarily. He had found it in a document the marshals left unguarded. He used his telephone credit card, another serious violation of security precautions.

When she answered, he could tell she still surrounded herself with a wall of ice. She said hello and nothing else.

"I've been thinking. I'm really sorry for the bad things I've done. Really sorry. You know how you're a Christian and all that. I want to be a Christian again too. Will you help me? Will you forgive me?"

There was a long silence. Finally, she said, "Of course, Jesse."

"Not just for me, but for the kids." There was no response. "Let's just forget about all that has happened between us. We'll start all over." Again, only silence. He whispered to her, "Look, to hell with this crap about hiding out. I'll tell these guys to hit the road and I'll grab the next flight back. We'll go away together."

"You know you can't do that, Jesse." She laughed feebly. "Not right now. There'll be time." Then she hung up.

While Jesse was elated at the thought of renewing his marriage to Carolee, his family with his paramour was a lingering problem. He wasn't sure how to handle that. It always was a major bone of contention between Carolee and him.

He knew God didn't look kindly on such relationships and He spoke out specifically against adultery. Forgiveness was assured with repentance and appeal to Jesus, but only if Jesse vowed to discontinue such immorality. How could he do that when he continued to live adulterously? Lies to the Lord didn't work.

He and the two marshals caught the flight to Boston, where they stayed in a two-bedroom suite. He found a Gideon Bible in the nightstand in his room. He paged through it, promising himself to soon begin reading it. He wanted it to be the foundation of his new life.

The Mob In Turmoil

Turmoil began stirring the underworld two weeks after Jesse disappeared. Berne and Trupiano were concerned. Jesse had said he was taking a week's vacation in Florida and would check in with them while he was gone, but no one heard from him. It wasn't like him. He was a man of his word. They worried he had been hit.

On September 6, three weeks after Jesse disappeared, the mob's worry turned to rage. The federal grand jury in East St. Louis returned the first of many indictments. Bramlet and Politte were among the first arrested by FBI agents. They were considered the most dangerous. It didn't take long for the first sparks of suspicion to flare into a raging conflagration.

Bramlet immediately suspected Jesse was a snitch. Agents found in his wallet a recently post-marked envelope addressed to Jesse. It was returned stamped, "No forwarding address." When arrested as he left his home, he was wearing combat fatigues and boots and had automatic weapons and hand grenades in the trunk of his car. Bramlet told the agents, "You don't have to tell me who did it to me. It was that (expletive) Stoneking."

Brazil was impassive when he was arrested. "You know how we got you, don't you?" Fox said. "Jesse Stoneking."

"No way," he said, shaking his head in disbelief.

"Would I lie to you?"

"I'm telling you there's no way Jesse's a snitch."

As the agents finished processing him, a marshal said Jesse wanted to talk to Fox or Bohneneier. After a few minutes, Fox handed the telephone to Brazil. "Here, you want to talk to Jesse?"

"It ain't you, is it, Jesse?" Brazil asked desperately.

"You got it right, Lucas. It's the happiest day of my life to tell you I'm the one who did it to you, you little fruit."

Brazil gave the receiver back to Fox. "That (expletive) should have died." The agents didn't know what he meant. He obviously was referring to his failed attempt to hit Jesse.

Hours after the first arrests, the underworld realized it had been betrayed by one of its most trusted and respected operatives. The ripples of shock grew to thunderous upheavals. FBI agents and police intelligence detectives observed small groups of hoods gathered on street corners and at Produce Row. Conversations were animated, heads shook violently in disgust, feet stomped in anger, fists raised. Trupiano and Berne went into seclusion.

In Chicago, Aiuppa was furious. Someone he had trusted and permitted to get close to him turned out to be a snitch. He blamed Berne. Retribution had to be swift. Jesse had to be made an example.

Life in the Witness Protection Program with its stringent restrictions soon became unbearable for Jesse. He was back in a prison. Once again, he couldn't be his own person. He rebelled.

"I couldn't move without the marshals right beside me. I couldn't even go to the bathroom without one of them tagging along. They told me I wasn't the easiest person to babysit. It was like being under a magnifying glass. I was arguing with them all the time. I called them the wardens. They just laughed. They were just doing their jobs. They really were good guys for having to put up with me."

He was worried about Carolee. He couldn't deny the possibility she had abandoned him when he was told she had left the motel. The marshals knew where she was, but kept it a secret. One finally agreed to call her.

He asked her if she wanted to talk to Jesse. Her response was blunt. She never wanted to see or talk to him again. He couldn't believe it until he heard it from her personally, but he realized he never would. She was gone forever. He could blame only himself. Fox and Bohnemeier refused to call her, claiming they were prohibited.

Jesse made a fateful decision. He had been in the Witness Protection Program only a few weeks, but it was time to walk away from it. "That did it. I wasn't getting any help from nobody, just a lot of bull. Don't they realize it's my family, my wife and my kids? I'm out of there."

An Escape Fund

The next morning he told the marshals he was going to the lobby for a pack of cigarettes. Instead, he took a large envelope with $50,000 in cash from his hotel safe deposit box. It was all the money he had except his government stipend.

It was the "escape fund" he had amassed in the days before he went into hiding. The thief in Jesse hadn't been totally sedated. He and Mark committed several thefts, including $25,000 gotten from Berne in a scam and the theft from Bramlet.

Jesse wrote a note to the marshals that he was leaving the program and for them not to worry. He put it in an envelope and told the clerk to deliver it to their room.

He bought a new Toyota Corolla. It was the cheapest car he had owned in years. He didn't take time to dicker over the price. An hour out of Boston, he called Fox and Bohnemeier and told them he had walked away from the program and was on his way home.

"You crazy, Jesse?" Bohnemeier said angrily.

"I know what I'm doing."

"No you don't. You can't run around the country on your own without any protection. It's too ..."

Jesse cut him off. "I don't care what you think. I just did it."

He rented a room in a motel 100 miles from the East Side. He caught himself registering in his real name. Dorothy was waiting his call. They agreed she, too, should leave the program and join him. He rented a small house in southern Illinois far from the metropolitan area.

Jesse still was concerned about Carolee. He had to make one more effort to settle their differences, as futile as he suspected it would be. At least they could be friends if not partners. The agents agreed to call her. He again wouldn't know where she was.

Her response was emphatic. She and the children still wanted no contact with him. He was out of their lives forever. The marriage was over. She planned to soon divorce him for desertion. She said she hoped he wouldn't contest it. Jesse laughed at the irony of that. How could he protest when he didn't know where she was?

The divorce was granted quickly. Jesse couldn't be served with papers because his location still was listed as unknown. He demanded a copy of the decree. It would disclose where she was. The agents saw through his request and refused. A few weeks later he married Dorothy.

He never would see Carolee or their children again. He eventually considered it an appropriate penalty for what he had done to them.

Under Fire In Court

Jesse spent the next two years in courtrooms. It was his baptism by fire. In pre-trial hearings, defense attorneys tried to discredit him to have the tape recordings and his testimony excluded as evidence on the grounds they were tainted, his words unreliable and the defendants had been entrapped. The government's cases would be severely damaged if not lost without that evidence. Two years of work hung precariously in the balance.

Jesse was on public display, his soul bared for all to see. It was punishing. The defense probed every weakness and tried to create others. Some of the intimate secrets of his private and criminal life were exposed. His credibility was a major issue. Self-control and poise were essential and there could be no outbursts of anger, no arguing with the defense that would depict him as arrogant, impetuous and unreliable.

The tapes and Jesse's testimony were admitted as evidence. His credibility and veracity as well as the integrity of the government's cases were intact.

At trial, Jesse, often the principal witness, again was verbally assaulted hour after hour, case after case. His credibility had to be invalidated. Accusations, some truthful, were the defense's sledge hammers. You have killed before, haven't you? Didn't you lure the defendants into committing crimes? You committed felonies while working for the FBI, didn't you? You lied all your life, haven't you? Did snitching on your friends make you feel good? Did you become a traitor just to get out of prison?

Jesse held up under the fierce barrage of cross-examination, denying accusations and answering questions succinctly, but respectfully. He made no excuses for his past or apologies for going undercover. He neither was insensitive nor boastful about those he caused to be arrested. He only was doing his job.

He was reminded continually of the contempt in which he was held. The icy stares and grim smiles from those who once had been his partners and friends. The not-so- veiled threats. The thumb and forefinger resembling a pistol being cocked. He ignored them all. What else could he expect?

And then in mid July 1986 it finally was over. For almost two years he had been in and out of courtrooms on both sides of the Mississippi River. "I had been through four years of hell and it was over at last. I was going home. I was going to start a new life. It was all that mattered anymore."

It was then I got to know Jesse Stoneking, the "Stone Killer" now the Christian.

CHAPTER THIRTY-TWO

Twenty-Five Reasons To Die

Jesse Stoneking's ties with the federal government might have been severed, but not with the mob. It wasn't a fraternal relationship, only a deadly, revengeful one. Nor was it profitable except potentially for his enemies.

Twenty-five men, some once his close friends and associates, had been stung by Scorpion and were languishing behind bars. There now were 25 reasons to kill him. The underworld sought its justice with a $100,000 contract on him. Its hound dogs were constantly on the prowl, seeking heroic stature in the underworld and money in their pockets.

That Jesse would be Number One on every hood's kill list was foreseen. He knew that the moment he signed on as a snitch. What he hadn't perceived was the damage he would do to the underworld in just two years.

He wreaked havoc on the mob, leaving it in chaos and demoralized. Organized crime in the traditional sense was being relegated to the trash heap of history after Jesse's ambush and the juggernaut of the FBI and U. S. Attorneys on both sides of the river.

With most of the leaders ruling from prison cells, the mob had few power bases and lucrative sources of income. Many of the construction labor unions were being cleansed of underworld influences. Those operatives who escaped the government's wrath were on their own, but suspicion possessed them. If Jesse Stoneking had been a snitch, then who else was one? Who could be trusted? Where could business be conducted away from the government's prying eyes and ears?

The streets, once a battlefield littered with broken bodies and demolished cars, were quieter and safer now. From 1962 to 1984 there had been 22 car bombings, most gang related, but by the turn of the century there were none. St. Louis lost its title of the "bomb capital" of the nation.

The Chicago and Kansas City Outfits were of little help. They, too, were in disarray. FBI wiretaps and snitches also decimated their leadership. Aiuppa, the Civella brothers and some of their operatives were either dead or under long prison sentences.

The Leisures were the catalyst that brought the downfall of organized crime. They had set out to build a powerful, ruthless criminal empire in the image of the old Capone gang, but it imploded with their own bullets, bombs and mayhem.

Had the Leisures not chased revenge, had they been prudent and discrete rather than tactless and impetuous, and had they resorted to persuasion with words and threats rather than with violence, they might today enjoy the criminal monarchy they sought. Had they not brandished their criminal virility, Jesse might not have turned into the devastating informant he was and he likely would have carried out his massacre.

It was the new life in the straight world awaiting Jesse that now occupied his thoughts and ambitions. What kind would it be? Would it be the one of comfort and serenity he envisioned? Peace of mind at last? He was in desperate need of that. He confided in me the freedom he craved.

"Tom and Terry were always telling me to be careful. They'd say, 'We got a vested interest in you, Jesse'. I said I had a bigger interest in me than they did. I told them, 'What are you guys, dummies or what? I'm done with this. The FBI doesn't own me no more. We're even. You got what you wanted'. And Tom asks, 'You got what you wanted'? I told them, 'Yeah, I'm free from you guys and everybody. I don't owe anybody anything anymore'."

For awhile, he had come out of the shadows where he lived so long and became the center of attention, the star witness, the subject of news stories. It was a tremendous ego trip. He was the mystical, sinister gangster on whom all eyes inside and outside the courtroom were focused. But the hero status he savored so much was waning, the limelight dimming. Now he welcomed that. He needed to get on with his new life, the one where no one saw or knew him.

From Source To Friend

I eventually abandoned the mandate of investigative reporting that relationship be on a professional, impersonal level. I allowed it to become personal and over time Jesse and I became close friends and confidants. He was a man who needed help returning to the Christian faith and I couldn't turn my back on him. That was as important to me as the sensational stories he gave me.

His problems at times seemed insolvable. He might elude the killers hunting him, but escaping himself seemed another matter. He didn't want to become a prisoner of his past, but at times it had a stranglehold on him.

Although not a made member of La Cosa Nostra because he wasn't of Sicilian heritage, early in his criminal career he adopted the Mafia's code of silence punishable by death and applicable to all hoodlums. He couldn't escape his belief he had violated that by committing the ultimate act of disloyalty. A paid snitch at that. I wondered if he would he be able to extinguish those false fires of shame burning in him.

It was difficult at first for him to understand and accept that God had to destroy the old, evil Jesse Stoneking to build the new one. I told him the Lord already had done the groundwork and drawn the specifications for the new, pious Jesse. The conversion now was in progress.

Jesse believed he had an equally dangerous adversary as the mob. Bohnemeier had asked him why he seemed so distrustful of most people.

"You think I trust anybody? Let me tell you something. I don't even trust my own people. Somebody in my family is trying to find out where I am."

"What's wrong with that? Sure, they would want to know where you're at. Who wants to know?"

"My father, " he said abruptly.

"So what? He's your father. He wants to help you?"

Jesse laughed sarcastically. "I haven't heard from him for so long I don't remember when the last time was." He again lapsed into silence. Bohnemeier knew he had more to tell him. He finally spoke. "There's something I never told you guys before. My father knows Art Berne's brother."

An awkward silence hung heavily. Fox tried to evaluate the threat without sounding an alarm. "How could he find out where you're at?"

"He can't. I haven't even told my mom or my sister where I'm at. It's for their own good. I call them, but they don't know where I'm calling from. I tell them I'm a thousand miles away."

Bohnemeier told him there was no immediate cause for worry. "Look, this is paranoia time for all of us."

"Yeah, but you guys aren't worth a hundred thousand dollars."

CHAPTER THIRTY-THREE

Divine Intervention

Had Jesse gone to the service station a few minutes earlier or later that Thursday in November, the chain of events that almost climaxed with his and the family's assassination would not have been set in motion.

The $100,000 contract on him came within minutes of being collected and the mob's craving for revenge satisfied. There would have been glee, instead of desperation and anger, in the prison cells his victims now called home.

There was nothing suspicious about the two men who drove into the service station lot. They were getting gas for their car as was Jesse. Their maroon Chrysler bore an Illinois license plate, but that was of little concern. Paducah, Kentucky, where Jesse was beginning his new life, was just across the state line and many Illinois motorists passed through the area.

One of the men was about Jesse's age, the other older and balding. Jesse glanced at them as he walked to the station office to pay his bill. There was an instant of recognition by the older man. Jesse didn't know him, but he for sure wasn't an outfit guy.

Jesse watched them as he paid his bill. The older man was pointing in his direction and talking excitedly to the other man. As Jesse walked outside, the older man stepped forward, grinning.

"Well, I'll be darned. Jesse Stoneking. I've been reading about you. How you been?" He extended his right hand.

Jesse couldn't acknowledge anything. "Sorry, pal. You got me mixed up with someone else."

The old man waved at Jesse as he walked away. He didn't think any more about it. They weren't a threat. He had spent many days testifying in courtrooms, often with many observers, and that obviously was how he was recognized.

It was just a few months after Jesse finished testifying. The obscurity now so necessary to survive seemed to be working, except for that minor incident at the service station. He had shed his celebrity cloak and donned one of anonymity to become a nobody. He didn't have to keep looking over his shoulder any more for that mob face from the past, a gun aimed at him.

Paducah was near where he began his flight two years earlier and where he last saw Carolee and their children. It was here he wanted to spend the rest of his life. The agents advised against that. It was too close to St. Louis, making him vulnerable. Jesse argued it was far enough from the danger zone, yet close enough to his mother with whom he wanted to mend fences and his brother to whom he had grown close.

A few nights later his older daughter returned home from visiting a friend. She ran into the living room, breathless and terrified. A maroon car with two men was parked near their house. The passenger got out and headed toward the back yard. He was carrying something she couldn't identify.

Jesse immediately ordered Dorothy and the children to the basement. He peeked out the window. It was the same car at the service station. He could see the dim outline of a man behind the steering wheel. The passenger seat was empty.

He grabbed his guardian angel from a drawer in the night stand and hurried to another bedroom where he could view the rear of the house. A man with a rifle or a shotgun was on the back porch. He was the older man at the service station. He reached for the doorknob of the kitchen door.

Jesse raced to the kitchen, knocking over a chair. Heavy footsteps ran across the porch and the man was gone. He heard the car speed off. He stayed awake that night, sitting in a chair in the darkened living room, the pistol on his lap, even though he believed they wouldn't return so soon.

It wasn't coincidental. Jesse was puzzled how they knew where he lived. He had made sure he hadn't been followed while in Paducah. Then he realized his car's license plate was registered in his cover name at his house's address. Jesse McBride now was exposed.

Bohnemeier believed they were thieves. That wasn't the way a hit comes down, he argued. "Only amateurs would do it that way."

"It's the amateurs I worry about," Jesse said.

"Maybe you ought to think about moving if you're that worried."

"No way. I'm not going to run."

Jesse knew it wasn't a heist. "No burglar would try to come into a house when the lights were on and people were inside. We lived in a poor neighborhood and most people didn't have anything worthwhile stealing. They were after me. Not anything I had. I knew what they would have done to my family, too."

"They're Going To Kill Him"

Two days later, Bohnemeier took a call in his office from a woman, her voice hesitating. "I heard my boyfriend and another man talking the other night. They said they knew where Jesse Stoneking is and they are going to kill him. Shoot him for what he did and get the reward money."

"Where did you hear them say this?" Bohnemeier asked.

"What difference does that make?" she asked, her voice tensing.

Bohnemeier couldn't lose her now. "It could be important, ma'm. What exactly did they say?"

"I told you. They're going to kill him. They said they tried before, but it went bad."

"Did they say where he lived?" he asked cautiously..

"They knew the exact address. I heard the other man say it, but I don't remember. It was in Paducah, Kentucky."

"Give me a description of the men, ma'm. Their names."

The phone went dead. Bohnemeier would have passed it off as a crank call if she hadn't said Paducah and they had tried before. It was cause for alarm. He called Jesse. There was a long silence as Jesse pondered what he was told. The security he had built around himself and his family had been penetrated so quickly. There wasn't the safety in Paducah he had thought. Would there be anywhere?

Bohnemeier suggested Jesse move his family. He now didn't have a choice. He reluctantly agreed to relocate, but he wouldn't go far. He and his family moved to a small community in southern Illinois about 150 miles from the East Side where he once again hoped they would be safe. It was remote and not near any major highway where travelers might see him.

Over time, Jesse understood why he escaped death. It wasn't merely good fortune. Lady Luck hadn't smiled on him and given him a free pass. It was Divine intervention. God had saved him and his loved ones.

Jesse recalled what he had learned at church and reading the Bible as a youngster. "I remembered them talking about God running your life and taking care of you all the time. I thought that makes sense. Wasn't that what God was really all about? But then, I got to thinking, 'Jesse, what makes you think God's will take care of you of all people'? That's when I thought I could take care of myself. Now I know how wrong I was. God was taking care of me."

Prince To Pauper

Jesse's new life in the straight world came at a high cost. The evolution from the shadowy, intoxicating life of crime to the one of legitimacy he once scorned but now was so appealing was more challenging and painful than he had anticipated. Now he saw how distorted and destructive was the sophistication of the underworld that lured him there. The elegance he once savored was fantasy and so addictive.

He didn't regret leaving all that behind, but changing course wasn't as easy as just crossing the street to the other side. He made an irrevocable mistake walking out of the Witness Protection Program so soon. The marshals abandoned him, throwing him to the wolves and forcing him to fend for himself.

He had sat in the lap of luxury for many years, relishing the intoxicating sweet smell of success, driven by the insatiable craving for more and better material things. But now, as God was cleansing him, he was hunkered down on the cold, barren floor of indigence and broken dreams. The prince of crime was a pauper.

Prosperity once the foundation of his life had evaporated. The extravagance he had cherished was replaced by the bitter pangs of destitution. He was near dead broke and friendless. He drove inexpensive, older cars. The gourmet dinners in fashionable restaurants were replaced with macaroni and cheese out of a box in cheap, rented houses. He barely was able to feed his family, a blow to his pride. Instead of the thousands of dollars of spending cash he once carried, now all he had was pocket change.

He had to make sacrifices that before were alien, even humorous. He sold his expensive jewelry for cents on the dollar, the ultimate humiliation. Gone, too, was his guardian angel that accompanied him for so long. It brought him some money, but his vow to God of peace instead of violence precluded even owning a weapon. That was a condition of his parole to God.

The intrigue he once wove so deftly now was his nemesis. The power he had possessed and the prestige his money and reputation brought him now were a Sword of Damocles hanging over his head, ready to wreak retribution on him.

All that bred increasing uncertainty about his future. Not knowing whether tomorrow would bring promise or catastrophe, hope or fear, was draining his soul and his willpower. In what kind of bed would he lie next week? A year from now? Would he even have a bed? He had been a survivor, but now he wondered how long he could last in this alien world.

There were no legitimate jobs requiring a hoodlum's skills and talents. Crime and violence were his only qualifications. He had no credible references other than gangsters he had betrayed and who wanted him dead.

Jesse's health seemed to be failing. His doctor suspected his spine was deteriorating and there might be a malignancy. Costly tests and treatment were needed, but he had no insurance or money to pay for them. Welfare was unavailable because Jesse McBride didn't exist in official records. His past life under that name couldn't be confirmed because there was none. He had left the Witness Protection Program before it could be completed.

In desperation, Jesse drifted back to the fringes of crime, hustling cheap jewelry and counterfeit Rolex watches. His street jargon and smarts were a magnet. Street punks and petty thieves sensed his knowledge of crime and gravitated to him. He began fencing their stolen goods. For awhile he earned enough money to take care of his family's needs, but the stigma became intolerable.

I suspected his new life was falling apart or perhaps he was dismantling it. He explained: "I didn't care anymore. I was back where I used to be. Fate was playing those terrible games with me again. I had to keep fencing because I needed the money. It was all I had. I knew it was dragging me back to my old life, but what was I to do? I kept telling myself it wasn't like I was stealing. But deep down I knew there wasn't any difference."

God At Work

I encouraged Jesse to talk about the necessity of faith in God. I wanted to comfort him as tactfully as I could without sermonizing. A preacher I certainly wasn't. He wondered why God allowed him to have such bad times when he was trying so desperately to go straight.

He said after he returned from Boston he bought a Bible and stayed up late at night studying it. He attended church services regularly and talked with church leaders. Prayer now was becoming a part of his daily life. He was finding the answers to some of the questions disturbing him.

Jesse conceded God sometimes rescues us by chastening and strengthening us with adversities to get our attention. He said the Bible told him with pain comes hope and faith and He wants us to reach out to Him for help. I told him I knew that from personal experience.

I suggested God likely was replacing the material things to which he had been addicted, the idols of his former life, with His riches, the divine, eternal ones. To survive, he must build his faith on the solid rocks of God's words, not on the shifting sands of his own wisdom.

Jesse said Jesus told him about that in Matthew. "It says right there in the sixth chapter what you got to do. It says you got to get rid of all that stuff." He closed his eyes and began quoting the passages from memory. "'Do not lay up for yourselves treasures upon earth, where moth and rust destroy, and where thieves break in and steal. But lay up for yourselves treasures in heaven, where neither moth nor rust destroys, and where thieves do not break in or steal; for where your treasure is there will your heart be also'."

He laughed. "I don't have any treasures to get rid of. God's already taken them from me."

Jesse's surely seemed to be heading in the right direction. That he could quote such Bible passages from memory was proof positive. I sensed he had found peace of mind that before was illusive. He said he now realized he had to totally hand over his life to God. He made a mess of it by himself because he was his own worst enemy. I told him I would help him however I could, but God was the only real source of assistance and comfort.

God came to Jesse's rescue. The FBI gave him a $30,000 bonus. It was the last money he was to get from the government. It was just in time. He had only a few hundred dollars.

Jesse got to know his neighbors. They were simple people whose lives seemed uncomplicated. They were suspicious at first of this stranger who suddenly appeared in their midst. He wasn't like them and his ways were those of the big city, his sophistication out of place. He told them he was from the East Coast and had gotten tired of that lifestyle

It seemed to be the sanctuary he needed to begin his new life. Perhaps at last he would find security there.

A neighbor gave him part of that, a pit bull named "Duke." It became Jesse's constant companion and his body guard. It went on full alert when a stranger came near his master, standing rigidly in front and growling. It was a symbol of what Jesse once was.

CHAPTER THIRTY-FOUR

Family As Ransom

Because of my affiliation with Jesse Stoneking, I came within minutes of being forced to decide who would die - he or my daughter and infant granddaughter. I was unaware murder was lurking so nearby until one morning early in 1988 when it came calling in disguise.

After almost four years of stalking Jesse, the mob's attack dogs finally were closing in on their prey. Their ravenous appetite for revenge and the $100,000 bounty on his head finally would be satisfied. His debt to the underworld would be paid in full, reparations made with his blood.

By then, the kill squads apparently had run out of leads and had no trails to follow. No one had come close to finding Jesse except the amateurs who tried to whack him in Paducah and failed, but then he had disappeared. There was no trace of him anywhere.

Except through me. I was their best - maybe their only - opportunity to find Jesse.

It was by chance I learned of the plot to use me to find him. Only I didn't know it would involve the life-or-death situation. A Post-Dispatch employee wanted to talk to me privately the day before. The tone of his voice suggested it was about something serious. I assumed he had a tip about a potential story, but that wasn't what he wanted to tell me. It was more personal.

As he placed a bet with a mob bookmaker that morning, he overheard a man he knew was a gangster talking about me. He was discussing my stories based on interviews with Jesse and the $100,000 contract on him. I surely knew where he was, the hoodlum insisted. He hinted they intended to use me to find him, but he didn't say how.

I was to meet Jesse the next day. Would we both be walking into a trap with the mob killing two birds with one stone? The hit men no doubt would open fire the moment they saw him. No talking. No negotiations. They wouldn't kill him in my presence and let me live. Witnesses weren't left behind. Besides, I wasn't looked upon with friendly eyes by the underworld. Good riddance of that nuisance!

Another question haunted me. Were they aware of the meeting and if so how did they find out? Only two editors knew of it and I trusted them. Perhaps the mob was unaware of the meeting and it just was coincidental. I didn't believe much in coincidences, but I accepted that possibility.

Perhaps my home telephone was bugged. I communicated with Jesse from home and not the office because I feared the calls there could be monitored and his number recorded. During an earlier investigation of police corruption, my home phone was tapped by a ranking police official.

Two police intelligence detectives were concerned I was being watched. One warned me, "Don't stop looking over your shoulder, buddy. You know how these mob guys are. They'll take you out if they need to. You're not exactly a hero with them."

There was one way to find out if the mobsters were watching me. The detectives followed me as I drove from downtown 30 miles into the far southwestern suburbs. There was no mobile surveillance of me. There would be no need for the hoods to tail me today if they knew of my meeting with Jesse. They would do it tomorrow.

I called Jesse from a public telephone and canceled the meeting. I told him why. He was concerned about my welfare. His wasn't an issue. He had been dodging the mob's kill squads for a long time now.

Ransom Time

I was late for work the next morning. My wife already had left. Our daughter and granddaughter, just one year old, who lived with us were in the kitchen. As I was leaving, the telephone in the kitchen rang. I thought about letting my daughter answer it, but I did instead. It might be the office calling.

The male caller spoke hesitatingly. He said the dishwasher would be delivered between 10 and 11 o'clock that morning and gave our address. It almost was 9 o'clock. He seemed surprised when I answered and hung up before I could respond. We hadn't ordered any appliances. I called the store he said sold the appliance. It confirmed no delivery to anyone with my name at any address in our subdivision or anywhere nearby was scheduled for that day.

Something was wrong. I wasn't paranoid and I considered it a threat. It was well known our daughter and granddaughter lived with us and were alone in the house during weekdays while my wife and I were at work. The detectives assumed it was an attempt to kidnap them and hold them hostage to force me to disclose Jesse's whereabouts. I didn't dispute that.

The telephone call likely was to confirm our daughter and her child were there alone when she answered. It also would induce her to respond to a knock on the door, believing it was the delivery. My wife and I parked our cars inside the garage and it wouldn't be known if they were gone as there were no windows. Watching the house in a residential neighborhood could expose them. Surprise had to be a key element in the abduction.

The kidnapers probably would have grabbed their hostages as soon as it was confirmed they were alone. When I answered the telephone they assumed I would be home that day and they couldn't pull it off. I was curious why the caller didn't just say he had the wrong number when I answered. That would have aroused no suspicion. What was most frightening was kidnap victims not always are released alive, regardless if the ransom is paid. They could identify those who snatched them.

I took our daughter and granddaughter to a friend's home for the day. Detectives casually watched our house, but no one came there. The kidnapping apparently had been aborted.

I didn't take my usual route to the office downtown. There was the possibility I would be followed. I drove circuitously and occasionally made sudden turns into side streets without signaling. I had no tail. I did the same returning home that evening. I was convinced the hit team was unaware of my meeting with Jesse. Had they known they merely would have followed me when I left home and wouldn't have bothered setting up the kidnapping.

The decision I would have been forced to make was paralyzing. I certainly wouldn't have allowed our daughter and granddaughter to be killed if I could stop it. But then I essentially would have signed Jesse's death warrant. That would have haunted me and tormented me for the rest of my life. Fortunately, the door had been slammed shut on murder that came calling on me that day.

A newspaper editor offered to have a bodyguard escort me for several days, but I declined. A loaded semi-automatic pistol was in my briefcase. It was illegal to carry a concealed weapon then, but I had to under the circumstances.

The True Protector

This was one more proof of Divine protection. God was the bodyguard protecting my family and Jesse from tragedy. In this crisis, as in all others, He interceded in His usual method. He was why I was late leaving for work. He made me answer the telephone. He was why the newspaper employee overheard the conversation. He was why the kidnapping didn't happen. He wouldn't allow it. What better guardian can one have?

I described God's intervention to Jesse. He wrote several Bible passages on a piece of paper and handed it to me. That night I looked up the Bible verses. One was from the book of Samuel in which David describes his near-death experience and how God helped him.

"For the waves of death encompassed me; the torrents of destruction overwhelmed me; the cords of Sheol surrounded me; the snares of death confronted me." (22: 5-6)

David didn't panic and run and hide. He asked God for help.

"In my distress I called upon the Lord, yes, I cried to my God; and from His temple He heard my voice, and my cry for help came into His ears. He delivered me from my strong enemy, from those who hated me, for they were too strong for me. They confronted me in the day of my calamity, but the Lord was my support." (22: 7, 18-19)

In First Chronicles, David passed his wisdom on to his son, instructing him to trust only in God when threatened.

"Then David said to his son Solomon, 'Be strong and courageous, and act; do not fear nor be dismayed, for the Lord God, my God, is with you. He will not fail you nor forsake you until all the work for the services of the house of the Lord is finished'." (29: 20)

Jesse obviously had read those Bible passages and understood their message of reliance on God. I hoped he would practice what they told him. In times of trouble that might lie ahead, not to rely totally on God surely would increase his peril.

CHAPTER THIRTY-FIVE

A Judas Kiss

For reasons Jesse at first couldn't understand, he suddenly was the center of attention in the small Illinois town where he believed he had anonymity and safety. And he now was a stranger to his new friends.

"It was a parade in front of my house, people driving by and gawking. Pick-up trucks, cars, kids on bicycles. Even motorcycles. Nobody talked to me anymore. One man had offered to loan me money to help pay my bills, but then he refused. I was supposed to work for another guy. Instead, he spent the whole day taking me around town, kind of showing me off."

But to Jesse, his one true friend remained loyal. Mark Stram showed up a few days earlier. He and I were the only persons other than Fox and Bohnemeier who knew his location. Jesse was elated. They hadn't seen each other for more than two years, although they stayed in telephone contact. Stram and his wife were roaming around the country. Jesse wondered if they were on the run from something or someone.

The agents had warned Jesse not to trust him. He scoffed at them. They had been together too long and had been through too much for any distrust to come between them. They were soul brothers and once crime comrades.

Still, Jesse was concerned about Stram. He wasn't the carefree guy he used to be, joking and teasing. He was preoccupied and moody, rarely looking Jesse in the eye and then only fleetingly. It was as if he was embarrassed or deeply concerned about something. He angrily denied to Jesse he was using drugs.

He was even more indignant when Jesse asked if he was doing any scores. Jesse told him it was time to walk away from crime if he already hadn't and begin an honorable life. Stram insisted he had gone straight. Jesse wanted to believe him because he never had caught him in a lie, but now he wasn't sure.

Stram's frequent trips to St. Louis also concerned Jesse. The mob was in chaos, but it still had shooters and he also might be on everybody's hit list. But he could be worth more alive than dead. The price of forgiveness for the little damage he had done would be high: his life exchanged for Jesse's whereabouts. How much pressure and physical abuse could he endure? How solid was he? What price disloyalty? Was that why he showed up? They were ugly thoughts Jesses needed to suppress.

A Friend In Greed

Stram stayed several days and left as suddenly as he arrived. He didn't tell Jesse where he was going. It was then the cavalcade by his house began. It soon got worse. Sheriff's cars were in the area more often, driving slowly by his house. He wasn't concerned at first. Their presence offered protection. The last time he saw so many police cars in his neighborhood was before he was arrested in 1981.

Jesse's curiosity grew when an unmarked car with two casually dressed men parked in the morning within sight of his house and then followed him when he left. They weren't hit men. They were too obvious. They had to be cops.

That was too much. Jesse reacted the only way he knew. He confronted the sheriff. He told Jesse they were looking for Stram. He had been questioned earlier and they needed to talk to him again, but he couldn't be found. Officers had seen him with Jesse. The sheriff said Stram told them they had been partners in crime.

Jesse insisted they were friends, but not partners. The sheriff showed him a photograph of the two of them together at Jesse's house deputies had taken. As he continued denying their partnership, the sheriff showed him newspaper clippings about his undercover escapades.

"Big city gangsters aren't welcome in my county, Stoneking," the sheriff told him in no uncertain terms.

His cover as Jesse McBride again was blown. Too many emotions - fear, hatred, confusion and emptiness - slammed into him as he drove home. A dozen questions screamed at him, one the loudest of all: "Had Mark come in on me? I didn't want to even think about that. He was the only real friend I had. But how else would the cops have known about me? There was no one to connect me to my real name. It had to be Mark. He double-crossed me."

Jesse had been betrayed by his best friend he had trusted with his life. He was fully exposed now and everyone in town probably knew it. Jesse was stunned but not furious.

Jesse couldn't hate Stram. Vengeance no longer was a virtue, a compelling emotion, for him. After all, he had been a snitch and had brought trouble and discontent into many lives, even though justifiably. Not long ago he would have killed Stram for such disloyalty, a matter of honor. But now forgiveness was paramount.

"Those cops must have had something on him, maybe dealing drugs. I guess he agreed to spy on me and then he took off. If they had caught him dirty they wouldn't have let him go unless he snitched. I did the same thing when I got busted. I turned and came in on my good friends."

What Jesse hadn't comprehended was the nature of a small country town. There were few secrets among its people. Gossip was a way of rural life, a diversion from boredom, the news media of the community. Especially if law enforcement divulged a juicy tidbit. Like a big time hoodlum living in their midst. That encouraged suspicion, fear and chatter.

As Jesse related his forgiveness, my trust in him, already at a high level, increased. Would I have granted clemency to someone who betrayed me like that? I experienced that in my professional life and it took me a long time to forgive and forget. He did it quickly.

Over time, Jesse slipped back into despondency, this time more crippling. Was he giving up his struggle for spiritual survival? Had he convinced himself he was beyond help or salvation? Had he surrendered to Satan and given up on God helping him? Those possibilities troubled me.

As we talked over the next months, he unsealed more secrets of his criminal life to me, some of them quite horrifying. I assumed this was his way of purging his soul, but there were other, more current issues confronting him.

A Breath Of Death

The new year 1988 offered little encouragement for Jesse. He still had no full-time job. His finances again were dwindling. By summer he would be broke. It was a continuing struggle he had with himself. And with God. He insisted he still was clinging to God for help, but it appeared he might be losing his grip. His life was a yo-yo, up to a new high, down to a new low. Then he told me just how far down he had gone.

"Things weren't working out. Everything was getting messed up. The peace of mind I thought I'd have wasn't there. I didn't have much money, no friends, nothing. I felt sorry for myself. Guilty about what I was doing to my family. Not being able to take care of them. I was a total failure. I didn't want a lot of money. I just wanted to get by. Where was God? I prayed a lot but God didn't seem to be listening to me. I wondered if He had forgotten about me.

"The Bible says Jesus died so my sins would be forgiven, but I figured I was being punished for mine. I talked to Him about that a lot. God wasn't letting me forget them. My life was over as far as I was concerned. What was there to live for? God was playing terrible games with me again. How can you beat those odds? It's a loser."

Jesse drove north and when he got near the East Side he called the FBI office. Fox had just retired and Bohnemeier was out. Jesse met with another agent, Don Taylor, and handed him an envelope, telling him not to open it until that night. Taylor unsealed it as Jesse drove off. It was a suicide note! Jesse was going to kill himself. There was no way Taylor could stop him.

To Jesse, suicide was honorable, the only way out of his crushing failures. The world and his loved ones would be better off without him. They might miss him for awhile, but not for long, and then he only would be a memory, a bad one at that. He would give them a new life free of the troubles he brought them.

He drove to a deserted country road and parked with the engine running. He sat and thought for a few minutes. Freeing himself of these burdens of the past and the present soothed his troubled mind. Asphyxiation was the best way, quick and neat, a painless death. No blood splatters to clean up. No head blown apart. It was his way of atonement, answering for his sinful past life. It probably was what God wanted, he thought.

He took a six-foot length of vacuum hose from the trunk. He put one end in the exhaust pipe and secured it with tape. He rolled down the rear window on the driver's side a few inches, pushed the other end of the hose inside and closed the window until the hose was securely in place.

He sat behind the steering wheel. He could smell the exhaust fumes. In just a few moments his problems would be solved. He leaned the back of his head on the head rest and closed his eyes, ready to die. Then a strange sensation came over him.

"I really can't describe it. I kept asking myself, 'What are you doing'? I realized what a stupid jerk I was. I turned the engine off and opened the door. I prayed like I never did before. I got to tell you, I cried. Jesse Stoneking crying? That wasn't supposed to ever happen. Well, God answered me. He told me to quiet down and stop this nonsense. He helped me right there on the spot. I know that for a fact."

Taylor called Fox. They suspected the suicide threat was Jesse's way of seeking sympathy, but they couldn't ignore he might be serious. Fox waited until early in the evening to give Jesse enough time to get home before calling him. Dorothy answered. He asked for Jesse and held his breath. If he wasn't there he probably was dead. She said she would get him.

Jesse's despair was evident to Fox. They met the next afternoon in a restaurant in Mt. Vernon east of the metropolitan area. Fox hadn't seen him for some time and he was shocked at the broken, defeated man. The swagger was gone and he shuffled. Once robust and erect, he now was gaunt and stoop-shouldered. His hair was speckled with gray and his face was eroded with deep wrinkles.

Fox was puzzled about the encounter with the sheriff. Jesse said nothing about Stram. "No idea how it happened?" Fox probed.

"Yeah, I got an idea, but I can't prove it."

"Mark Stram?" Fox asked.

"I don't want to talk about it."

"You have to, Jesse. Get it all out. Let me help you."

Jesse told him everything. When he finished, his eyes glistened. Fox always had thought he was incapable of shedding tears. "I don't see that you have much choice," Fox said bluntly. It was the best way to deal with Jesse.

"I don't know what to think anymore. What to do. It's all over with, isn't it?"

"It's only over if you say it is, Jesse. Now, I'm going to tell you what you have to do, not what you want to hear. Get out now! Walk away from it. You've been set up. Go home and get Dorothy and the kids. Pack up and leave. And never go back."

Jesse nodded his head. He understood all too clearly.

"And I don't mean tomorrow or the next day," Fox continued. "Tonight! Do it late so no one sees you."

"Where will I go. I don't have any money left?"

"As far as you can go." He paused. "I almost forgot the good news. I talked with the people in the Belleville office and they're going to get you a few thousand dollars. You should have it the day after tomorrow. One other thing. Stay away from Mark. Don't tell him where you're at. It's obvious he came in on you."

Jesse now felt unburdened, elated for the first time in months. "I couldn't believe it. Out of the clear blue sky I got the answer I had been praying for. God had come through after all. I was going to get out of this mess in one piece. Jesse Stoneking, you just got a new life."

Jesse told Dorothy everything and she was understanding. It was with a new excitement they packed their few belongings. They would leave the furniture behind. It wasn't worth much. Neither talked about their hopes for the future. There were no plans beyond that day.

They would go wherever intuition took them. It first would take them back to St. Louis. Jesse had to see his mother and try to mend the differences, the animosity that had alienated them for so many years. It was then he almost reaped what he had sown and barely escaped assassination.

My heart was troubled, as Jesse told me about his attempt to end his life. How could a man who had such strong, although sometimes misdirected, inner strength sink so deeply into self-degradation and despair? I knew he was sincere and wasn't he faking it to gain my sympathy? Never would he lie about something that made him appear so weak.

At least, Jesse knew where to go in a time of great trouble. Instead of leaping over the precipice of life into the depths of death, at the last moment he held his hand out to God, who rescued him. What a lesson that must have been for him, one he would remember the rest of his life, I thought.

I suggested to Jesse the Lord probably took him so near death to break his resistance and then reclaimed him. That was why He didn't let him die. Perhaps God wasn't finished cleansing him. Jesse didn't disagree.

A Prisoner of Paranoia

I was sure Jesse would be engaged in more battles in his war with himself. It was becoming obvious he still hadn't buried his terrible past and was allowing it to command his new life.

His former criminal life seemed to becoming a terrible burden. Stealing and swindling would be enough of an encumbrance, but could he ever erase the memories of his violent side? He might have ambiguously admitted killing Don Ellington as a way of cleansing his conscience and described in detail the attempted hit on Hickey to satisfy his vanity, but were those memories still punishing him? Was his conscience taking control?

How many murders had he actually committed? How much blood had he caused to be spilled? How many tears were shed because of him? Did he envision the carnage his massacre would have wreaked? Men he knew screaming in agony as they died, their blood gushing from them? Were the memories of his conflicts with Carolee and the disappearance of that family haunting him, punishing him? Were the panic-stricken eyes of Manion and the dope dealer he beat up for Kowalski staring back at him?

Were his words - "Yeah, that's the way you become a man. By cracking people"- echoing in his mind like thunder? Pointing an accusing finger at him? Did killing not make a man of him in the end, but a wimp?

It wouldn't be easy for Jesse, or anyone, for that matter, to overcome all of that without God's assistance. No longer was he a man to be feared, but a man who feared himself. He apparently was beating himself up over his past. He was a breeding ground for paranoia when he opened up to me about what he feared would happen to him.

He feared that stranger who suddenly appeared in his life might be the executioner he assumed lurked nearby? Would there be a sudden crack of a gun the instant he died or the deafening roar and consuming fire when the bomb detonated under his car? Maybe the police officers he saw were hit men in disguise. They had a license to kill, just as he had years earlier when he was a cop. Was there anyone in his life he could trust now? The chilling reality came to him that he was not immune from death, that it was as certain as the sunrise. Maybe tomorrow's.

Jesse's words, his face and his gestures reflected his mental torment. We all entertain paranoia at times. It is a crack in the armor of faith the Lord provides us. Satan wants us to entertain delusions and become fearful because that separates us from God. He obviously was becoming captive of his conscience that was putting him in a strait jacket of shame over deeds long past so he no longer could not think or act freely. I was concerned whether he could cast it aside and live his life in peace with himself and with God or if it eventually would do him in

Jesse asked me what I thought were his problems. I wasn't sure I wanted to explore that. I wasn't a counselor or a psychologist and didn't want to be. I tried to answer him simply, in a way he could comprehend, without being accusatory. I said it was a matter of where he wanted to live - in the darkness of his sinful past or in the bright light of Jesus' forgiveness today. He shouldn't let his conscience dictate his present life, but he should learn from it so as not to repeat past sins.

I eventually could tell Jesse still was sincerely struggling to return to God and walk the right path. But he had done that before, only to turn in the opposite direction.

God's word is a telescope through which to see the real truth, especially about ourselves. Jesse said he now was reading the Bible from cover to cover. I had no reason to doubt that. He could quote more Bible passages than a preacher. Sometimes he walked into the desert night and talked to God. He attended church services. My heart rejoiced for him. I hoped he was looking forward and not backward.

He called me one night. He was excited. He had made a monumental decision. This one, he said, also was written in stone. "I've decided I'll just put my life and all my problems in God's hands. For sure this time. Definitely. What do I have to lose? I've made a mess of my life and I finally realize I can't do myself any good anymore. I mean, who else can I turn to? Now I'm free."

"Congratulations, Jesse," I said. "I'm proud of you."

"I know I screwed up a lot, haven't I"

I laughed. "If you have ten or twelve hours to kill, I'll tell you all the times I have."

"This time, it's for good. I mean it. Trust me."

Even though Jesse's faith was uplifted, I detected he still was struggling with his past. He said he still had to keep looking over his shoulder because there always was someone waiting to do him in one way or another. What happened after he left his mother's house proved that.

I urged him not to worry. I didn't believe there was anyone in Arizona where he now lived who knew about his past who would come in on him. I didn't know how wrong I was.

CHAPTER THIRTY-SIX

Suicide By Cop

Without warning, two uniformed police officers barged into the room, their hands on their service revolvers in their holsters, ready to take Jesse down if they had to. They knew who he was and how dangerous he could be.

Jesse was confused, then angered. He wasn't a threat to anyone, least of all his wife, Dorothy, in the hospital bed nearby or his son standing by the window.

"You're not supposed to be here, Stoneking," one of the officers said. He stepped toward Jesse. The other officer stood in the doorway.

"What are you talking about?" Jesse growled, glaring at the officers.

"You're violating the restraining order, Stoneking. You aren't supposed to come near your wife. We know who you really are. A gangster. We're taking you into custody."

"How'd you know I was here? Who I am?"

"It doesn't matter. You're where you're not supposed to be."

Jesse lost it. Police in Arizona knew his true identity! How could that be? And he hadn't done anything wrong. He assumed it was his time to die. Even if it was suicide.

He pulled the .22 caliber pistol from his back trouser pocket. Dorothy stifled a scream. His son crouched.

"This is it. I'm ready to die," he shouted at the patrolmen, moving away from Dorothy's bed.

The officers froze. Jesse pointed the revolver at the nearest one and then at the other. They slowly removed their hands from their pistols and held them up to show they weren't resisting. They backed out of the doorway into the hallway.

Jesse heard one of the officers talking, but he couldn't make out what was being said. He assumed he was talking on his radio or a telephone. "The next thing I know the place was full of cops. They got their guns drawn. They're aimed at me. The cops cuffed me. I felt like a fool. This isn't the way I was anymore. That just wasn't me. I knew I blew it big time. They were going to book me and I'd have to do time. I didn't want my wife to see me like that."

Fear seized Jesse as officers led him handcuffed out of the hospital. Was he going to jail or somewhere else where he would be killed? Did a fate worse than a prison sentence await him? At first, he assumed the police had tailed him. How else would they know he was there? But why did they follow him? Perhaps his worst fear about a hidden enemy was coming true. How else would they know his background? Were they officers of revenge, not of the law? Maybe his paranoia was reality after all.

Another Judas Kiss

Jesse's arrest wasn't a hit coming down. He was booked and released on bond. The next day he learned why he was arrested and his world came crashing down on him. His son confessed and implicated his sister. Once again, Jesse was a victim of treachery by someone close to him.

His son said because they feared him, knowing he had the pistol, they believed he intended to kill his mother. Jesse and Dorothy were separated and she had obtained a restraining order preventing him from coming near her, claiming he was a threat. Insisting he never harmed her, intended to or made any threats, he filed suit for divorce.

His son accompanied him to the hospital. He stayed outside while Jesse went inside and called his sister, telling her to summon police. She not only told them he was going to kill her mother but he was a notorious hoodlum and killer from St. Louis. Dorothy confirmed that to police.

Jesse brought Dorothy a get-well card and a bouquet of flowers as a good will gesture. He wanted to try to reconcile their differences and resume their marital relationship. The .22 in his pocket was for a friend, but he had forgotten to leave it in his car.

This was betrayal far worse than by Stram. His own children were traitors. He could understand why they erroneously believed he intended to harm their mother and maybe forgive them for that. But why did his daughter tell the police about his past? That was unforgivable. Did she also tell them about the good he had done as an undercover informant? He knew she hadn't.

Jesse had tried to bury his evil past, but now it had been yanked out of the closet and exposed for all to see. His shallow cover identity was worthless. There was no more Jesse McBride. Only the real Jesse Stoneking. His paranoia was becoming reality, just as he knew it would one day. Maybe it was an omen of worse times to come. He was tired of fighting it. He gave up once again.

"I didn't care what happened to me then. Even if I went to the pen. Even if it was suicide. Or I got hit. I mean, when your kids come in on you like that! Like that guy in the Bible, Judas. I could maybe understand my wife telling them, but my own children? My own flesh and blood? If you can't trust them, who can you trust? I still loved them, but I didn't want to have anything to do with them anymore. I figured that's how they wanted it, anyhow."

Out Of Reach

The confrontation was why Jesse suddenly went missing for a year. He was serving time in the infamous - or famous, depending how you look at it - Maricopa County Jail in Arizona. There was not a trace of him. Only I didn't know why.

After a month of silence, I tried to call him, but the telephone number no longer was in service. I was worried. Was he fleeing from something or someone, real or imagined? Maybe his conscience still tormented him. Where was Dorothy? She must be with him. Perhaps they were just roaming around the country on an extended vacation.

The last time I talked to him was not long before he disappeared. He didn't tell me about his arrest, but I detected he again was on the roller coaster careening downward. He was more delusional than before. Peril was everywhere and there still were past and current enemies plotting to do him in. Despite being deeply troubled, he insisted he was holding fast to his trust in God.

Jesse finally called me after more than a year. I asked him where he had been. "I've just been hanging around," was all he said. He was upbeat, chuckling and teasing, but I sensed his cheerful demeanor was false. Was he hiding something tragic or embarrassing?

I flew to Arizona to see him a month after the tragedy of September 11, 2001. He was his gracious, generous self, permitting me to pay for nothing, even my motel room. The roller coaster seemed to be heading back upward and his faith had taken hold again, this time hopefully more securely. St. Paul was a role model, second only to Jesus. He read all his epistles several times and was quick to quote from them.

He likened himself to Paul, once a non-believer and an unrepentant sinner who harmed people. Jesus came into Paul's life and turned him around. That's what Jesse believed the Savior was doing with him. What made Paul so captivating was he always told the truth regardless of his adversities and circumstances. Jesse said that was what he had to do with me and then he told me about the confrontation in the hospital.

I asked if it was another attempt to take his own life, this time suicide by cops. He didn't deny that. There was a benefit in the prison sentence, he said. The year in jail gave him time to thaw the ice in his heart and replace it with forgiveness. "Like Jesus tells you to do, I forgave my children in my heart. If He could forgive that thief on the cross next to him who didn't do anything to Him, I guess I could forgive them."

Jesse then told me of his planned massacre. I was astonished. Why had he disclosed that 20 years later? Could he be so troubled by almost killing that many men he had to get it off his chest? I had to believe that was at least a partial motive.

I couldn't help but wonder if that was his first lie to me. His eyes and his speech didn't suggest he was being untruthful. I doubted he would have contrived something as atrocious as that. To make sure he wasn't lying, I later twice asked him to go over it. Every detail was exactly the same, not one variation. I knew he hadn't fabricated it.

A Curious Friendship

Jesse's divorce petition was granted while he was behind bars. When he was released, he was alone in the world. No friends, no wife, no home. Little to look forward to, still much to look back at.

He preferred the simple life - all he knew now - and he rented a mobile home. He befriended a man named Howard, not his real name, and let him and his son live with him. A number of items, including collectibles, were stolen from Jesse. Had they done that to the old Jesse they might have lived another hour. If they were that lucky. The new Jesse read to them from the Bible as punishment.

Howard was a homosexual and had been arrested for related offenses. A bit sarcastically, I asked Jesse about him. I was concerned he might have gone to that lifestyle. His explanation was a bit surprising. He said he hoped he could turn Howard around and convert him to a Christian.

"You know what it says in the Bible about that?"

"Tell me," I said, challenging him.

"Well, it says you got to forgive the sinner and condemn the sin." He chuckled. "That simple."

"Then I suppose those hoods back in St. Louis should forgive you."

"That'll be the day."

"Have you forgiven them yet?"

He grinned and rolled his eyes. "What do you think? How could I believe in Jesus if I didn't?"

My admiration for Jesse increased. In his earlier days, he wouldn't have tolerated homosexuals, least of all shared his residence with one. And he obviously still was studying the Bible.

Jesse moved to Chester, Illinois, not far south of the metropolitan area. Howard accompanied him. I wondered why he chose to live so near the metropolitan area that still should be considered dangerous. He didn't explain. We stood on the sundeck of the small house he rented. In the distance was the Illinois Maximum Security Penitentiary at Menard. He chuckled and said he should be living there instead as a free man.

Jesse said he had been diagnosed with colon cancer. He couldn't seek treatment because, as before, he had no medical insurance and he still couldn't get indigent coverage. I told him even the poorest could receive medical treatment of some kind. He replied he would have to use his real name and that surely would get him killed. I said his true identity already was known. He just shrugged his shoulders.

His voice and his eyes didn't conceal the distress still gnawing at him. Was he again trying to take his life, this time suicide by disease? His attitude seemed indifferent, but I could tell it was false. Fear was beginning to dominate him.

He left after a few months and called me in the spring of 2002. He didn't say where he was. The caller identification on my telephone showed he was using a cell phone. He seemed despondent, almost desperate. I suggested he come back to the St. Louis area so we could talk. He laughed but it was flimsy and tentative. "There's nothing there for me anymore."

I started to ask him what he meant, but he said, "Goodbye, my good friend," and hung up. I thought I heard a slight sob. There was a hint of finality in his words. To this day, they remain in my mind as if he was speaking them now.

Then, he again disappeared. I suspected he once more was fleeing his past, but was he running fast enough? And did he have the necessary endurance to see it through?

I tried to reach him for several weeks, but I couldn't. I decided to wait for him to call me. It was to be a long wait.

CHAPTER THIRTY-SEVEN

Die By The Sword

S hortly before 10 o'clock Sunday night, January 19, 2003, Jesse stopped running from his past. The demons chasing him for so long finally caught up with him and he surrendered, no longer able - or wanting - to resist them. Paranoia became reality, as he feared it would.

He was driving Howard's car near Surprise, Arizona, not far from his home in Wickenburg. He couldn't avoid debris in the road and a tire went flat. Several other vehicles also were disabled.

As a sheriff's squad car approached, its red and blue lights flashing, Jesse apparently believed his worst fears finally were coming true. The officer was the executioner he had been expecting. He told Howard what to do.

"Police are here," he said calmly. "Don't be scared. They're after me. Just do what they say. They're going to tell you to put your hands on your head and lay on the ground. Do what they tell you."

Howard got out of the car. He was confused. Why should he do that? The officer was there to help, not to arrest or kill. Why didn't Jesse talk to the officer? He was driving.

As Howard and the deputy talked, a gunshot cracked in the night. They found Jesse slumped over in the seat, blood flowing from a wound in his head. His right hand rested on a .38 caliber revolver. It was Howard's gun, but he didn't know Jesse had it.

I was stunned, then heartbroken, the next day when I learned what happened. A close friend was gone, never to be seen. My respect for him didn't lessen because he took his own life. He was a man for whom forgiveness became a way of life, replacing one of violence. He had humbled himself beyond what most men could, or would want to, endure. I wanted to attend his funeral and say goodbye, but his body was cremated.

Howard offered one possible motive to authorities. Jesse's brother in Illinois had died of colon cancer. It was exactly nine months to the day - April 19, 2002 - and Jesse still grieved.

Jesse's last words to me - "Goodbye, my good friend" - echoed in my mind. I didn't remember the date he spoke them, but it was about the time his brother died. Was that why he said there was nothing remaining for him in St. Louis and why there seemed to be finality to his words? Had he been there when his brother passed on? Did he know then what he was going to do and why he was silent for so long? It wasn't for me to know. Only God did.

His words after he almost was killed leaving his mother's house now seemed weirdly prophetic. Had he reaped what he had sown after all? Had he died by the sword because he had lived by it, as the Bible foretells? He was convinced he would because the Bible told him so. But does God punish like that? Only He knows.

There no doubt were those who found joy and sarcasm in Jesse's death. The "Stone Killer," the big bully, in the end was a loser, a weakling who killed himself, the ultimate act of desperation and failure. He had put out a contract on himself. The underworld, what was left of it, certainly celebrated. Only no one would collect the $100,000 bounty for his death. He had cheated them out of that.

Jesse's death left a void in my life probably never to be filled. I doubt I ever will know anyone quite like him. Sometimes, I tended to accuse myself. Had I abandoned him when he needed someone? If only I had been there to help him more, to talk to him, to pray with him. If only I had not waited all those months in silence for him to call. If only …

Jesse's life was an education for me. I gained a new perspective of life I hadn't seen up close and personal until I came to know him. My own faith was enriched because of him. I watched a man who groveled in the depths of sin and depravity for so long try to cleanse himself with God's word and help, a Herculean task for anyone.

Suicide Or Murder?

After an autopsy, the medical examiner ruled Jesse's death was a suicide. He lived 54 years, five months and 13 days. The autopsy report didn't establish if he had cancer. I assumed that could be another reason he took his own life.

The autopsy report indicated Jesse's corpse reflected his faith and his conflicted life. On his right shoulder was a tattoo of prison bars and praying hands. I had an idea what message that was meant to convey. Sketched on the back of his right forearm were the words, "The Outlaw," which I assumed he considered himself, not derogatorily, but proudly. On his left leg was an image of an angel. Two tattoos of doves were elsewhere on his body. Were they symbols of the peace he craved or perhaps of his former wives?

Being a skeptic, I questioned if he actually killed himself despite conclusive evidence of suicide in the autopsy report. Had someone from his past satisfied the lingering grudge after almost 20 years? The shooter would assume Jesse was armed. He probably wouldn't have come that close and would have fired from a distance. Howard, a witness, also would have been killed. To make an assassination appear a suicide would be too difficult under the circumstances. It would have required the complicity of Howard, the officer, the medical examiner and others.

Some suggested Jesse faked his death with another body to escape his past and begin a new life. That was so far removed from reality I laughed. Too many people, including officials, would have to be involved in such a cover-up. Too many loose tongues. Too much money changing hands.

I read and reread copies of the police and medical examiner's reports. There was nothing suspicious, unexplained or unsupported factually. There was no gunshot residue on Howard's hands, proving he had not pulled the trigger. Jesse, indeed, had taken his own life. That he left no note was the only curiosity, but I understood why.

It would have been more proof of his weakness and failure. He wouldn't want to leave that legacy.

Consumed By Fear

I later learned the truth about Jesse's last days, leaving absolutely no doubt he killed himself. His paranoia was more pernicious than I had assumed. Time hadn't healed his old wounds. It apparently caused new ones.

One of his daughters told me of his mental degeneration. "When we went shopping he would think people were following him and he would drive like a mad man up and down the streets trying to lose them. He was convinced people undercover were watching him all the time. He would tell me that there always were helicopters over his house. He'd say, 'They're coming for me and I won't let them get me'."

She had her weekly Saturday lunch with Jesse the day before he died. He promised to have a birthday cake and barbecue for her the next weekend. She didn't know she wouldn't be able to enjoy that.

She confirmed Jesse's continuing faith in God. Much of their weekly conversations were about that. "We would talk about God and he would read the Bible to me. I would ask questions and he would always have the answers. He kept saying Jesus forgives our sins. He talked a lot about St. Paul."

That was conclusive proof of what I already believed. Jesse hadn't abandoned his redeeming faith in Jesus in his last days. He had nourished it.

Howard told her there were power failures at their mobile home and that terrified Jesse. It reached a climax the Sunday he died. "He told me my dad said, 'I think something's going to happen tonight and we need to leave'."

It was obvious why Jesse had Howard's pistol. Even though he believed he was in constant danger and hit men stalked him, he still wouldn't permit himself to own a gun. He told me it was a symbol of his terrible past and he wasn't a killer anymore. I assumed he also feared what he might do to someone - even himself - if he owned one.

It also explained why he didn't shoot the officer he assumed was his assassin. He no longer could harm another person even one he believed was trying to kill him. He had held fast to his vow to God to no longer commit violence, at least not against others. But his resolve apparently didn't apply to himself.

I still wondered if Jesse was in conflict with himself and Satan, not with God, and that somehow prevailed. Paul, in his epistle to the Romans, tells of his daily contention with the evil spirits dwelling in him. It is the same combat we all wage daily and not always successfully, as perhaps with Jesse.

"For we know that the Law is spiritual, but I am of the flesh, sold into bondage to sin. For that which I am doing, I do not understand; for I am not practicing what I would like to do, but I am doing the very thing I hate. So now, no longer am I the one doing it, but sin which dwells in me. For I know that nothing good dwells in me, that is, in my flesh; for the wishing is present in me, but the doing of the good is not.

"For the good that I wish I do not do; but I practice the very evil that I do not wish. But if I am doing the very things I do not wish, I am no longer the one doing it, but sin which dwells in me." (7: 14-15; 17-20)

Paul knew how to overcome his constant torment, but suicide wasn't the answer.

"Wretched man that I am! Who will set me free from the body of this death? Thanks be to God through Jesus Christ, Our Lord! So then, on the one hand I myself with my mind am serving the law of God, but on the other, with my flesh, the law of sin." (7: 24-25)

I certainly cannot answer one outstanding question – Why did Jesse not turn to God as his hero, Paul, stressed? There are questions regarding God's will and wisdom for which we have no absolute answers or insight. It is the way He wants it.

Forgiven Or Not?

I had seen victims of homicide, suicide and accidents in my career. Death, even my own, had troubled me for years until I resolved it through God's word. I accepted that death is not the end, but the beginning if you believe in Jesus. You leave a corrupt habitat for a pure one with Him.

But is suicide forgivable by God? What are the Scriptural implications of suicide? The Sixth Commandment is clear in condemning taking a life, but does that prohibition include your own? If so, does that mean Jesse was doomed to eternal hell for that sin in the last moments of his life?

The Bible doesn't mention the word suicide, but in the Old Testament it discusses those who considered it during times of trial and tribulation, with God disapproving. They were strong-willed men of God, among them Job, Jonah and other prophets, who suffered terrible adversities and who questioned Him.

Some wished they never were born and asked God to take their lives, but He refused. Jesus and the Apostles were persecuted, tortured and even put to death. They didn't take the easy way out and kill themselves when the going got tough. They hung in there and relied on God.

That still didn't explain much about Jesse. My research showed there are a number of causes of suicide, some interwoven, but what motivated Jesse? I was sure his conscience played a part in his mental instability. Was it also depression caused by feeling isolated and rejected, believing no one cared for him? Did he believe his life was without purpose or meaning?

One school of thought about suicide and Scriptural implications concerning forgiveness believes it is an unpardonable sin because it is an act of rebellion against God. It contends it not only violates the Sixth Commandment, but God doesn't condone the taking of one's life to escape even under the most terrible of circumstances. Suicide destroys the very life God gave us, it says.

I have no doubt Jesse violated the Sixth Commandment, but was what he did an unforgivable sin, punishable by consignment to hell?

We all in one way or another violate the Commandments every day. And more than just once a day! I certainly do.

Further research of the Bible, particularly the New Testament, answered the questions I had about whether Jesse was forgiven or condemned to hell for his suicide. I believe Jesse met the requirements to receive his place in Heaven.

There only is one sin unforgiveable by God which leads to eternal death – blasphemy against the Holy Spirit, which I never detected in Jesse. Mark quoted Jesus as telling us:

"Truly, I say to you, all sins shall be forgiven the sons of men, and whatever blasphemies they utter, but whoever blasphemes against the Holy Spirit never has forgiveness, but is guilty of an eternal sin." (3: 28-29)

Uncompromising faith in Jesus, which I know Jesse possessed, assures us of eternal life with Him. John confirms that:

"For God so loved the world that He gave His only begotten son, that whoever believes in Him should not perish, but have eternal life. For God did not send the Son into the world to judge the world, but that the world should be saved through Him. He who believes in Him is not judged; he who does not believe had been judged already, because he has not believed in the name of the only begotten son of God." (3: 16-18)

Still, I grieve for Jesse, but I know without a doubt our Savior, Jesus Christ, has delivered him from the turmoil of his troubled mind and has taken him home to live with Him forever. Jesse no longer dwells in the darkness of his sinful past, but in the light of the saving grace of Jesus. The true life. The beginning. Not the end.

Paul, in his epistle to the Ephesians also assured me Jesse is in his true home:

"In Him, you also, after listening to the message of truth, the gospel of your salvation, having also believed, you were sealed in Him with the Holy Spirit of promise, who is given as a pledge of our inheritance, with a view to the redemption of God's own possession, to the praise of His Glory." (1: 13-14)

That Jesus forgives sinners and opens the gates of Heaven for them is indisputable. Luke tells us that as Jesus was being crucified one of two criminals also being slain appealed to him.

"And he was saying, 'Jesus, remember me when You come into Your kingdom'. And He said to him, 'Truly, I say to you, today you shall be with Me in Paradise. (23: 42-43)

Enjoy it, Jesse. You finally are at peace!

EPILOGUE

Another Mob War

B y 1985, with the mob in turmoil because of Jesse's exposures, Ray Flynn saw an opportunity to empower himself. It was time to launch his own conflict to gain control of the underworld.

He would fill the vacuum created by the absence of the Leisures, who were in prison for the rest of their lives. And he was home free. He hadn't been arrested for his participation in the Leisures' hits. Berne had made him his agent in Missouri while he awaited trial. When Berne went to prison, as he obviously would, Flynn would take over his outfit, even though it was decimated. That would help elevate him to power.

Flynn's main target in his power play, as was the Leisures', would be the Mafia, particlarly Trupiano, who had fallen into disrespect for his ineffective leadership. Intelligence sources said Trupiano was unable to consolidate power after the demise of the Leisure Outfit. Co-existence between Trupiano's outfit and the rest of organized crime was gone.

Trupiano's crumbling dynasty caught the attention of New York City's five-family underworld. Intelligence officials reported members of the Profacci Family visited him several times. He also had to make sudden, urgent trips to Detroit. The Mafia there had been aligned with the St. Louis Family.

Flynn's plot to gain mob dominance never reached fruition. The government hadn't forgotten him and he wasn't home free. On July 24, 1986, he was indicted for involvement in the murders of Spica, Michaels and Faheen. He also was charged with receiving $400,000 in stolen property from the Lordo's score and with buying the $6,500 in stolen jewelry from Jesse.

After he was indicted, he offered to become a snitch against Jesse, but the FBI turned him down.

Flynn pleaded guilty to the receiving stolen property charges and was sentenced to two 10-year concurrent sentences. Judge William Beatty, in passing sentence on the federal charge, said he regretted having to do so. Flynn, he mused, had a "great deal of talent" and a "number of leadership skills." But he said he had no choice but to send him to prison.

For his part in the Leisure War murders, Flynn was convicted of a Racketeering Influenced and Corrupt Organization (RICO) charge and sentenced to 45 years in prison. The sentence later was reduced to 30 years. He died on May 22, 2002, while in prison.

Following is a summary of the disposition of charges against others discussed in the book.

- Innes Anderson, the telephone repairman who assisted the Leisures in attempting to monitor phones, was granted immunity from prosecution in return for his testimony.

After testifying, he entered the Witness Protection Program.

- The crux of Lucas Brazil's defense was Jesse was the culprit, not he. He was tried in U. S. District Court under his true name, Robert Allen. Taking the witness stand in his own defense, he claimed when he refused to make the bomb Jesse threatened to kill his sister. It was the bomb Brazil came within minutes of detonating to kill Jesse.

"He was a master of imitating my voice," Brazil testified, asserting Jesse faked his incriminating statements that were recorded. The jurors didn't believe him. It took them only 45 minutes to find him guilty of making and selling the bomb. He was sentenced to 15 years in prison.

- Fernando "Nando" Bartolotta was sentenced to five years after his conviction of conspiracy to transport stolen money across state lines in the aborted of Venture robbery.

His guilty pleas to charges of being part of Trupiano's gambling ring and credit card fraud added six more years. He plea bargained on a charge of extorting money with Berne and Trupiano from Dennis Sonnenschein, owner of the topless night club, and was given a six-year sentence to run concurrently with the other terms.

But Bartolotta didn't abandon his crime career. A U. S. District Court jury convicted him in March 1997 of participating in a bank robbery, of driving the getaway car used in an armored car robbery and of transporting goods stolen in a burglary in Illinois across state lines. He was sentenced to 18 years in federal prison.

- Art Berne timidly admitted he used intimidation and threats to extort money from Sonnenschein. He pleaded guilty of extortion and interstate travel in aid of racketeering. He was sentenced to six years in prison and placed on three years' probation, although the prosecutor recommended a 14-year term. He could have been sentenced to 25 years and fined $20,000. He was paroled in the spring of 1989 and died not long afterwards. The East Side Outfit essentially disintegrated.

- The jury rejected Clinton Bramlet's defense of insanity in committing the robberies of the banks in Bartelso and Irvington. He testified he suffered from "organic brain damage" resulting from the beating by the union thugs. He was found guilty of nine charges – the two bank robberies, six weapons violations and one of conspiracy. He could have been sentenced to 115 years and fined $90,000, but he received 45 years.

He plea bargained a murder charge in the Billy Belt slaying down to voluntary manslaughter in Illinois state court and was sentenced to 15 years to run concurrently with the federal term. He also pleaded guilty to four counts of mail fraud and received five years in prison on each count to run consecutively with the bank robbery convictions.

- After Ronald Broderick was indicted for involvement in the Leisure War, he agreed to testify for the government against the Leisures and pleaded guilty to a single RICO count. He was sentenced to 18 years in prison. His family went into hiding under the federal Witness Protection Program and he joined them when he was released from prison.
- Joseph Brooks' gamble with a guilty plea paid off and he was sentenced to two concurrent four-year terms on the bank robbery charges and four years' probation for weapons violations. He was ordered to make restitution to two banks.
- Judge Beatty concluded George Eidson was a "career criminal beyond rehabilitation" and sentenced him to five years after he pleaded guilty of helping fence $1 million in jewelry stolen in a robbery of a downtown St. Louis store. The term was to run consecutively with a 25-year sentence he was serving in Missouri for a burglary Jesse helped solve.
- Shortly after Paulie Leisure was bombed, Jack Issa became a fugitive. Despite an extensive search, he couldn't be located. He had died of heart disease shortly after disappearing.
- Stanley Kowalski pleaded guilty of involvement in interstate transportation of stolen property. Because he was 70 years old, he was placed on five years' probation.
- Anthony Leisure showed no contrition at his sentencing after his conviction in U. S. District Court on numerous charges in the bombings. Standing erect, his words rambling, he told the judge: "I find it very hard to show compassion for anybody who would blow up my brother and harm my mother whom I considered a saint. I don't feel I'm greedy or power hungry."

He then focused his attention to Fred Prater, a former associate and principal witness against him and the others. "I feel sorrow for the community in which they are letting Fred Prater go. He's a monster on the loose."

He was sentenced to 40 years in federal prison. A state court a jury convicted him only of manslaughter, although the prosecution sought the death penalty. It recommended 10 years in prison and the judge concurred. Prosecutors and investigators still consider the verdict an anomaly.

- David Leisure was convicted on similar charges as his cousin, Anthony, in federal court. At his sentencing, he had one request of the judge. "I would like to have my health checked." The judge, without comment, sentenced him to 55 years.

He fared worse in state court. He was convicted on two counts of capital murder - one in the death of Sonny Faheen, the other in the bombing of Jimmy Michaels. For Faheen's death, he was sentenced to life imprisonment without parole. He was given the death penalty for killing Michaels.

After his conviction and sentencing on the state charges, he was evaluated by psychiatrists, who found he had an I. Q. of 74 and was "mildly mentally retarded."

While on death row, he granted an interview to a St. Louis Post-Dispatch reporter. While declining to discuss the crimes for which he was convicted, he gave a vivid insight into himself. He admitted he was delusional. His mother had died, he believed, because he had broken a mirror. And he was responsible for the murder of his brother, Richard, because he had seen a white pigeon, a bad omen.

In the 1970s, he began using drugs, including speed and cocaine. He would drink a case of beer or a fifth of whisky a day.

Nicknamed "Bozo" by Paulie and Anthony, David Leisure was the butt of many jokes because of his blind obedience. When in his pre-teens, they coaxed him into a wooden crate. "They would wind the crate up in the air and let me swing for a while. It scared me. They'd let me down and they would talk me into doing it again. There were times when a guy would be riding his bike down the street and they'd say, 'Hit the guy'. So, I'd hit the guy. I was trying to be big."

Shortly after midnight on September 1, 1999, he was given a lethal injection. He achieved prominence in criminal history. He was one of few, if any, gangsters in recent memory to be executed.

- Paulie Leisure, confined to a wheelchair, made some accusations after his conviction in federal court on similar charges as his brother. The professional hit man whose life almost ended with a hit asked to address the sentencing judge.

Speaking barely above a whisper, he said: "The men who did this to me have led lives of crime. They have been murderers all their lives." He accused the FBI of not warning him he would be bombed. "It is a bad precedent when the FBI acts as judge, jury and executioner. I would ask this court not to let this happen again. I ask the court to see that this never affects another U. S. citizen."

Leisure's attorney, Albert Krieger of Miami, made an impassioned plea for leniency. "Paul Leisure lost his emotional balance that has been only partially given back with anti-depressants. He suffers the tortures of the damned – literally and figuratively – every day. There is no punishment worse than the punishment he suffers. The few hours of sleep he gets – drug induced – is the only respite he has. The only respite he will get until he meets his maker."

The judge wasn't impressed. He sentenced Leisure to 55 years.

Three years later, Leisure, on a change of venue, was convicted in state court in St. Joseph, Missouri, of the Michaels' murder. Moments after the verdict was announced the police department received a threat of a bomb at the motel where the jury was quartered. No bomb was found. Leisure was sentenced to life imprisonment without parole, although the prosecution sought the death penalty.

On Monday, July 17, 2000, Paul Leisure died of heart disease in the U. S. Medical Center for Federal Prisoners in Springfield, Mo.

It was disclosed during the trials of the Leisures that the FBI had monitored Paulie Leisure's telephones for six months beginning in February 1982. More than 750 hours of conversations were recorded.

- Charles Loewe was sentenced to 35 years in federal court for his part in the Leisure War. A Missouri Circuit Court jury convicted him of two counts of first-degree assault in the shooting of John Michaels and his friend. He was sentenced to 50 years to run concurrently with the federal term.
- Patrick McAtee saw no advantage in fighting a charge of illegally possessing the dynamite he gave to Brazil and he

pleaded guilty. Because of his old age, he was placed on five years' probation.

- On the day William Politte was to have gone to trial, he pleaded guilty to four charges – bombing a union hall, transferring a hand grenade to Jesse, mail fraud and conspiracy to fraudulently dispose of his car in an insurance scam with the help of Jesse.

He was sentenced to 13 years plus another year for parole violation. He could have received 40 more years in prison. He died not long after being paroled.

- Fred Prater's and Jesse's testimonies were crucial in the prosecution of Flynn in the Spica hit. The once close associate of the Leisures turned government witness when Anthony and David Leisure, suspecting he would tell all when subpoenaed to a federal grand jury, asked him to take a car ride with them. He knew he would be killed.

A slender, small man with a raspy voice, Prater called U. S. Attorney Dittmeier late one night, saying he wanted to cooperate. He was granted immunity from prosecution in return for his testimony and immediately disappeared with his family in the Witness Protection Program. The Leisures searched frantically for him when they discovered his house was abandoned.

- It required a federal indictment to force John Ramo to turn on the Leisure Outfit. In return for his cooperation, he was permitted to plead guilty to a single RICO count and was sentenced to 15 years. He and his family went into Witness Protection. He later died.
- When the judge refused to allow Theodore Rousseau, the deputy sheriff, and his attorney to interview Jesse, he pleaded guilty to one charge of bank robbery and received a seven-year federal prison sentence.
- Milton R. "Russ" Schepp, the former police chief who was a fugitive for 19 months after the Paulie Leisure bombing, was convicted of conspiracy, making a bomb and using a bomb to blow up a car. He was sentenced to one five-year sentence and two 10-year terms to run concurrently in federal prison.

- Frank Termine Jr. was the first Leisure Outfit member to become a snitch. He told investigators how the Faheen hit came down. Based on his information, FBI agents began monitoring conversations in Paulie Leisure's home. For his part, Termine was sentenced to 16 years in prison to run concurrently with a 16-year-term in Illinois for burglary.
- Matthew "Mike" Trupiano, the Mafia capo, first went to trial in U. S. District Judge John F. Nangle in St. Louis on charges of running the handbook ring. The jury, unimpressed by his claims that although it was a million-dollar-a-year operation he lost money, found him guilty. He became the joke of the underworld when it became known he actually had lost money, unheard of for bookies. His greed hadn't permitted him to lay off bets to protect himself.

He was sentenced to four years in prison and fined $30,000. Before entering prison, Trupiano asked Judge Nangle to permit him to take a brief vacation with his wife in Las Vegas because the trial had been a "severe strain." Assistant U. S. Attorney David M. Rosen argued the vacation would permit him to "continue his illegal activity." The request was denied.

He was paroled after serving a year and a half. A condition was he not associate with convicted felons or persons of ill repute. It hampered his ability to lead his outfit, what was left of it.

Unlike Berne, Trupiano pleaded not guilty of extortion of the topless bar operator and went to trial. The federal trial lasted eight days and the jury after four hours of deliberation acquitted him. He could have been sentenced to 20 years in prison and fined $25,000.

Among Trupiano's many shortcomings, he was a compulsive gambler. The FBI, which had placed him under continual surveillance, caught him operating a gin rummy game in a back room of a used car dealership in 1991. He also was charged with embezzling from Laborers' Local 110, of which he still was president. He was running the card game while on union time. It was a cheap charge, but it worked. He was convicted and sentenced to two and a half years in prison. The judge admonished him to "shun gambling in all forms."

A year after Trupiano's arrest, members of Local 110 voted him out of office. He died on October 22, 1997, after suffering a heart attack. To the end he denied he was a made member of the Mafia.

Investigators in the St. Louis Police Department tentatively identified one of the officers who had fed information to the Leisures. He was of lower rank and was stationed in the Third District on the city's near south side which embraced the Leisures' home territory. He voluntarily resigned.

By the turn of the century, there was no recognizable, traditional organized crime in St. Louis. Most mob figures were dead or too old to continue their criminal activities. The only gangs that existed were street thugs and those dealing in narcotics, resulting in even higher annual murder rates.

CPSIA information can be obtained at www.ICGtesting.com
Printed in the USA
LVOW05s1151021114

411652LV00016B/340/P

9 781619 042971